Youth Diversion

Using New South Wales as a case example, this book engages with central themes of discretionary decision-making processes regarding youth diversion away from court and the broader political and policy constraints that impact implementation to full potential.

Drawing on mixed quantitative and qualitative data, including interviews with experienced police officers, magistrates and youth justice personnel, this study examines discretionary decision-making processes under the *Young Offenders Act 1997* (NSW). While focusing on the Australian experience, the shared colonisation history with other Commonwealth countries such as New Zealand, Canada, and the United Kingdom allow for the insights to be globally applicable. Readers will gain insights into implementing diversionary justice, understand theoretical frameworks shaping contemporary youth justice and access evidence-based analysis for improving outcomes internationally.

Youth Diversion will be a valuable resource for students, scholars and practitioners of criminology, legal studies, sociology and social policy.

Estrella Pearce is a lecturer in Criminology at the University of Sydney, Australia.

Routledge Frontiers of Criminal Justice

Education in Youth Detention Homes
An Ethnographic Study of Schooling Against the Odds
David Wästerfors

The Use of Algorithms in Criminal Law
A central European perspective
Edited by K. Burdziak, I. Ambrus

The Structural Exclusion of Rape Complainants in South Africa's Criminal Justice System
Justice through Participation
Jameelah Omar

Cross-border Victims in Europe
Legal and Practical Barriers to Free Movement of Victims in Europe
Edited by Elżbieta Hryniewicz-Lach and Michael Kilchling

Legal Implications of Taser Use and Prone Position on Excited Delirium Subjects
Vidisha Barua Worley

Through the Distorted Lens
Constructing Truth and Reality with Legal Narratives
Fiona C. Hum

Youth Diversion
Exploring Criminal Justice Perspectives through An Australian Case Study
Estrella Pearce

For more information about this series, please visit: www.routledge.com/Routledge-Frontiers-of-Criminal-Justice/book-series/RFCJ

Youth Diversion

Exploring Criminal Justice Perspectives through An Australian Case Study

Estrella Pearce

Routledge
Taylor & Francis Group
LONDON AND NEW YORK

First published 2026
by Routledge
4 Park Square, Milton Park, Abingdon, Oxon OX14 4RN

and by Routledge
605 Third Avenue, New York, NY 10158

Routledge is an imprint of the Taylor & Francis Group, an informa business

Funded by University of Sydney Library.

British Library Cataloguing-in-Publication Data
A catalogue record for this book is available from the British Library

ISBN: 9781032746746 (hbk)
ISBN: 9781032746753 (pbk)
ISBN: 9781003470366 (ebk)

DOI: 10.4324/9781003470366

Typeset in Times New Roman
by KnowledgeWorks Global Ltd.

Contents

List of Tables

Acknowledgements

I am grateful to the many people who provided valuable feedback on the material presented here, including Stephen Tomsen, Selda Dagistanli and Ana Rodas. The research upon which this book is based was made possible by an Australian Postgraduate Award and the generous support of the School of Social Sciences and Psychology at Western Sydney University during my doctoral studies.

I extend my sincere appreciation to the NSW Children's Court, the NSW Police Force and Juvenile Justice NSW for recognising the necessity and importance of this research. Special thanks to Judge Peter Johnstone, former President of the Children's Court NSW, and to each of the twelve magistrates who generously shared their experiences and insights.

I am particularly grateful to Dr. Chris Devery of the NSW Police Force, who was instrumental in facilitating access to the organisation, and to the police officers who participated in this study, sharing the complexities of their work with candour and professionalism.

My appreciation extends to Dr. Eric Heller, Victoria Perry and Carolyn Newbigin from the Research and Information Unit at Juvenile Justice NSW (now Youth Justice NSW) for their support in facilitating access to respondents. I also wish to thank the Assistant Managers in Juvenile Justice and the Aboriginal Legal Services solicitor who took time from their demanding schedules to participate in interviews.

Finally, to my family, for their unwavering love and support throughout this journey.

I acknowledge permission granted by Taylor & Francis as the section 'Legislative constraints to diversion: "admission of guilt"' in Chapter 4, has been partially published before in:

Pearce, E. (2021). Why "admission of guilt" is not working in youth diversionary schemes in NSW – exploratory findings from interviews with police officers. *Current Issues in Criminal Justice*, *33*(3), 285–299. https://doi.org/10.1080/10345329.2021.1874625

List of Acronyms

ACT	Australian Capital Territory
AIHW	Australian Institute of Health and Welfare
ALRC	Australian Law Reform Commission
ALS	Aboriginal Legal Service
AVO	Apprehended Violence Order
BOCSAR	NSW Bureau of Crime Statistics and Research
CCYP	Commission for Children and Young People
COPS	Computerised Operational Police System
DAGJ	The Department of Attorney General and Justice
DCJ	NSW Department of Communities and Justice
DPP	Director of Public Prosecutions
DVO	Domestic Violence Order
FGC	Family Group Conferencing
JHFMHN	Justice Health and Forensic Mental Health Network
JJ	Juvenile Justice NSW
LAC	Local Area Command
MACR	Minimum age of criminal responsibility
MAPP	Multi-Agency Public Protection Arrangements
NISATSIC	National Inquiry into the Separation of Aboriginal and Torres Strait Islander Children from Their Families
NSW	New South Wales
NSWLRC	NSW Law Reform Commission
PANSW	Police Association of New South Wales
PAS	Protected Admission Scheme
PC	Police Constables
PCYC	Police Citizens Youth Clubs
POI	Person Of Interest
RCIADIC	Royal Commission into Aboriginal Deaths in Custody
SYO	Specialist Youth Officer
UK	United Kingdom

UNCRC	United Nations Convention on the Rights of the Child
US	United States
YCJA	Youth Criminal Justice Act (Canada)
YJC	Youth Justice Conference
YLO	Youth Liaison Officer
YOA	Young Offenders Act 1997 (NSW)

1 Introduction

Introduction

It is well recognised in international human rights jurisprudence that most children do not need to be in, nor belong to, the criminal justice system (United Nations Convention on the Rights of the Child (UNCRC), 1989; United Nations General Assembly, 1985 (Beijing Rules)). Internationally, many youth justice systems aim to divert young people away from court through mechanisms such as police cautions and restorative youth justice conferencing (YJC). Among other things, diversion avoids potentially criminogenic effects of formal contact with the criminal justice system. However, tension between the desire to reform or discipline and the need to contain, deter and punish remains, and diversion has not reached its full potential.

This book engages with central themes of discretionary decision-making processes around youth diversion away from court and broader political and policy constraints impacting youth diversion implementation to its full potential. The research takes the case example of youth diversion in New South Wales (NSW), Australia's most populous state, while presenting rival perspectives on YJC underutilisation to understand the failure to divert to full potential. Drawing on mixed quantitative and qualitative data—particularly in-depth interviews with experienced police officers, magistrates and youth justice personnel—this study examines discretionary decision-making processes involved in youth diversion under the *Young Offenders Act 1997* (NSW) (YOA). It grounds these processes in critical theoretical thinking about colonisation processes and the historical arrangement of criminal processing systems established in NSW.

The book aims to confront how institutional and individual actors perform gatekeeping functions around diversionary practices. Firstly, it examines attitudes and understandings of diversion by individual criminal actors, within their roles in particular institutions, including police, courts and juvenile justice personnel. Secondly, it moves from exploring individual attitudes that both reproduce and depart from prevailing institutionalised cultures to identifying broader political and policy constraints and opportunities surrounding existing youth diversion forms. It situates these issues in continuing tensions between welfare and justice, social

DOI: 10.4324/9781003470366-1

control, shame and reintegration as punishment, risk management theories and police culture(s).

Deploying interdisciplinary approaches, this work sits at the intersections of critical criminology, sociology and cultural studies, rethinking how individual responsibilisation, risk-based strategies (focusing on intervention) and punitivism form a significant backdrop to decisions shaping law and order. This work contributes to several fields: current policy initiatives to divert young people from criminal justice systems, understanding criminal justice perspectives on diversion and contextualising challenges in implementing youth diversion.

The book focuses on the Australian experience, though this is not unique as it draws law from England and reflects colonisation and post-colonisation history shared with other Commonwealth countries, such as New Zealand, Canada and England. Furthermore, exploring youth justice governance development and discretionary decision-making approaches on diversion by judges, magistrates, police officers and criminal justice personnel, this book provides insights into this subject area which is of considerable academic and practical interest internationally. What follows is an overview of the minimum age of criminal responsibility (MACR) in Australia, followed by brief background to the research, clarification of terminology, description of theoretical approach and research design, and finally outline of chapters that follow.

The minimum age of criminal responsibility (MACR)

In Australia, the age at which children can be legally held accountable for their criminal actions is a matter for each state and territory, as criminal law is not one of the powers conferred on the Commonwealth Government under the Australian Constitution. However, all jurisdictions have adhered to the traditional common law approach of two age levels (Crofts, 2015). At the first age level, there is an absolute irrebuttable age, a MACR, below which a child is *doli incapax*—that is, a child lacks sufficient capacity to be guilty of crime. Historically, the MACR was set at the notably low threshold of seven, but between 1976 and 2000, this age was progressively increased to ten years across all Australian jurisdictions (Crofts, 2018). From that point onwards, and up until very recent changes—soon to be discussed—the MACR remained set at ten years across all Australian states and territories (Pearce, 2025). The second age level introduces a rebuttable presumption of *doli incapax*—which applies to children aged 10–13 (Crofts, 2018). Not a defence, but a rebuttable presumption, *doli incapax* is applied to all Australian jurisdictions, but the principle has been criticised for being inconsistently applied, difficult to prove and potentially leading to unjust outcomes (Fitz-Gibbon & O'Brien, 2019; Law Council of Australia, 2020). Thus, although *doli incapax* is intended to serve as a legal safeguard for children under 14, many argue that it offers limited practical protection in its current application (Australian Human Rights Commission, 2020; Australian Law Reform Commission (ALRC), 1997; Crofts, 2022; Cunneen, 2020; Fitz-Gibbon & O'Brien, 2019).

Australia has long faced criticisms for maintaining one of the lowest MACRs among developed nations. Over the past two decades, sustained domestic and international pressure has kept the issue at the forefront of legal and human rights debates. The scrutiny intensified in 2016 following the broadcast of an *ABC Four Corners* investigation, which exposed systemic abuse and mistreatment of vulnerable children in detention facilities in the Northern Territory—a sparsely populated jurisdiction located in central and northern Australia. These revelations prompted the establishment of a Royal Commission into the Protections and Detention of Children in the Northern Territory, significantly amplifying calls—both nationally and international—for Australia to raise its MACR. Subsequently, the Northern Territory briefly raised its MACR to 12 in 2022, which took effect in August 2023. However, this reform was reversed in November 2024 following a change in government within the Territory. The Australian Capital Territory (ACT) currently maintains the highest MACR at 12, having implemented a change in 2023, and has committed to increasing it further to 14 by July 2025. All other jurisdictions continue to maintain a MACR of ten years (Pearce, 2025).

Determining the age at which a child possesses the necessary cognitive and moral capacities to be held criminally responsible is inherently complex. However, an extensive growing body of research in neuroscience and development psychology indicates that children under the age of 14 generally lack the requisite capacity for criminal culpability (Crofts, 2022; Pearce, 2025). In 2012, the UNCRC stated that a MACR below 12 years is not internationally acceptable and recommended raising it to at least 14, or preferably 16 (2012, [84(a)]). This position was reaffirmed in 2019, when the UNCRC issued a general comment on children's rights in the child justice system, advocating for a global MACR of no less than 14 years—the most common MACR internationally (2019, [24]).

The criminogenic nature of the criminal justice system and its detrimental effects on children and young people who come into contact with it have been extensively documented (Amnesty International, 2018; Goldson, 2013; Law Council of Australia, 2020; McAra & McVie, 2007). Notwithstanding this evidence, the Australian government has demonstrated a degree of reticence in raising the MACR, often citing the need to balance community safety with the protection of vulnerable children. A key argument for maintaining the MACR at ten years is the perceived necessity of holding children accountable for serious offending. This position is often supported by reference to existing legal safeguards for vulnerable children, such as the rebuttable presumption of *doli incapax* (Crofts, 2022; Pearce, 2025). Additionally, diversionary mechanisms—such as those provided under the YOA—are presented as alternatives to punitive measures, allowing children to be redirected away from the criminogenic effects of formal proceedings and into rehabilitative or community-based interventions (Crofts, 2022; Pearce, 2025). However, the existence of such diversionary alternatives cannot be used to justify maintaining the current MACR (Pearce, 2025). As discussed throughout this book, evidence indicates that discretionary biases within the justice system can limit access to diversion, leading to the unintended exclusion of certain populations—particularly First Nations children, who are significantly over-represented in the criminal justice system yet are less likely to be diverted by police (Allard et al., 2010; Cunneen et al., 2021; Papalia et al., 2019). Furthermore, research on court-based diversion has raised further concerns about the exclusions of young people with cognitive and mental health impairments from diversionary pathways (NSW Law Reform Commission (NSWLRC), 2012, 2013). These disparities raise serious concerns about the equity and effectiveness of diversion as a safeguard for all children. It is critically important to get diversion right—especially while the MACR remains as low as 10—because diversion serves as one of the few protective mechanisms available to mitigate the harms of early criminalisation.

Exploring youth 'diversion'—brief background

Diversion away from court is increasingly used in various jurisdictions as a mechanism to avoid formal interaction with criminal justice systems. Given the criminogenic nature of criminal justice systems, diversionary practices such as cautions and YJC have become particularly prominent for children and young people, with Australia and New Zealand becoming world leaders in conferencing programs during the 2000s. While these alternatives hold promise, critical scrutiny has highlighted their pitfalls, including concerns about whether diversionary programs are discriminatory due to inconsistent decision-making patterns on youth diversion.

Twenty-eight years have passed since the YOA's introduction in NSW, Australia. The Act was designed to reduce the number of children and young people entering the formal criminal justice system by promoting diversionary measures such as warnings[1], cautions and YJC. Central to the YOA is the principle that detention should be a measure of 'last resort'—a standard also articulated in Article 37(b) of the UNCRC (1989). Despite this legislative commitment, the practical application of the YOA has been inconsistent and in many respects inadequate. The current landscape reveals a longstanding reticence within the criminal justice system to fully apply the YOA.

The YOA emerged from a decade of juvenile justice inquiries, legislative reviews and community consultation throughout the 1990s (Chan, 2005; Hennessy, 1999). It introduced a structured hierarchical approach to youth offending responses, with diversionary options intended to precede court involvement. The Act was initially lauded for aligning with restorative justice principles and was seen as progressive for juvenile justice in NSW. Despite these aspirations, the YOA's outcomes have not materialised as expected. Empirical evidence and scholarly commentary indicate that, following implementation, young people in detention began rising. A key contributing factor was increasing numbers of young people remanded in custody due to bail refusal (Stubbs, 2010). Simultaneously, First Nations children's over-representation in court and custody persisted, and by the late 2000s, NSW recorded the highest proportion of First Nations young people in court and detention nationally (Taylor, 2009).

The over-representation of First Nations children in juvenile detention is a well-documented and persistent issue, having been subject of numerous inquiries. In June 2011, the *House of Representatives Standing Committee on Aboriginal and*

Torres Strait Islander Affairs reported that the over-representation of Indigenous youth in detention had worsened compared to levels observed two decades earlier, when the *Royal Commission into Aboriginal Deaths in Custody* (RCIADIC) (1991) was released. This increase is likely attributable, at least in part, to a decline in the incarceration of non-Indigenous young people (see Australian Institute of Health and Welfare (AIHW), 2017). Nevertheless, this disparity remains stark: in 2022–2023, First Nations young people accounted for 65% of those in custody in NSW, despite comprising approximately 7.5% of the state's youth population (AIHW, 2024).

The principle of detention as a last resort, central to the YOA, is grounded in the recognition that custodial detention is generally not in the best interest of the child. This principle is also enshrined in Article 37(b) of UNCRC (1989), which states:

> The arrest, detention or imprisonment of a child shall be in conformity with the law and shall be used only as a measure of last resort and for the shortest appropriate period of time.

As a signatory to the UNCRC, Australia is expected to uphold this standard. However, in practice, this commitment has often failed to translate into consistent application. Reviews of the YOA have identified significant implementation issues that have undermined its core objectives—particularly detention as a last resort. For instance, the NSW Ombudsman's submission to *Justice Wood's NSW Child Protection Inquiry into Child Protection Services*, highlighted:

> We found significant discrepancy in the use of diversionary options between (police) commands, and on occasions between different sectors of the same command. This suggests that use of the YOA (NSW) depends heavily on the views of an individual officer rather than the application of more general criteria. In our view, the issue should be closely monitor by NSW Police to identify how referrals rates (to conferences) might be improved.
>
> (Ombudsman, as cited in Justice Wood, 2008, p. 563)

These concerns were echoed in the Noetic Solutions Review (2010), which concluded that the juvenile justice system in NSW had lost its strategic direction. This review noted that early gains in promoting diversion and limiting detention had been eroded, and the outlook was poor. It attributed this decline to a political climate increasingly dominated by 'law and order' rhetoric and 'tough on crime' policy shifts (see Hogg & Brown, 1998). Between 2000 and 2011, for example, the *Bail Act 1978* (NSW) was amended more than 18 times, reflecting this punitive turn. The Noetic Review also found that these legislative changes had unintended and adverse consequences for children and young people. Restrictions on bail eligibility, combined with a lack of community-based resources accommodation, led to increased remand rates—even in cases where a custodial sentence was unlikely upon conviction. As a result, the principles of the YOA have been undermined by conflicting legislative frameworks in NSW, including the *Bail Act 1978*, the

Children and Young Persons (Care and Protection) Act 1998 and the *Children (Criminal Proceedings) Act 1987*.

This pattern reflects a broader, long-term failure to apply the YOA to its full extent. A review of the literature reveals that limited scholarly attention has been directed towards the decision-making practices of various institutional actors responsible for granting access to diversion. The NSW Police Force and the magistrates of the Children's Court hold significant discretionary power in determining whether a young person should be dealt with by way of a warning, caution or YJC. Under Sections 14 and 20 of the YOA, these authorities may deny diversion on the basis that, in their 'opinion' and having regard to the 'interests of justice,' it is more appropriate not to deal with the matter by the way of diversion under the Act. This discretionary framework, coupled with a lack of transparency and accountability, raises critical questions about the consistency and equity of diversionary decision-making.

Despite a substantial body of criminological research on youth justice in Australia, a few studies have examined the implementation of diversionary policies or the institutional dynamics that shape access to diversion. In Australia, most of the criminological research on juvenile justice has focused on historical and contemporary practices of youth justice policies and the impact of such policies on specific groups of young people. Notable contributions include Chris Cunneen's work on Indigenous juvenile justice (see, for example, Cunneen, 1997, 2001, 2008a, 2008b, 2011; Cunneen et al., 2006), Rob White's research on young people and public space (1997, 1998, 2009), and Kelly Richards' extensive research on restorative justice (see, for example, Richards, 2005, 2006, 2010a, 2010b, 2014; Richards et al., 2017). Other scholars, such as Christine Alder (2000) and Kerry Carrington (1993), have focus on young girls and crime, while broader analyses of juvenile justice legislation and courts have been offered by John Seymour (1997) and Allan Borovski and James M Murray (1985) and, more recently, Rosemary Sheehan and Allan Borowski (2013). However, this literature does not specifically focus on the operationalisation of diversion and the institutional factors that constraint its use.

The background and broader impact of the YOA have been examined by Janet Chan (2005) and by Noetic Solutions (2010). Yet, these works do not engage with the specific factors that enable or inhibit diversion in practice during decision-making, as encountered by those determining access to diversionary measures. This book seeks to address that gap by examining how institutional *decision-makers*—namely NSW Police Force, Children's Court Magistrates and youth justice personnel—interpret and apply the YOA. By focusing on the social, structural and institutional impediments to diversion, this research aims to provide a deeper understanding of the tensions that surround diversionary practices and youth justice governance in NSW.

Methodological pluralism

The research adopts a critical criminological approach. Taking this perspective does not imply adherence to 'critical criminology' as the exclusive framework. Instead, the research employs mixed-methods design incorporating historical and sociological insights into socio-economic differences and inequalities without being wholly embedded within the critical criminology paradigm. Although there is debate over what precisely defines critical criminology compared to other paradigms, no universally accepted formulation exists (Stubbs, 2008). Furthermore, critical criminologies are diverse and subject to continuous development, often 'likely to be influenced by borrowings from and dialogue with allied disciplines, and innovations generated by inter-disciplinary work' (Stubbs, 2008, p. 13). Despite differences in origins, methods and political beliefs, a shared concern with 'the unequal distribution of power and material resources within contemporary society provides a point of departure' (Friedrichs, 2009, p. 2010). There is consensus among critical criminologists that major social inequalities—particularly those related to class, gender, race and ethnicity—are significant in understanding crime aetiology, criminalisation processes and criminal justice responses (DeKeseredy & Dragiewicz, 1996, 2011). Accordingly, critical criminologists advocate for policy approaches addressing socio-economic and political factors contributing to crime while challenging the status quo and opposing punitive approaches that view crime as individual deviancy or pathology manifestation. They emphasise how criminal justice systems may perpetuate crime through development, enforcement and application of laws, policies and institutionalised practices (DeKeseredy & Dragiewicz, 2011). A critical and reflexive orientation is essential for engaging with crime and justice issues in a manner avoiding reductive interpretations and uncritical 'truth' claims. Such claims often obscure complexity and interdependence of systems under scrutiny. The nuances of 'diversion' can be examined through several frameworks while integrating theoretical knowledge from diverse disciplinary fields to pose fundamental questions about order, power, authority and social justice.

The research presented in this book is situated within critical criminology, with a specific focus on interrogating structural inequalities within the youth justice system, particularly regarding diversionary practices. It engages with key tensions between punitivism and welfarism (Graham & Moore, 2006; Van der Laan, 2006), social control (Cohen, 1985), net-widening (Cohen, 1985; Seymour, 1998), risk management (Feeley & Simon, 1994) and the racialisation of criminal justice discourses (Keith, 1993). Among these, occupational culture offers a particularly productive analytical lens through which to interpret the findings. This includes the study of police culture(s) (Chan, 1996; Delahunty, 1998; Durivage et al., 1992; Goldsmith, 1990), police attitudes towards diversion (Marinos & Innocente, 2008; Shafiq et al., 2016) and magisterial perspectives on youth conferencing (Bazemore, 1998; Bazemore & Leip, 2000; Camilleri et al., 2013; Naudé & Prinsloo, 2005; Richards et al., 2017; Spiranovic et al., 2015; Stephens, 2007; Tilbury & Mazerolle, 2013).

Research design

I am a migrant woman from Spain, living and working in Australia. As a criminologist researching First Nations over-representation in the criminal legal system, I acknowledge my position of privilege and status as an outsider to the communities most affected by this system. My racial and cultural identity has afforded me advantages within institutions that have historically marginalised First Nations peoples and perpetuated the systemic inequalities this research examines. I recognise that my experience fundamentally limits my understanding of colonisation's impacts, systemic racism, and ongoing dispossession experienced by First Nations communities. I am deeply committed to critically examining the structures and practices that contribute to the over-representation of Aboriginal and Torres Strait Islander young people in the criminal legal system.

This research is grounded in a recognition of the historical and ongoing impacts of colonisation, and the need for justice responses that are culturally informed, equitable and accountable. I acknowledge the limitations of my own standpoint and have sought to approach this work with humility, reflexivity, respect and a commitment to amplifying the voices and experiences of those most affected by youth justice policies. My aim is not to speak for Indigenous communities, but to interrogate the institutional mechanisms—particularly within policing, the courts, and youth justice—that shape access to diversion and contribute to systemic inequality.

The NSW case study

Ethical approval for this study was granted by the Western Sydney University Human Research Ethics Committee, protocol EC00314. Additionally, approval was obtained from the NSW Police Force which provided access to relevant representatives—namely the Youth Liaison Officers (YLOs) and Youth Policy Officers.

The overreaching question guiding this inquiry is: Why has there been a failure to refer young people to diversion in NSW? To address this, the research examines the barriers hindering the effective implementation of diversionary practices under the YOA. In doing so, it seeks to illuminate the complex interplay between policy, discretion, social and political context, institutional culture(s), and both individual and structural impediments to youth diversion.

To explore these issues, a mixed-methods approach is adopted. Official sources materials, such as legislation and policy documents governing youth diversion in NSW, provide essential contextual grounding. The quantitative component employs time-series correlation analysis using data obtained from the Bureau of Crime Statistics and Research (BOCSAR) to examine trends in diversion over time. However, the primary emphasis is placed on qualitative interviews with key stakeholders in the criminal justice system who are involved in diversion-related decision-making. Youth justice personnel—including representatives from Juvenile Justice (JJ) and Aboriginal Legal Services (ALS)—along with NSW Police and magistrates of the Children's Court, were identified as key informants for achieving the objectives of this study. The interviews aimed to explore:

- the attitudes of the police and magistracy towards diversion;
- how key practitioners interpret diversionary policy and act in accordance with legal policies and practices;
- the decision-making processes, as perceived by participants.

Each method associated with each data source is now described.

Official source material

The Noetic Report (2010) was a key document in identifying system issues in the application of the YOA, particularly the inconsistent use of diversionary options across NSW. It found that while some LACs were making substantial use of YJC, the majority were under-utilising this option. Alongside other reviews of the YOA, the Noetic Report highlighted the need for a closer examination of how diversion is implemented in practice. Analysis of these documents provided essential contextual grounding for the research.

Another important source of official data was databases published by DCJ and JJ, allowing for quantitate comparative insights into police-referred and court-referred YJC trends. In addition, access was obtained to de-identified data from BOCSAR. This dataset included recorded crime statistics for persons of interest (POIs) 10–17, who were dealt by the NSW Police by way of warning, caution, YJC or referral to court—covering the period from 1998 to 2017, which was the most current data available at the time of data collection. BOCSAR later provided an updated dataset incorporating more recent trends extending to 2024. BOCSAR remains the most comprehensive and reliable source for tracking the use of diversionary measures by NSW Police since the YOA's introduction.

Together, these data sources enabled analysis of trends in police and court diversion practices, with particular attention to how frequently NSW Police employed diversionary options in line with the YOAs principle that court should be a last resort. These findings are integrated throughout the analysis chapters of this book.

Qualitative interviews

The book draws on qualitative research undertaken with criminal justice professionals considered the 'gatekeepers' to diversion under the YOA. The so-called 'gatekeepers' are involved in the diversionary decision-making processes that determine whether a young person is dealt with under the Act. These stakeholders are NSW Police representatives (n = 6), Magistrates of Children's Court (n = 13), youth justice personnel—including JJ and ALS representatives (n = 6). Thus, the total participating sample is n = 25. Interviews were semi-structured, involving a core set of questions that were asking about the participant's general experience in the criminal justice system before moving to specific questions relating to their experience towards diversion and with the diversion processes.

The qualitative information was subject to critical grounded theory and qualitative content analysis. Constructivist grounded theory emphasises interpretation and comparison, rejecting notions of emergence and objectivity (Mills et al., 2006). Four iterative coding stages initial, focused, axial and theoretical coding—allowed for multiple readings of data and identification of discursive themes (Charmaz, 2006). Initial coding involved line-by-line examination and labelling of patterns in official source materials and interviews. Focused coding categorised codes based on meaning and relationships to each other and other data, while contradictions and silences of codes were also noted. Axial coding, the third stage, identified 'central axes' (Saldaña, 2009, p. 115) and integrated categories into a theoretical framework. Theoretical coding collapsed categories with similar conditions and consequences into themes, reaching theoretical saturation when further analysis no longer produced new codes or data (see Phillips & Hardy, 2002; Saldaña, 2009). The relationships existing within themes, between and across narratives were fundamental in completing the next methodological stage, which was qualitative content analysis.

The focus of content analysis lies in examining the characteristics of language and communication, with particular attention on the content and contextual meaning of text (Hsieh & Shannon, 2005). Content analysis initially focused on quantifiable aspects of text (Titscher et al., 2000). Critics argued that this approach neglected unique text qualities and underlying contexts (Glaser & Laudel, 2013). Qualitative content analysis overcomes these limitations by examining hidden meanings, themes and patterns within the text (Zhang & Wildermuth, 2005). The study employed an interpretive qualitative content analysis, focusing on the meaning produced by text and the influences shaping diversionary decision-makers' interpretations of their social worlds. Texts are not isolated entities but rather products of cultural contexts that inform values guiding social life (Hesse-Biber & Leavy, 2011). This approach provides a deeper understanding of the reality being studied. In applying qualitative content analysis, each set of interview data was reviewed sentence by sentence to determine meaning. Data analysis began with repeated readings of the manuscripts to achieve immersion and understand the whole. Labels and codes emerged, reflecting multiple key ideas, which were sorted into categories based on relationships. Categories were used to organise group codes into meaningful topics. Relationships between topics were analysed for strength, direction and meaning to identify attitudes, values, motivations and tones within the data. Data were then segmented by topic, with each interview organised into major themes or categories. Meaningful themes related to decision-makers' perceptions of youth diversion, its concepts, importance and process. Theme and code matching, condensation and finalising were performed, collating in-depth information and accommodating diversity in experiences, attitudes and perceptions. Similar data analysis procedures were repeated across the three fields of study. Emerging themes between fields were compared, resulting in a list of finalised themes and sub-themes supported by verbatim data. This methodological approach enabled exploration of diversionary decision-making and identification of social/political, structural and institutional impediments to youth diversion in NSW.

Terminology

Diversion: For this research, 'diversion' refers to pre-court and court-initiated alternatives that divert young people away from the criminal justice system as legislated by the YOA, unless specified otherwise.

First Nations: This research primarily uses 'First Nations people' to refer to Aboriginal and Torres Strait Islander people. To maintain fidelity to the terminology used by original document authors, sources and research participants, specific terms such as 'Indigenous,' 'Aboriginal' and 'Aboriginal and Torres Strait Islander' are preserved in certain contexts or citations, reflecting nuanced language of the cited works.

Youth Justice/Juvenile Justice: At the time the research was conducted, the relevant department for children in the youth justice system was called Juvenile Justice (JJ). This term is used as it was the one used by the research participants. The department is now known as Youth Justice, a division of the Department of Communities and Justice (DCJ).

Young Offenders Act 1997 (NSW): In the book, the terms 'YOA,' 'legislation' and 'the Act' are used interchangeably to refer to the *Young Offenders Act 1997* (NSW).

Youth diversion: exploring criminal justice perspectives

The early chapters of this work provide a robust critical analysis of historical research and documentary material, contextualising diversion through a comprehensive historical overview of juvenile justice in Australia. This analysis traces the tensions between welfare and justice paradigms before extending to examine theories and practices of risk management and neoliberalism ideologies—particularly their emphasis on individual responsibilisation—characteristic of youth governance in the United Kingdom (UK), Australasia and North America. The later chapters focus primarily on the experiences and perspectives of experienced police officers, magistrates and youth justice personnel—the key discretionary decision-makers often referred to as 'gatekeepers' to youth diversion. Through qualitative interview analysis grounded in critical theoretical frameworks—colonisation processes and the historical configuration of criminal processing systems discussed in the earlier chapters—and contextualised within quantitative data, this work suggests that the success of diversion depends upon systematic change that, to some extent, entails an overhaul and rebuild of the youth justice system.

Chapter 2 examines different concepts and understandings of 'diversion' across various fields. The variability of meanings within different institutional contexts results in different aims for diverting young people across multiple domains. These aims can sometimes focus on crime prevention and early intervention, and at other times on sentencing options or alternative pathways for offenders to non-court institutions. As will be explained in this chapter, within this book, 'diversion' refers to pre-court and court-initiated alternatives away from the criminal justice system as legislated by the YOA. Within this context, diversion provides a process intended to minimise intervention and ensure the use of detention as a 'last resort.' Throughout the chapter, diversion is contextualised through a historical overview of the juvenile justice system in NSW—criminal law in Australia is the responsibility of individual states and territories, but they are many similarities across jurisdictions. This overview recognises the progression from punitive 'welfare-focused' responses for socially unacceptable behaviours during the first half of the 19th century, to an early form of diversion by the second half of the 19th century. This shift marked the beginning of progressive reforms in the criminal justice system, which increasingly differentiated children from adults. Such reforms laid the foundation for diversionary thinking, leading to the handling of children away from the adult system. This was achieved through the establishment of a separate court system specifically designed for young people with the aim of protecting them from the stigmatisation of the adult system. This period encapsulated the birth of the distinct concept of the 'young offender' and, more significantly, the dichotomy of welfare and justice that defines juvenile governance today. The existing tensions and overlaps between these paradigms are discussed throughout the account of juvenile policies and practices, up to the establishment of the YOA. It is within this context that consideration is given throughout this book to the role of NSW Police and magistrates as institutional decision-makers in youth justice governance. The role of discretion is of particular interest in determining whether a young person would or would not be processed under the YOA diversionary scheme, and if so, at what level—ranging from warnings or cautions to YJC referrals. A brief overview of international restorative conferencing practices in Aotearoa New Zealand, Northern Ireland and Canada offers a comparative perspective before concluding the chapter.

Chapter 3 addresses risk as a management and assessment tool that influences youth governance. It traces the tensions between welfare and justice paradigms. The governance of youth justice—especially within the UK, Australasia and North America—appears increasingly subsumed by concepts of 'risk' management. This chapter explores the theories and practices of risk management. It begins by contextualising 'risk' in contemporary society and then moves on to discuss the relationship between risk and neoliberalism—'a particular project designed by and developed by an increasingly transnational elite that has radically transformed the character of the spheres of economic, social and penal interventions' (Carrington et al., 2016, p. 15). Within this context, particular attention is given to the emphasis on individual responsibilisation in relation to crime. The chapter then advances to examine this issue specifically within the context of the YOA in NSW, exploring how 'risk management' and institutional cultures—including 'police culture(s)'—can result in certain groups being directed *into* the traditional criminal justice system rather than being diverted from it through the schemes of the Act. This failure to divert occurs in context-specific ways within the NSW Police Force and the NSW Children's Court, which are the primary focus of this book.

Chapter 4 analyses the significant role of the NSW Police Force in the decision-making process concerning the diversion of young people under the YOA. It draws on findings from interviews with YLOs and a youth policy officer, unveiling police perspectives on a range of issues. These include their motivations for becoming YLOs, their understanding of the role (both personally and as perceived by non-YLO officers such as general duties/arresting officers), their views on the strengths and weaknesses of the YOA, and their practices in implementing diversion under the Act. The analysis unveils internal police dynamics, including power conflict and disparities in knowledge and attitudes towards diversion between different groups within the police force. This chapter argues that, in this context, discretionary decision-making often serves to reproduce the norms and cultural tendencies of an organisation that leans towards conservatism, law enforcement and punitive practices. Drawing on critical ideas of police culture(s), the chapter shows how punitive discourses influence the arbitrary interpretation of legislation. In practice, the seriousness of the offence and the offender's history often outweigh the eligibility of the offence in the decision-making process. Similarly, occupational culture—such as a tendency to favour interventionist approaches—combined with punitive attitudes leads decision-makers to arbitrarily impose an informal cap on the YJC referrals, limiting them to a maximum of two (as a norm), despite no such restriction in the legislation. Building on the discussion of individual responsibilisation of young people in Chapter 3, this chapter demonstrates that the Act's admission of guilt requirement continues to undermine diversion. The findings show that the Protection Admission Scheme (PAS), recently introduced to overcome this issue, is viewed with scepticism and resistance by most police officers, and the scheme is rarely used. More significantly, it is argued that the overall resistance to the scheme stems from a police culture where the traditional value of an admission of guilt as evidence is protected at all costs. The chapter argues that policymakers while intending to protect young people are divorced from the realities of youth situations and the attitudes that young people encounter from police when they are brought into the station. Thus, rather than being used as a protective measure—and despite its other flaws, such as issues of due process—the PAS generates further hostility from police, who view it as something that undermines their role. Finally, by revealing the YLOs' frustration with the incoherence of the legislation—particularly regarding certain unwarranted offence exclusions that prevent the diversion of children in cases they consider appropriate—the chapter begins to highlight how these exclusions neglect children's welfare, are punitive in nature, and ultimately undermine the legislation's very own key principle of detention as a 'last resort.'

Chapter 5 focuses on judicial understandings, views and practices in relation to decision-making processes determining whether young people will be diverted under the YOA by the Children's Court. An analysis of interviews with specialist Children's Court magistrates, Local Court magistrates and the President of the Children's Court in NSW provides a judicial perspective that unveils magisterial thinking on matters of diversion. This chapter reveals that the NSW Children's Court magistrates are generally supportive of the use of YJC. However, objections discussed throughout the analysis place doubt on the readiness of the magistracy to *fully* embrace diversionary alternatives. The findings indicate that high expectations of diversionary practices and a focus on recidivism lead to reluctance regarding further referrals for young people. For instance, there is an unspoken arbitrary decision among most magistrates that, in most cases, a maximum of two YJC referrals per individual is acceptable. The findings show that YJC is perceived as a sentencing tool rather than a true alternative to diverting children away from the court system. Furthermore, the chapter highlights a city versus rural divide whereby justice modes of operation, as well as differences in training, education and resources, are factors that undermine diversion further in rural areas. It is also revealed that community expectations are at the forefront of judicial decision-making, and there is a general claim that communities view YJC as a 'soft' approach, in turn undermining the opportunity to divert young people. The findings on NSW judiciary perspectives also show that YJC referrals might be undermined by the perception that outcome plans (as part of the YJC) are not sufficiently demanding of young people. Finally, the magistracy also expressed frustration at the preclusion of numerous offences, considering it unwarranted and a direct barrier to diverting children in what they believe to be appropriate cases. Taken as a whole, this chapter demonstrates how commitment towards the ethos of the YOA—to divert children and young people away from the traditional court system—is at times difficult to maintain when other priorities take precedence.

Chapter 6 contributes to a deeper understanding of decision-making processes that determine whether young people are diverted under the YOA by incorporating the perspectives of youth justice personnel—namely Assistant Managers from JJ (who manage referrals to YJC) and solicitors from ALS. The findings in this chapter corroborate some of the concluding remarks in the previous two chapters. Interviews with youth justice personnel indicate that, although there is a general commitment to the Act among practitioners, resistance remains among police and some magistrates. The success of diversion in each LAC hinges on support for diversionary alternatives at the management level. Additionally, success depends on the attitudes and commitment of YLOs to the principles of YOA. However, with the competing interests of welfare and justice approaches once again forming the backdrop of decision-making, the findings suggest that some YLOs are less committed than others. The discussion in this chapter also suggests that localised approaches to diversion management by JJ result in varying levels of engagement with police and magistrates across different localities. Interviews indicate that consultation and information sharing are consistently identified as effective informal training tools through which JJ can advocate to the courts and NSW Police for diversionary alternatives. However, the strength of relationships between JJ and other institutional actors appears to vary across police LACs and court jurisdictions. As such, internal discussions aimed at strengthening these relationships are needed to maximise the use of diversion.

Chapter 7, the conclusion, synthesises the key themes and perspectives that have emerged throughout this book, addressing the overarching question of why there has been a failure to refer young people to diversion in NSW. Decision-making around diversionary alternatives by gatekeepers—namely, police and the judiciary—takes place within organisational microworlds (i.e., the internal structures, cultures and politics of institutions), which are themselves embedded in a broader macro-level social and political context. In an environment increasingly characterised by social control, individual responsibilisation, risk management, youth intervention and concerns about recidivism, the tension between punitivism and welfarism persists—ultimately hindering the use of diversion. The findings suggest that those responsible for making diversion decisions have internalised the institutional cultures, politics and practices of their respective organisations, and these are reproduced in their decision-making processes. Individual responsibilisation, risk-based strategies (with a focus on intervention) and punitive logics form a dominant backdrop to decision-making, shaping law and order responses. These dynamics undermine and contradict the principle of diversion and the notion of court as a last resort. The implementation of diversion is thus deeply embedded in a system of youth governance shaped by competing paradigms of welfarism and justice. The chapter concludes by discussing the theoretical and policy implications of these findings. It proposes an alternative approach to diversion in NSW and identifies directions for future research.

Note

1 Warnings were not examined in this study as the data were not deemed to be reliably recorded by NSW Police prior to January 2010. In addition, BOCSAR advice that while YJC and cautions under the YOA are often given instead of laying a formal charge and proceeding against the young person with a Court Appearance Notice, this is not the case with warnings. Therefore, warnings are not included when focusing on the use of the YOA.

References

Alder, C. (2000). Young women offenders and the challenge for restorative justice. In H. Strang & J. Braithwaite (Eds.), *Restorative justice: Philosophy to practice* (pp. 105–120). Ashgate.

Allard, T., Stewart, A., Chrzanowski, A., Ogilvie, J., Birks, D. J., & Little, S. (2010). *Police diversion of young offenders and Indigenous over-representations* (Trends and Issues in Crime and Criminal Justice, No. 390). Australian Institute of Criminology.

Amnesty International. (2018). *The sky is the limit: Keeping young children out of prison by raising the age of criminal responsibility*. Amnesty International. https://www.amnesty.org.au/wp-content/uploads/2018/09/The-Sky-is-the-Limit-FINAL-1.pdf

Australian Human Rights Commission. (2020). *Review of age of criminal responsibility*. https://humanrights.gov.au/sites/default/files/ahrc_20200226_submission_cag_working_group_macr.pdf

Australian Institute of Health and Welfare. (2017). *Youth justice in Australia 2015–2016*. (Bulletin 139. March 2017). Australian Government. https://www.aihw.gov.au/reports/youth-justice/youth-justice-in-australia-2015-16

Australian Institute of Health and Welfare. (2024). *Youth justice in Australia 2022–23*. https://www.aihw.gov.au/reports/youth-justice/youth-justice-in-australia-annual-report-2022-23

Australian Law Reform Commission. (1997). *Seen and heard: Priority for children in the legal process*. (Report No. 84). https://www.alrc.gov.au/wp-content/uploads/2019/08/ALRC84.pdf

Bail Act 1978 (NSW).

Bazemore, G. (1998). Crime victims and restorative justice in juvenile courts: Judges as obstacle or leader? *Western Criminology Review*, *1*(1), 1–36.

Bazemore, G., & Leip, L. (2000). Victim participation in the new juvenile court: Tracking judicial attitudes toward restorative justice reforms. *The Justice System Journal*, *21*(2), 199–226.

Borovski, A., & Murray, J. M. (1985). *Juvenile delinquency in Australia*. Methuen Australia.

Camilleri, P., Thomson, L., & McArthur, M. (2013). Needs or deeds? Child protection and youth justice in the Australian Capital Territory. *Journal of Social Welfare & Family Law*, *35*, 193–206.

Carrington, K. (1993). *Offending girls: Sex, youth and justice*. Allen and Unwin.

Carrington, K., Hogg, R., & Sozzo, M. (2016). Southern criminology. *British Journal of Criminology*, *56*(1), 1–20.
Chan, J. (1996). Changing police culture. *British Journal of Criminology*, *36*(1), 109–134.
Chan, J. B. L. (2005). *Reshaping Juvenile Justice: The NSW Young Offenders ACT 1997*. The Sydney Institute of Criminology.
Charmaz, K. (2006). *Constructing grounded theory: A practical guide through qualitative analysis*. Sage.
Children (Criminal Proceedings) Act 1987 (NSW).
Children and Young Persons (Care and Protection) Act 1998 (NSW).
Cohen, S. (1985). *Visions of social control: Crime, punishment and classification*. Polity Press.
Crofts, T. (2015). A brighter tomorrow: Raise the age of criminal responsibility. *Current Issues in Criminal Justice*, *27*(1), 123–131.
Crofts, T. (2018). Prosecuting child offenders: Factors relevant to rebutting the presumption of 'doli incapax'. *The Sydney Law Review*, *40*(3), 339–365.
Crofts, T. (2022). Act now: Raise the minimum age of criminal responsibility. *Current Issues in Criminal Justice*, 118–138. https://www.tandfonline.com/doi/full/10.1080/10345329.2022.2139892
Cunneen, C. (1997). Community conferencing and the fiction of Indigenous control. *The Australian and New Zealand Journal of Criminology*, *30*, 292–311.
Cunneen, C. (2001). *Conflict, politics and crime: Aboriginal communities and the police*. Allen & Urwin.
Cunneen, C. (2008a). Understanding restorative justice through the lens of critical criminology. In T. Anthony & C. Cunneen (Eds.), *The critical criminology companion* (pp. 290–302). Hawkins Press.
Cunneen, C. (2008b). Changing neo-colonial impacts of juvenile justice. *Current Issues in Criminal Justice*, *20*(1), 43–58.
Cunneen, C. (2011). State crime, the colonial question and indigenous peoples. In A. Smuelers & R. Haveman (Eds.), *Supranational criminology: Towards a criminology of international crimes* (pp. 159–180). Intersentia Press.
Cunneen, C. (2020). *Arguments for raising the minimum age of criminal responsibility*. Jumbunna Institute for Indigenous Education and Research, University of Technology.
Cunneen, C., Luke, G., & Ralph, N. (2006). *Evaluation of the Aboriginal over-representation strategy report to the NSW Department of Juvenile Justice Sydney*. Institute of Criminology University of Sydney Law School.
Cunneen, C., Russel, S., & Schwartz, M. (2021). Principles of diversion of Aboriginal and Torres Strait Islander young people from the criminal jurisdiction. *Current Issues in Criminal Justice*, *33*(2), 170–190. https://www.tandfonline.com/doi/abs/10.1080/10345329.2020.1813386
DeKeseredy, W. S., & Dragiewicz, M. (1996). *Contemporary criminology*. Wadsworth.
DeKeseredy, W. S., & Dragiewicz, M. (2011). Introduction, critical criminology: Past, present, and future. In *Routledge handbook of critical criminology* (pp. 1–8). Taylor and Francis.
Delahunty, B. (1998). Taking 'kiddie cops' and 'care bears' seriously. *Alternative Law Journal*, *23*(1), 13–18.
Durivage, A., Barrete, J., Montcalm, L., & Laberge, M. (1992). Analysis of organizational culture: The key to strategic planning. *Canadian Police College Journal*, *16*(2), 94–134.
Feeley, M., & Simon, J. (1994). Actuarial justice: The emerging new criminal law. In D. Nelken (Ed.), *The futures of criminology* (pp. 173–201). Sage.
Fitz-Gibbon, K., & O'Brien, W. (2019). A child's capacity to commit crime: Examining the operation of doli incapax in Victoria (Australia). *International Journal for Crime, Justice and Social Democracy*, *8*(1), 18–33. https://www.crimejusticejournal.com/article/view/1047

Friedrichs, D. O. (2009). Critical criminology. In J. M. Miller (Ed.), *21st century criminology: A reference handbook* (Vol. 1, pp. 210–218). Sage.

Glaser, J., & Laudel, G. (2013). Life with and without coding: Two methods of early stage data analysis in theory-guided qualitative research aiming at causal explanations. *Forum: Qualitative Social Research, 14*(2). https://doi.org/10.17169/fqs-14.2.1886

Goldsmith, A. (1990). Taking police culture seriously: Police discretion and the limits of the law. *Policing and Society, 1*(2), 91–114.

Goldson, B. (2013). "Unsafe, unjust and harmful to wider society": Grounds for raising the minimum age of criminal responsibility in England and Wales. *Youth Justice: An International Journal, 13*(2), 111–130.

Graham, J., & Moore, C. (2006). Beyond welfare versus justice: Justice in England and Wales. In J. Junger-Tas & S. H. Decker (Eds.), *International handbook of juvenile justice* (pp. 65–92). Springer Science and Business Media.

Hennessy, N. (1999). *Review of gatekeeping role in Young Offenders Act 1997 (NSW)*. Report to Youth Justice Advisory Committee.

Hesse-Biber, S., & Leavy, P. (2011). *The practice of qualitative research* (2nd ed.). Sage.

Hogg, R., & Brown, D. B. (1998). *Rethinking law and order*. Pluto Press.

House of Representatives Standing Committee on Aboriginal and Torres Strait Islander Affairs. (2011). *Doing time – Time for doing: Indigenous youth in the criminal justice system* (Report). Parliament of Australia. https://www.aph.gov.au/binaries/house/committee/atsia/sentencing/report/fullreport.pdf

Hsieh, H., & Shannon, S. E. (2005). Three approaches to qualitative content analysis. *Qualitative Health Research, 15*(9), 1277–1288.

Keith, M. (1993). From punishment to discipline. In M. Cross & M. Keith (Eds.), *Racism: the city and the state* (pp. 193–209). Routledge.

Law Council of Australia. (2020). *Council of attorneys general – Age of criminal responsibility working group review*. https://lawcouncil.au/resources/submissions/council-of-attorneys-general-age-of-criminal-responsibility-working-group-review

Marinos, V., & Innocente, N. (2008). Factors influencing police attitudes towards extrajudicial measures under the Youth Criminal Justice Act. *Canadian Journal of Criminology and Criminal Justice, 50*(4), 469–489.

McAra, L., & McVie, S. (2007). Youth justice? The impact of system contact on patterns of desistance from offending. *European Journal of Criminology, 4*, 315–345.

Mills, J., Bonner, A., & Francis, K. (2006). The development of constructivist grounded theory. *International Journal of Qualitative Methods, 5*(1), 25–35.

Naudé, B., & Prinsloo, J. (2005). Magistrates' and prosecutors' views of restorative justice. In T. Maepa (Ed.), *Beyond retribution: Prospects for restorative justice in South Africa* (pp. 53–65). Institute for Security Studies.

Noetic Solutions. (2010). *A strategic review of the New South Wales juvenile justice system: Report for the Minister for Juvenile Justice*. New South Wales Department of Human Services.

NSW Law Reform Commission. (2012). *People with cognitive and mental health impairments in the criminal justice system: Diversion* (135). NSW Law Reform Commission. https://lawreform.nsw.gov.au/documents/Publications/Reports/Report-135.pdf

NSW Law Reform Commission. (2013). *People with cognitive and mental impairments in the criminal justice system: Criminal responsibilities and consequences* (138). NSW Law Reform Commission. https://lawreform.nsw.gov.au/documents/Publications/Consultation-Papers/CP06.pdf

Papalia, N., Sheperd, S. M., Spivak, B., Luebbers, S., Shea, D. E., & Fullam, R. (2019). Disparities in criminal justice system responses to first-time juvenile offenders according to Indigenous status. *Criminal Justice and Behaviour, 46*(8), 1067–1087.

Pearce, E. (2025). Australia's push to raise the minimum age of criminal responsibility: Is 12 years old enough? In G. Martin & E. Pearce (Eds.), *Research handbook on youth criminology* (pp. 298–323). Edward Elgar Publishing.

Phillips, N., & Hardy, C. (2002). *Discourse analyses: Investigating processes of social construction*. SAGE.
Richards, K. (2005). Cause and effect? Failings of the contemporary penal system and the emergence of restorative justice. In J. Gaffey, A. Possamai-Inesedy, & K. Richards (Eds.), *The chameleon and the quilt: A cross-disciplinary exploration in the social sciences* (pp. 44–54). University of Western Sydney.
Richards, K. (2006). Not directly to blame? Considering the role of parental responsibility in the emergence of restorative justice practices for juveniles. In W. Tie, S. Jülich, & V. Waters (Eds.), *New frontiers in restorative justice: A reviewed selection of conference papers*. Centre for Justice and Peace Development, School of Social and Cultural Studies, Massey University.
Richards, K. (2010a). Police-referred restorative justice for juveniles in Australia. *Current Issues in Criminal Justice, 398*, 1–8.
Richards, K. (2010b). Restorative justice and "Empowerment": Producing and governing active subjects through "Empowering" practices. *Critical Criminology, 19*(2), 91–105.
Richards, K. (2014). A promise and a possibility: The limitation of the traditional criminal justice system as an explanation for the emergence of restorative justice. *Restorative Justice: An International Journal, 2*(2), 124–141.
Richards, K., Bartels, L., & Bolitho, J. (2017). Children's court magistrates' views of restorative justice and therapeutic jurisprudence measures for young offenders. *Youth Justice, 17*(1), 22–40.
Royal Commission into Aboriginal Deaths in Custody, & Jonhston, E. (1991). *National report*. Australian Government Publishing Service. https://www.naa.gov.au/sites/default/files/2020-06/research-guide-aboriginal-deaths-in-custody_0.pdf
Saldaña, J. (2009). *Discursive analysis: The sociolinguistic analysis of natural language*. Basil Blackwell.
Seymour, J. (1997). Children's Courts in Australia: Their current role and functions. In A. Borovski & I. O'Connor (Eds.), *Juvenile crime, justice and corrections* (pp. 292–306). Longman.
Seymour, J. (1998). *Dealing with juvenile offenders*. Law Book Company.
Shafiq, N., Ohlsson, I., & Mathias, P. (2016). Predictors of punitive attitudes among police officers. *Journal of Forensic Practice, 18*(1), 76–86.
Sheehan, R., & Borowski, A. (Eds.). (2013). *Australia's children's court today and tomorrow*. Springer.
Spiranovic, C., Clare, J., Bartels, L., Clare, M., & Clare, B. (2015). Aboriginal young people in the children's court of Western Australia: Findings from the national assessment of Australian children's courts. *University of Western Australia Law Review, 38*(2), 86–116.
Stephens, M. (2007). Lessons from the front line in Canada's restorative justice experiment: The experience of sentencing judges. *Queen's Law Journal, 33*, 19–78.
Stubbs, J. (2008). Critical criminological research. In T. Anthony & C. Cunneen (Eds.), *The critical criminology companion*. Hawkins Press.
Stubbs, J. (2010). Re-examining bail and remand for young people in NSW. *Australian and New Zealand Journal of Criminology, 43*(3), 485–505.
Taylor, N. (2009). *Juveniles in detention in Australia, 1981–2007*. Monitoring reports no. 5. Australian Institute of Criminology. https://www.aic.gov.au/publications/mr/mr5
Tilbury, C., & Mazerolle, P. (2013). The children's court in Queensland: Where to from here? In R. Sheehan & A. Borovski (Eds.), *Australia's children's courts today and tomorrow* Springer.
Titscher, S., Meyer, M., Wodak, R., & Vetter, E. (2000). *Methods of text discourse analysis*. Sage.
United Nations. (November 20, 1989). *United Nations Convention on the Rights of the Child* (UNCRC). https://www.unicef.org.au/united-nations-convention-on-the-rights-of-the-child

United Nations Committee on the Rights of the Child. (2012). *General comment no. 84 (a) on Concluding Observations: Australia*. https://www.refworld.org/document-sources/un-committee-rights-child-crc

United Nations Committee on the Rights of the Child. (2019). *General comment no. 24 (2019) on Children's Rights in the Child Justice System*. https://www.ohchr.org/en/documents/general-comments-and-recommendations/general-comment-no-24-2019-childrens-rights-child

United Nations General Assembly. (1985). *United Nations Standard Minimum Rules for the Administration of Juvenile Justice ("The Beijing Rules"): Resolution/Adopted by the General Assembly* (A/RES/40/33). http://www.refworld.org/docid/3b00f2203c.html

Van der Laan, P. H. (2006). Just desert and welfare: Juvenile justice in the Netherlands. In J. Junger-Tas & S. H. Decker (Eds.), *International handbook of juvenile justice* (pp. 145–170). Springer Science and Business Media.

White, R. (1997). Police practices, punishment and juvenile crime prevention. In A. Borovski & I. O'Connor (Eds.), *Juvenile crime, justice and corrections* (pp. 254–269). Addison Wesley Longman.

White, R. (1998). Contemporary comments: Hassle-free policing and the creation of community space. *Current Issues in Criminal Justice*, *9*(3), 312–324.

White, R. (2009). Ethnic diversity and differential policing in Australia: The good, the bad and the ugly. *Journal of International Migration and Integration*, *10*(4), 359–375.

Woods, J. (2008, November). *Report of the Special Commission of Inquiry into Child Protection Services in NSW*. NSW Department of Premier and Cabinet.

Young Offenders Act 1997 (NSW).

Zhang, Y., & Wildermuth, B. M. (2005). Qualitative analysis of content. *Analysis*, *1*(2), 1–12.

2 Juvenile Justice and the Aims of Diversion

Introduction

Research on diversionary decision-making must recognise the multifarious understandings of diversion. This conceptual ambiguity creates significantly different aims across social and institutional contexts. Diversion operates at various levels: as crime prevention, diversionary scheme, sentencing option, or alternative pathway steering offenders from court, custody, criminal justice systems, or reoffending (Richards, 2014, p. 6). Sometimes diversion combines crime prevention and early intervention strategies. Diversion is contextualised across multiple domains, serving multiple aims. This complexity means existing evidence is often limited, incomplete, contradictory and ambiguous, addressing varying interpretations. This has significant implications for justifying diversionary schemes and evaluating their effects.

This chapter addresses these implications by first examining the historical context of youth justice in Australia, with a specific focus on NSW. The governance of young people is traced back to the early colonial government's engagement with welfare policies. This discussion reveals that colonial welfare practices and policies have been—and continue to be—instrumental in the criminalisation of First Nations young people and their over-representation in the criminal justice system. The historical narrative then traces the first example of diversion to the separation of children from adults in the criminal justice system, through the establishment of the Children's Court in NSW in 1905. This development signalled the birth of a distinct 'young offender' category. The new legal regime for youth was justified by recognising children's immaturity and vulnerability, warranting a distinct criminal process from that of adults. Even at the height of the welfare model's influence, justice elements were never fully abandoned, with the Children's Court retaining features of the adult court system. This chapter demonstrates that Australia's juvenile justice system represents a hybrid of welfare and justice principles, never fitting exclusively into either category. The fallacy of assuming a strict dichotomy between these models becomes apparent as the chapter examines further developments leading to the current legislative framework for youth justice conferencing (YJC): the YOA. Finally, in alignment with the core focus of

DOI: 10.4324/9781003470366-2

this book, the chapter discusses the roles of police and magistrates as key actors within the politics of diversionary discretion and decision-making that control access to YJC.

The ambiguities around 'diversion'

The importance of diversion for young people in conflict with the law is emphasised by several international legal frameworks. In accordance with the UNCRC and The Beijing Rules, Australia's juvenile justice system—which addresses youth in conflict with the law—is underpinned by the requirement to treat children and young people with greater leniency than adults. It also seeks to divert them from formal criminal justice processes wherever possible (Cashmore, 2013; Richards, 2011b). This approach is also adopted in other jurisdictions, such as the US, the UK, Canada and New Zealand, reflecting a global trend towards rehabilitative, restorative practices and the consideration of detention as a *last resort*. However, the legal force of United Nations conventions, international law and human rights remains uncertain—particularly in Australia. Without a Bill of Rights, Australia lacks an enforceable charter of rights (Kirby, 1999).

International law significantly influences the development of both common law and constitutional law in Australia (Kirby, 1999). Consequently, the importance of diversion for young people in conflict with the law—as emphasised by international law—is evident in Australia's youth governance. At the federal level, this emphasis on diversion is reflected in the National Youth Policing Model (Attorney-General's Department, 2010), the Juvenile Justice Standards (Australasian Juvenile Justice Administrators, 2009) and the Principles of Youth Justice in Australia (Australasian Juvenile Justice Administrators, 2014). At the state and territory levels, each jurisdiction's juvenile justice system theoretically emphasises diversion, either through legislation or through policy (AIHW, 2024; Jordan & Farrell, 2013). In youth justice, 'diversion is omnipresent' (Richards, 2014, p. 9). While specific schemes receive attention, the concept itself receives little scrutiny, resulting in conceptual ambiguity (Richards, 2014). Nejelski (1976, p. 394) emphasised that overuse has made the term 'a coin of debased value.' Richards (2014) argues diversion is amorphous, taking different meanings depending on context and institutional actors.

Kelly and Armitage (2015) identify five understandings: diversion from crime; into alternative services; from the youth justice system; from custody; and from prosecution or court proceedings. Each carries ambiguities. For example, diverting from the youth justice system depends on how boundaries are defined, while 'diversion from crime' depends on where 'interventions sit within the broader landscape of support provisions' (Phoenix & Kelly, 2013, p. 117). Richards (2014) further notes that diversion operates at three levels: crime prevention strategies, diversionary schemes and sentencing options. It encompasses varied aims, making it unclear what young people are being diverted from—and towards. Sometimes diversion means pathways from court to non-court institutions, community services or treatment programs. Other times, it refers to diversion from court, custody, the criminal justice system, or reoffending. Although literature often refers to crime prevention and early intervention, diversion spans multiple domains with varied meanings.

The conceptual confusion over whether diversion refers to diverting away from the criminal justice system or away from offending itself is evident in both local and international contexts. Almost all actors interpret diversion differently, which in turn affects how diversion schemes are justified and how their effects are evaluated (Richards, 2014). As Richards argues, 'the ill-defined ethos of "diversion" is used to legitimise criminal justice measures that seek more and less intervention in young people's lives' (2014, p. 4). Consequently, evidence on diversion remains limited, incomplete, contradictory and ambiguous.

In Scotland, McAra and McVie (2007, p. 183) argue policymakers have selectively drawn on 'what works' and 'risk factors paradigms,' leading to 'a reconfiguration of power between key elites and a recasting of system ethos into a somewhat conflicted and contradictory set of rationalities' (McAra & McVie, 2010, p. 184). This approach overlooks that young people involved in serious offending are often the most victimised and vulnerable. Their study found prior system contact was the strongest predictor of future offending, concluding youth justice should 'maximise diversion wherever possible' as diversion fosters desistance (2010, p. 202).

In contrast, Australian research by Weatherburn et al. (2012) on diversion towards restorative justice processes suggests limited evidence of positive recidivism impacts. They argue there's no evidence of stigmatising and labelling effects from court systems. Rather than advocating a *hands-off approach*, they recommend risk-based diversion to treatment programs using existing risk tools—prior system contact, gender, age at first contact, and offending-related factors. This model differs from diversion away from the system, as such risk-based diversion would 'undoubtedly increase the number of young offenders coming before the Children's Court' (Weatherburn et al., 2012, p. 808).

Using recidivism rates to measure diversion effectiveness is problematic for two reasons. Firstly, the positivistic approach places undue burden on diversion schemes to demonstrate reduced recidivism despite difficulty producing such evidence, fuelling scepticism. Secondly, demanding concrete proof of stigmatising effects while claiming objectivity has real-world consequences for public and political diversion support. Moreover, focusing on recidivism shifts attention from protecting young people from the traditional justice system's criminogenic effects. Ultimately, diversion should prioritise steering young people away from traditional justice harms.

Jordan and Farrell (2013, cited in Richards 2014) draw on labelling theory and the youth justice system's capacity to stigmatise young people. They advocate for robust systems directing young offenders away from adverse criminal justice outcomes like custodial sentences, emphasising diversion away from the system rather than offending itself. While offending often leads to criminal justice contact, certain groups encounter the system not through continual offending but because they're highly visible to police and justice agencies, resulting in greater scrutiny (Richards, 2014). Evidence supports this for First Nations young people

(Blagg et al., 2005; Cunneen, 2008b), young people on bail (Richards & Renshaw, 2013), and those from sex and gender diverse communities (Dwyer, 2011). Richards (2014) argues that while connections exist between offending and system contact, it's more nuanced than some authors suggest (e.g. Weatherburn et al., 2012). Distinguishing between diversion from the criminal justice system and diversion from offending is crucial for understanding diversion's aims and applications (Richards, 2014).

This distinction is vital because diversion from the criminal justice system focuses on minimising criminogenic effects of contact, while diversion from offending targets behavioural change and structural factors influencing system involvement (Richards, 2014). These different aims produce distinct responses: diversion from the system advocates less intrusive intervention, whereas diversion from offending calls for more intensive measures (Richards, 2014). *Real diversion* should prioritise steering young people away from the criminal justice system, particularly from custody, prosecution and court—this should be its core meaning.

These issues highlight diversion's inherent complexities. The rise of restorative practices and diversion has coincided with neoliberal governance in contemporary Australia (Cunneen, 2012), marked by an increasing emphasis on individual responsibility, accountability and risk management in youth justice responses (Cunneen, 2012; Muncie, 2006). Simultaneously, traditional welfare notions have evolved into mechanisms of classification, control and coercion (Muncie, 2006). Responsibility and accountability have shifted from social structures to individuals, families and communities (Cunneen, 2012). Through 'governing at a distance,' responsibilisation transfers from state to community-based and non-state actors (Garland, 1996). Diversion aligns with this politicisation and responsibilisation demands. In YJC, victims, offenders and communities become co-responsible for crime control. Diversion supports neoliberal values by promoting self-help and individual responsibility.

In the neoliberal regime, privatisation of crime control services, rising inequalities and fears related to terrorism, illegal immigration and moral panics surrounding race, religion and ethnicity have impacted criminal justice systems. Demands for authoritarian 'law and order' responses have prioritised deterrence and incapacitation, intensifying punishment. This trend has occurred alongside the introduction of diversion and restorative justice practices. Consequently, restorative justice elements (such as diversion), retribution, just deserts, rehabilitation and incapacitation now operate concurrently.

The focus on predicting risk has increased reliance on techniques for identifying, classifying and managing citizens (Feeley & Simon, 1994), resulting in incapacitation policies for those deemed *most* dangerous. Risk assessment becomes a tool for dividing populations. In diversion contexts, such techniques segregate individuals who benefit from diversion from those channelled into punitive processes like incapacitation (Cunneen, 2012). These issues, discussed further in Chapter 3, are pertinent to conceptual contestation around diversion, providing context for differing perspectives among criminal justice practitioners and their interpretations of what diversion entails.

Within this book, 'diversion' refers to pre-court and court-initiated alternatives away from the criminal justice system as legislated by the YOA. This process aims to minimise intervention and use detention as a last resort. Diversion from formal criminal justice benefits young people because:

- Young people should be treated differently to adults
- Diversion can incorporate restorative justice approaches
- Minimising detention contact aligns with international human rights frameworks
- Diversion addresses offenders' needs without stigmatising and criminalising
- Diversion reduces further court system contact, lowering detention risk
- Most young people naturally grow out of crime

Young people should be treated differently due to limited life experience, maturity and responsiveness to positive interventions (Richards & Lee, 2013). While crime is committed disproportionately by young people, offending peaks at ages 18–19—when individuals are no longer legally juveniles (Richards, 2011b). Most importantly, only a small proportion continue offending into adulthood (Skardhamar, 2009). Thus, 'left to their own devices, most juveniles grow out of crime…juvenile crime is for the most part transient and self-limiting' (Richards & Lee, 2013, p. 849).

Furthermore, brain development research shows decision-making competence doesn't fully develop until the second decade, with peer influence significantly impacting adolescent risk-taking (Steinberg, 2005). Young people generally commit less serious, more property-related offences, tend to be less experienced, offend in groups and public spaces and act unplanned and opportunistically—factors increasing vulnerability and detection risk (Cunneen & White, 2007; Richards, 2011a). Additionally, due to immaturity and peer reliance, young people face heightened risks including mental health challenges, substance use, peer pressure and victimisation by adults and peers (Richards, 2011b; Finkelhor & Hashima, 2001). Their over-representation as victims is critical, as victimisation is a well-established pathway into offending. Diversionary measures are premised on the belief in giving deserving individuals a second chance, while ensuring proportionality and participation in the criminal justice process, as reflected in UN youth justice frameworks (UNCRC, 1989; United Nations General Assembly, 1985 ("The Beijing Rules")). Restorative justice recognises children's vulnerability, especially with authority figures such as police and magistrates (Richards & Lee, 2013). Diversion holds young people accountable while providing opportunities for child, family and community involvement in decisions affecting their lives (Richards & Lee, 2013). In contrast, Court contact increases the likelihood of further criminal system involvement. Vulnerable groups—sex and gender diverse youth (Dwyer, 2011), those on bail or in out-of-home care (McAra & McVie, 2007), rural youth and First Nations young people—are particularly susceptible (Richards & Renshaw, 2013). This entanglement often stems from increased scrutiny once they're known to the system rather than reoffending (McAra & McVie, 2007; Richards & Lee, 2013). For instance, technical bail breaches can lead to increased surveillance and recorded offences that might otherwise go unnoticed. Young people in out-of-home care are especially vulnerable, as staff often lack skills to manage challenging behaviours and rely on police intervention. Diversion prevents detention, sentencing or remand, reducing court contact and incarceration risk (Richards & Lee, 2013).

Research shows prior charges are the strongest predictor of future police charges. Cross-national studies found increased sanctions have little deterrence effect and may worsen outcomes (Huizinga et al., 2004). McAra and McVie's (2007) study of 4300 Edinburgh youth revealed that individuals with prior charges were over seven times more likely to be charged at age 15—regardless of current serious offending involvement. Prolonged court involvement adversely affects family relationships, education and employment opportunities, and increases detention risk (Carrington & Pereira, 2009).

The effects of detention are notably harmful (DeLisi et al., 2011; Gatti et al., 2009). Imprisonment is widely recognised as fostering further criminal behaviour through peer interactions—an effect amplified in young people due to their immaturity and susceptibility to peer pressure (Richards, 2011b). Detention also negatively affects young people's mental and physical health, increasing the risk of depression, self-harm and suicide (Holman & Zeidenberg, 2006).

Additionally, research shows that many young people who experience youth detention later end up in adult prisons. In Australia, a 2010 survey found that 22% of adult entrants had previously been in youth detention, with half having been detained at least three times (AIHW, 2011). A longitudinal study by Gatti et al. (2009) of children born in Canada in 1984 also found that contact with the juvenile justice system increased the likelihood of adult criminal justice involvement by a factor of seven, with more intense interventions leading to more severe long-term consequences. These findings highlight the criminogenic effects of detention and emphasise the importance of minimising intervention, reserving detention as a *last resort*.

Diversion reduces young people's contact with the courts and thereby their risk of detention. As discussed, this approach aligns with international human rights principles, such as those outlined in The Beijing Rules (1985) and UNCRC (1989), to which Australia is a signatory. As a form of restorative justice, diversion promotes accountability, empowerment, participation and voice, while limiting contact with the criminal justice system. Rather than a reductionist approach, diversion reflects a normative stance on how society should respond to young people in conflict with the law (Richards & Lee, 2013). It considers factors such as vulnerability, age, maturity and cultural background (Richards & Lee, 2013). Accordingly, and as reflected in the principles of the YOA, diversion from the formal justice system is considered optimal for young people. To understand the origins of these principles, a historical overview of the juvenile system in NSW is now necessary.

Origins of 'diversion': juvenile justice and diversion in New South Wales

The governance of children in the criminal justice system has been shaped by profound beliefs about the state's responsibility to act in the 'best interests of the child' (Cunneen & White, 2007; Fernandez et al., 2014; Muncie, 2008; Sheehan, 2001;

Sullivan, 1993). These beliefs have emerged from broader social, political and economic developments (Coppins et al., 2011; Cunneen & White, 2007; Day, 2011; Fernandez et al., 2014; Seymour, 1997).

Australia's approach to governing children and young people has varied across time (Picton & Boss, 1981; Swain, 2014). Following the gold rush era, economic and demographic changes increased the visibility of children, particularly in urban centres (Scott & Swain, 2002). This period marked the beginning of the Australian colonial government's involvement in child welfare. However, for First Nations children, the colonial experience was markedly different. A central feature of colonisation was the so-called civilising mission, which involved the forced removal of First Nations children from their families and communities (Cunneen, 2011). As Cunneen (2011, p. 164) notes, 'the Australian removal policies rested on specific assumptions about race, "blood" and racial hygiene.'

Throughout much of the 20th century, First Nations people were constructed as dangerous, justifying regulatory regimes targeting them (Carrington, 2011). These regimes were enforced through immigration restrictions, protection Acts for First Nations people and child welfare measures, creating new criminality based on racial and exclusionary criteria (Carrington, 2011). The aim was to cleanse the social body of perceived contaminating influences and protect it from non-British elements. Under penal welfarism, justice institutions focused on the young person's character and family background rather than the offence (Carrington, 2011). This blurred the line between delinquency and neglect, turning the 'problem child' into an instrument for social control over non-normative families, particularly First Nations communities (Carrington, 2011, p. 33).

Deficit discourses enable social control through punishment and institutionalisation of those deemed unruly or unwanted (Carrington, 2011). These narratives construct non-normative populations as 'the Other,' overlooking colonialism's impacts, social background, inequities and exclusion forms that may influence young people's behaviour. Instead, the delinquent or neglected child is seen as symptomatic of deficits 'attributable to a maladjusted childhood, dysfunctional family, deficiencies of character or poor social background' (Carrington, 2011, p. 34).

The first half of the 19th century was marked by colonial efforts to intervene in the lives of children deemed at 'risk and a potential risk in their current situations' (Swain, 2014, p. 6). The removal of First Nations children—particularly those of mixed-blood parentage—was justified under this rationale, ostensibly for their protection and in the national interest (Carrington, 2011). In 1997, the National Inquiry into the Separation of Aboriginal and Torres Strait Islander Children from their Families (NISATSIC) found that most First Nations families continue to suffer the intergenerational effects of these removals. Today's disproportionately high incarceration rates of First Nations children reflect a systemic denial of Indigenous human rights (Cunneen & Libesman, 2000).

Although legislation allowing removals based solely on race was eventually repealed, new child welfare policies enabled continued interventions based on the so-called expert knowledge (Carrington, 2011, p. 35). These targeted destitute children in public spaces, those picked up under vagrancy provisions and incarcerated youth (Swain, 2014). Children living in socially unacceptable conditions were institutionalised in orphanages and asylums (Sheehan, 2013). Often, concern for the child was either not genuine or secondary to fears about social disorder. The *child-saving* welfare philosophy targeted impoverished children—particularly unsupervised children aged 2–16—who were seen as threats by respectable classes (Scott & Swain, 2002) and labelled 'original sinners' (Cunningham, 1995, p. 134).

Governance of First Nations youth was gendered and especially harsh for girls (Carrington & Pereira, 2009; Goodall, 1990). Girls were seen as subjects of moral reform and committed to institutions where they trained as domestic servants (Carrington & Pereira, 2009). Against bio-eugenicist ideology aimed at preserving Australia's white British purity, fears of interracial contamination led to disproportionate institutionalisation of First Nations girls (Carrington, 2011).

As Carrington and Pereira (2009, p. 2) observe, 'the punishment of children for non-criminal conduct under status or welfare offences, such as uncontrollable or exposed to moral danger, permitted the criminalization of immorality, poverty and cultural differences.' First Nations children were especially targeted. Extra-judicial welfare agencies had broad powers to sexualise girls' behaviour, remove children based on race, punish impoverished families and single parents and treat abused children as delinquents (Carrington, 1993). By linking coercive welfare assistance with punishment, penal welfarism drove disadvantaged, neglected and abused children from institutionalised care into juvenile detention for non-criminal behaviour (Carrington, 1993; Carrington & Pereira, 2009; O'Connor, 1997). Welfarism thus criminalised disadvantage through institutionalisation.

Australia's first legal recognition of the need to treat children differently from adults came with the *Juvenile Offender Act 1850* (14Vic No11) (Blackmore, 1989). The Act aimed to expedite trials for children and mitigate the harm of long-term imprisonment (Blackmore, 1989; Johnstone, 2014). Magistrates were granted broad sentencing discretion, including the power to sentence children under 14 years old for simple larceny to up to 'three-month imprisonment, or a fine of three pounds or dismissal on finding sureties for good behaviour' (Blackmore, 1989, p. 6). Despite these provisions, the law at the time remained markedly punitive.

In 1866, the *Reformatory School Act* (30Vic No IV) introduced alternatives to prisons through the establishment of reformatory schools, while the *Destitute Children Act 1866* (30Vic No11) enabled the provision of private and public industrial schools for the institutionalisation of vagrant and destitute children (Blackmore, 1989). These reforms were seen as a form of diversion, enabling the separation between two identifiable categories of children needing governance: 'those who were neglected, orphaned or vagrant, and those who were young offenders' (Blackmore, 1989, p. 6). In practice, however, these categories often overlapped, with poverty and orphanhood effectively criminalised through institutionalisation.

These developments mirrored legislative changes in England, where Parliament formally recognised juvenile delinquency as a distinct social phenomenon (Goldson, 2004; Hendrick, 2015; May, 1973). Key factors shaped the political context: compulsory education for 'dangerous classes,' fears of 'untutored savages'

(Lord Ashley, cited in Cunningham, 1991, p. 97) and social theories distinguishing childhood from youth (Hendrick, 2003). Central was whether children should be conceptualised as victims needing protection or threats to social order requiring control. Additionally, moral conceptions of need proclaimed that prisons had failed to obtain willing obedience—necessary for social stability and working-class compliance (Hendrick, 2015).

These trends marked early criminal justice reform, increasingly recognising the need to treat children differently from adults. Most significantly, these reforms emphasised age as key in penal justice and began 'to yield a structure of institutionalised surveillance and control' (Hendrick, 2015, p. 6), focused more on maintaining social equilibrium than addressing crime (Hendrick, 2015). This invested new meanings into crime and delinquency concepts, shaping juvenile justice attitudes ever since. These reforms laid the groundwork for diversionary thought and Children's Courts' creation.

The Children's Court—a historical overview

According to Polk (1993), Australia's earliest diversionary practices for juvenile offenders emerged in the late 19th century with the establishment of a distinct court system for young people. Although markedly different from contemporary practices, these early efforts marked the genesis of diversion as a concept.

In Australia, juvenile justice falls under the jurisdiction of individual states and territories, resulting in legislative and systemic variation across regions. The first Children's Court was established in South Australia in 1895 to address minor offences (Daly, 1999; Sheehan, 2013). In NSW, the first Children's Court was founded in 1905 under the *Neglected Children's and Juvenile Offenders Act 1905* (NSW) (Blackmore, 1989; Fernandez et al., 2013, 2014). Aimed at protecting children from the stigmatisation of the adult criminal justice system, discrete closed courts with two *specialist* magistrates were established in Sydney, Newcastle, Parramatta, Burwood and Broken Hill (Blackmore, 1989; Johnstone, 2014). In NSW, the Children's Court held jurisdiction over both care and protection matters and criminal cases (Crawford, 2005; Fernandez et al., 2014).

The approach was rooted in a welfare system or *needs-based* model (Bernard, 1992), recognising psychosocial factors contributing to child offending and children's capacity for reform and rehabilitation (Seymour, 1997, 1998; Wundersitz, 2000). These developments must be understood within the broader evolution of how *young offenders* have been conceptualised. The notion of the *juvenile offender* is relatively recent, emerging in the late 19th century amid growing anxieties around the discovery of *adolescence* (Donzelot, 1979)—defined as a 'period marked by puberty, sexual initiation and the loss of innocence, a period of responsibility' (Straton, 1992, p. 19)—not a child, not an adult, a *transition phase*.

Advancements in psychology highlighted factors such as immaturity, risk-taking propensity and peer influence susceptibility, plus environmental contributors such as intellectual disability, mental illness and victimisation—all increasing offending likelihood (Hay et al., 2004; Steinberg, 2005). Previously, childhood was relatively short, often ending when children became valued as cheap labour (Cunningham, 2020). These shifts in understanding childhood and adolescence coincided with major economic, socio-political and structural changes: compulsory schooling, child labour abolition, urbanisation and child health reforms (Stephenson, 2007). Under child-saving philosophy and state paternalism, a new legal regime for youth was justified, acknowledging children's immaturity and vulnerability (Crawford, 2005; Dickey, 1987; Fernandez et al., 2014; Seymour, 1998).

Despite adolescent psychology's influence, social class remained dominant in penal youth justice. Rather than replacing class-based anxieties, psychological insights fused them, reinforcing delinquency as a lower-class youth problem. The label of *delinquent* enabled the construction of lower working-class youth as the *Other*—subjects in need of constant surveillance, discipline and punitive treatment (Garland, 1985, p. 231). As this book argues, these ideas continue to shape the contemporary juvenile justice landscape and inform prevailing attitudes towards youth governance in Australia.

The 'child-saving movement' reforms introduced a welfare lens to youth offending (Crawford, 2005). The newly established Children's Court, presided over by a specialised magistrate, was intended to have 'somewhat of a parental, informal character rather than the severity, formality and possible terrorism of the ordinary courts of the land' (Golder, 1991, p. 127). In 1905, in response to criminal offences or neglect, children aged 5–16 could be declared state wards—placed under state welfare authority guardianship and institutionalised under the guise of protection and reform (Blackmore, 1998; Crawford, 2005; Dickey, 1987; Fernandez et al., 2014). The definition of a neglected child was broad, encompassing those without support, ill-treated, involved in dangerous public exhibitions, females soliciting men, children present where opium was smoked or those living in conditions suggesting risk of falling into crime (Crawford, 2005). Children placed under state care were among the most vulnerable, including First Nations youth, unruly girls and those perceived to have inadequate parenting. As Carrington (2011, p. 40) notes, state wards were 'neglected, orphaned, impoverished children or children stolen from their families and communities by virtue of their ethnicity, "poor" parenting, or mixed Aboriginal heritage.'

Unlike Britain, where reformatory institutions were predominantly operated by charities with government subsidies, churches in Australia largely managed reformatory and industrial schools until the mid-19th century (Swain, 2014). As child welfare in Australia is state, not federal, responsibility, legislation governing children has been described as 'a patchwork rather than a coordinated model' (Swain, 2014, p. 22). Principles underpinning Australian legislation were adapted from British models and disseminated by travellers and experts who had visited homeland institutions (Swain, 2014). However, child welfare was rarely ranked high on state legislative agendas, granting institutional administrators significant discretion in policy interpretation (Swain, 2014). Consequently, NSW reforms expanded social control over young people's lives and families—deemed non-normative by the colonial gaze—perpetuating class, race and gender-based power structures rather than advancing purely humanitarian child-saving agendas (see O'Brien, 1998; Seymour, 1998; Windshuttle, 1980).

Under the welfare model, diversionary programs were not deemed necessary, as the Children's Court was perceived to act entirely in the *best interest of the child.* It focused on rehabilitation and aimed to prevent contamination and penal identification, which could otherwise turn a child into a 'career criminal' (Seymour, 1998). For criminal matters, the court employed preventative and corrective strategies classified as non-punitive, intended to 'reclaim erring children' (Seymour, 1997, p. 294). In practice, however, these measures were often punitive. Nonetheless, the establishment of the Children's Court—equipped with special provisions for addressing youth offending—marked the final stage in creating a separate system for children.

The Children's Court was seen as specially equipped to assist rather than punish (Pratt, 1986). Consequently, delays in administering treatment caused by diversion were viewed as potentially harmful (Pratt, 1986). While police occasionally issued warnings, their diversionary powers were limited and tolerated rather than encouraged due to the absence of formal legislative support (Seymour, 1998). This approach led to significant Children's Court referrals over the following decades (Crawford, 2005; Pratt, 1986). Despite increasing prosecution rates, 'new sentences available, especially probation, is given as a reason for the decline in the number of those being committed to an institution' (Crawford, 2005, p. 13). Tensions emerged when administrative responsibility for welfare transitioned from the State Children's Relief Board to the Department of Public Instruction in 1905. This required magistrates to justify decisions under law, with rulings subject to clerk review and potential ministerial overturning—a process magistrates disliked (Crawford, 2005).

Throughout the 20th century, several legislative reforms were introduced to address these tensions. The *Neglected Children and Juvenile Offenders Act* of 1905 was repealed by the *Child Welfare Act 1923* (NSW), which underwent numerous amendments before being replaced in 1987 by a series of new Acts addressing young offenders and children in need of care (Blackmore, 1989; Fernandez et al., 2014). Significant changes included raising the minimum age of criminal responsibility from 7 to 8 years in 1939, and from 8 to 10 in 1977 (Blackmore, 1989; Fernandez et al., 2014). Despite these reforms, the underlying philosophy of the Children's Court remained largely unaltered until 1987 (Fernandez et al., 2014).

Over time, child-saving ideologies came under increasing criticism, leading to a shift in focus towards the *rights of the child* (Fernandez et al., 2014; Seymour, 1997). In the 1960s, the welfare system came under attack for its failure to rehabilitate children and protect their legal rights (Naffine & Wundersitz, 1994). Conflict theorists, particularly those focused on labelling and stigmatisation, adopted a critical stance towards the existing social order and its relationship with criminal justice institutions, including the courts. They argued that contact with the Children's Court often results in labels such as '*delinquent*' or '*criminal,*' leading to lifelong stigmatisation for vulnerable youth (Becker, 1963; Cunneen & White, 1996; Goffman, 1963).

Labelling theorists contended that negative labels become internalised, leading individuals to embrace their new identity as a delinquent, thereby fostering a propensity for crime (Lemert, 1969; Matza, 1964, 1969; Sykes & Matza, 1957). Accordingly, court involvement could lead to secondary deviance rather than rehabilitation (Cunneen & White, 2007; Farrington, 1977). However, labelling theory faced significant criticism. Scholars argue that it relies on problematic assumptions, including that political and socio-economic power solely determines what is labelled as deviant, and that labelling experience causes deviant behaviour (Bernburg & Krohn, 2003). Critics also point to theoretical inadequacies and empirical limitations (Paternoster & Iovanni, 1989). Despite these critiques, labelling and stigmatisation remain widely regarded as influential factors in shaping the criminal trajectories of young offenders, affecting their likelihood of desisting from crime (Richards, 2011b). Several studies support the idea that prior contact with the criminal justice system is a strong predictor of recidivism (Chen et al., 2005; Hua et al., 2006).

Evidence suggests that the detrimental effects of intervention and processing young people through the justice system outweigh any potential benefits (Bernburg & Krohn, 2003; Cunneen & White, 2007; Ericson & Vinson, 2010; McAra & McVie, 2007). Research indicates juvenile crime is predominantly 'episodic and transitory' (Jordan & Farrell, 2013, p. 419) with most young people naturally growing out of offending behaviours as they mature (Cunneen & White, 2007; Richards, 2011b). Even those who come into contact with the police once or twice are likely to desist from crime (Rose, 2006). These insights provide a compelling rationale for diversionary alternatives aimed at minimising young people's contact with criminal justice systems.

During this period, there was a notable shift towards deinstitutionalisation, decarceration and decriminalisation. As pre-court mechanisms, diversionary measures were introduced through 'formal' police cautioning in Victoria, Queensland, Tasmania and NSW, while Children's Panels were established in Western Australia and South Australia. A Children's Panel was pre-court diversion where a panel—typically consisting of a social worker and police officer—met with the child and parents in a local community welfare office for 20–30 minutes, with matters usually resolved through warning and counselling (Wundersitz, 1997). These measures aimed to minimise criminal justice intervention and mitigate associated harms. Thus, Australian police diversion history can be traced to the 1970s, characterised by emphasis on diverting young people out of the system (Polk et al., 2003). When young people come to the attention of the police, formal discretion allowed verbal or written cautions. This approach—described as 'true diversion' by Cressey and McDermott (1974, p. 3)—aligned with Schur's principle of 'leaving the kids alone whenever possible' (1973, p. 155). The rationale was that 'official intervention may interfere with the natural process of reform' (Waegel, 1989, p. 236), as most youths tend to desist from crime over time.

In 1985, NSW was the last Australian jurisdiction to adopt formal pre-court mechanisms influenced by *true diversion* principles (Wundersitz, 1997). However, early research showed that in NSW and Tasmania, diversionary measures were used conservatively, accounting for less than 12% and 5% of police matters, respectively (Polk et al., 2003). In contrast, Victoria—where police cautioning had been formalised as early as 1959—saw, by the 1980s, 70% of young people who came into contact with the police dealt with by way of cautioning (Wundersitz, 1997).

At this point, the juvenile justice system had begun shifting its focus from *needs* to *deeds*, transitioning from a welfare approach to a *justice-oriented model.* The objective was to balance increased accountability with less coercive methods (Polk et al., 2003). Consequently, the welfare model was largely abandoned in favour of proportional sentencing and enhanced legal protections for young people's rights (Naffine et al., 1991; Wundersitz, 1997). Simultaneously, a trend towards lesser intervention reflected growing recognition of the limitations of welfare-based rehabilitation strategies. This shift led to the adoption of a retribution or 'just deserts' model, which emphasised proportionate sentencing, accountability and due process, viewing juvenile offenders as rational agents (Pratt, 1993).

As previously noted, this transition coincided with a more punitive political stance and the rise of authoritarian law-and-order responses in the 1980s. By the 1990s, however, it became widely recognised that retributive approaches—often termed '*just deserts*'—had adverse effects on young people, including stigmatisation and amplification of deviant behaviour. This awareness challenged the welfare/justice nexus dichotomy (Carrington & Pereira, 2009; Cunneen & White, 2007).

Nevertheless, youth justice extends beyond the basics of social welfare, legal responsibility and punishment. It addresses both children *at risk* and those posing *a risk* (Muncie, 2004). Both penal paradigms have contributed to the stigmatisation of society's most disadvantaged and vulnerable members (Cunneen & White, 2007). These tensions are evident within restorative justice frameworks, where warnings, cautions or conferencing emerge as *potential options*—a point further explored later in the chapter.

By the late 1980s and early 1990s, international attention increasingly focused on *the rights of the child* and issues of due process, control and deterrence. This shift is reflected in the Beijing Rules (1985) and the UNCRC (1989), both of which advocate for minimal intervention in the lives of children and young people. For instance, the UNCRC stipulates that measures should be taken to address juvenile offences without resorting to judicial proceedings whenever appropriate and desirable, providing that human rights and legal safeguards are fully respected (UNCRC, 1989, Art. 40(3b)).

Indeed, diversion away from the criminal justice system is intended to avoid judicial proceedings. According to the UNCRC (2007), the best interests of children in conflict with the law are best served through restorative justice principles rather than punitive approaches. This perspective is grounded in the recognition that children's emotional, intellectual and psychological capacities, as well as their needs, differ significantly from those of adults. This uniqueness underpins their lesser culpability.

In Australia, this commitment is reflected in reforms introduced in the late 1990s. Notably, the introduction of the YOA in 1997 emphasised restorative justice and diversionary alternatives within the realm of youth justice. The following section will examine these developments in the historical context of youth justice in NSW.

Restorative justice, the development of the YOA and YJC in NSW

Throughout the 1990s, various Western jurisdictions, including parts of Australia, introduced broader sentencing options and alternative dispute resolution. Despite these advancements, tension persisted between reforming youth and containing, deterring and punishing them. From the 2000s onwards, diversionary and community-based responses evolved alongside restorative justice in juvenile justice systems. While *restorative justice* encompasses a range of practices, this section focuses specifically on the rise of conferencing within the juvenile system. Conferencing proves to be the lynchpin of restorative justice, which, borrowing Marshall's (1996, p. 37) widely accepted definition, is 'a process whereby all the parties with a stake in a particular offence come together to resolve collectively how to deal with the aftermath of the offence and its implications for the future.'

Restorative justice centres on victims, offenders and the community, seeking meaningful solutions to *repair harms* and *restore* the moral equilibrium disrupted by the harmful acts (Bazemore & Schiff, 2001; Daly & Hayes, 2001; Marshall, 1996; Richards, 2010b; Zehr, 2015). Motivations for adopting restorative justice vary across jurisdictions but generally emphasise addressing all parties' needs and perspectives. Australia and New Zealand are recognised as world leaders in implementing youth conferencing models grounded in restorative justice principles (Daly & Hayes, 2001; Marien, 2012b). Despite jurisdictional differences, conferencing typically serves as diversion to prevent court proceedings, encouraging young people to take responsibility through direct victim interaction and efforts to repair harm (Daly & Hayes, 2001).

Prior to the YOA, between 1991 and 1994, YJCs in NSW were conducted by police under the Wagga model (Strang, 2001). This was followed by a 1995 pilot scheme of Community Youth Conferences at six locations across NSW. The YJC scheme was formally implemented in 1998 under the YOA (People & Trimboli, 2007; Strang, 2001). The adoption of restorative policing was influenced by John Braithwaite's re-integrative shaming theory (1989), pertaining to the 'disapproval of a bad act…while sustaining the identity of the actor as good… and transmitting shame within a continuum of respect for the wrongdoer' (Braithwaite & Mugford, 1994, p. 142). This theory posits that offenders can be reintegrated through appropriate shaming practices (Braithwaite, 1989). During conferences, young people express shame for their actions and are welcome back into the community. Restorative justice conference serves as reintegration ceremonies, fostering responsibility, apology, restitution and forgiveness (Braithwaite, 1993), ensuring accountability among all parties.

Legally, accountability involves holding offenders responsible for their actions and imposing appropriate sanctions. The assumption is that pain 'administered to offenders for the pain they have caused' should make them accountable (Zehr, 1997, p. 68). However, this model often fails to foster understanding of the consequences of one's actions. Furthermore, traditional criminal justice processes and incarceration can exacerbate feelings of alienation among offenders (Zehr, 1997, 2015). In contrast, restorative justice emphasises that *crime is harm*, and accountability as taking responsibility. This includes confronting offenders with the impact of their actions through direct interaction with the victim and requiring proactive efforts to repair harm, such as expressing remorse or writing a letter of apology (Zehr, 1997, 2015).

While restorative justice doesn't exclude punishment, it seeks to address traditional justice shortcomings by promoting genuine accountability. However, assigning responsibility to young children—whether through traditional or restorative means—remains challenging, particularly where social responsibilities and rights are largely reserved for adults (Cunneen & Goldson, 2015; Goldson, 2013). Similar challenges exist in New Zealand, Canada, the US and European nations where legal frameworks define adulthood and responsibility based on age-specific criteria.

Braithwaite's re-integrative shaming model has been widely praised and critiqued. It involves public shaming followed by re-integration strategies, grounded in the belief that 'crime control is cultural commitments' to shaming (Braithwaite, 1989, p. 1). This requires cultures to be intolerant of crime in ways that are simultaneously forgiving and stern. Central to the model are emotions such as shame and guilt and the offender's repentance (Braithwaite, 1989, p. 162).

One criticism is the potential misuse of shaming against vulnerable minorities. For instance, shaming directed at First Nations peoples in Australia has intensified rather than reduced social control (Blagg, 1997). Another concern is cultural variability in how shame is understood and experienced, affecting the model's effectiveness across different contexts (Blagg, 1997). Despite these concerns, re-integrative shaming offers a communication platform focusing on disapproval of the act rather than the offender (Braithwaite & Mugford, 1994). This contrasts with traditional courts, which often involve rites of disapproval, degradation and stigmatising shaming practices that focus on the offender (Garfinkel, 1956).

Youth conferencing was formalised in NSW with the enactment of the YOA, which established procedures and guidelines for diverting young people from the court system. The Act legislates a hierarchical response to offending, beginning with warnings, followed by official cautions, YJCs, and ultimately court proceedings (YOA, s.8, pt. 2). Youth conferencing promotes community-based involvement of all parties and emphasises restitution through the acceptance of responsibility for one's actions, thereby addressing the needs of victims, offenders and the broader community. This approach aligns with the principles of the restorative justice paradigm (Coppins et al., 2011; Zehr, 2015). Consistent with the UNCRC, the YOA legislates for the least restrictive form of sanction and prioritises alternative modes of adjudication that uphold the best interests of the child.

However, the YOA does not evade the inherent tensions between reform and retribution. Building on earlier discussion of responsibility and accountability, YJC is available to children aged 10–17 who are required to admit guilt and consent to participate (YOA, pt. 5, d. 1:36). Yet, the requirement of consent raises concerns, as many young people fall below the age of legal consent as defined in other areas of law (Crofts, 2015; Richards, 2011b). In NSW, the MACR is 10 years old (see Chapter 1). Below this age, there is a conclusive legal assumption that children cannot form criminal intent or possess a guilty mind (*mens rea*) (*Children's (Criminal Proceedings) Act 1987*, s. 5). This principle, known as *doli incapax*, holds that children under 10 are incapable of crime. For those aged 10–13, a rebuttable common law presumption of *doli incapax* applies (see Chapter 1). This acknowledges the variability in children's cognitive and emotional development (i.e. uneven maturation rates among children), necessitating individual judgement of their capacity for criminal responsibility (Richards, 2011b; Crofts, 2015). Presumptions about children's capacity for responsibility also extend to their ability to communicate effectively—an ability often lacking in many children (Cunneen, 2010). Effective communication is also essential for restorative justice alternatives like cautioning or YJC to succeed (Cunneen & Goldson, 2015), and issue further explored in Chapter 3.

Returning to the YOA, contradictions between welfare and justice philosophies are evident in its selective application to certain offences. The YOA applies to summary offences, indictable offences dealt with summarily under the *Criminal Procedure Act 1986* (NSW), and other prescribed offences (YOA, s. 8, pt. 1). However, it excludes offences resulting in death, armed robbery, robbery in company, most sexual offences, domestic violence, traffic violations and serious drug offences (YOA, s. 8, pt. 2).

Various stakeholders have advocated for expanding the YOA's scope to include more serious offences, citing the Government's stated commitment to diversion (Noetic Solutions, 2010; NSWLRC, 2005). This advocacy often rests on the premise that certain offences considered serious in adult contexts may be relatively minor when viewed within a youth context. For example, breaches of Apprehended Domestic Violence Orders (ADVO) under the *Crimes (Domestic and Personal Violence) Act* 2007 (NSW) are currently excluded. However, many such orders involving young people are used by family members as behavioural management tools rather than in response to actual or threatened violence (Legal Aid NSW, 2012; McFarlane, 2015). In such cases, diversion into conferencing may offer more constructive outcomes by assisting in *restoring* harms and supporting family relationships.

Nonetheless, the decision to pursue a diversionary pathway under the YOA—provided the offence is not excluded—rests with police officers and magistrates. Consequently, their interpretation and application of the Act play a critical role in determining the extent to which diversion is utilised.

Police as gatekeepers: decision-makers on diversion under the YOA

Although the YOA permits YJC referrals to be initiated by the Department of Public Prosecutions (DPP), a trained Police Liaison Officer, or a Magistrate (YOA, s. 38, pt. 5, d.1), in practice, the DPP does not directly refer young offenders to YJCs. This is because the DPP only prosecutes serious children's indictable offences, while matters falling within the scope of the YOA are prosecuted by police (NSWLRC, 2005). At the time the legislation was developed, it was originally intended that the DPP would assume responsibility for prosecuting summary matters, this transition has not occurred (Hennessy, 1999; NSW Parliamentary Debates, Legislative Council, 27 August, 2002, p. 4227). Therefore, in practice, the power to divert people to YJCs rests solely with NSW Police and the Courts.

Unlike New Zealand, where youth conferences are mandatory, NSW legislation grants police considerable discretion in determining eligibility for YJC (Prenzler & Hayes, 1999; Richards, 2010a). This discretionary power is arguably the most contentious feature of the YOA. Low referral rates from police have been identified as undermining the diversion to YJC, with courts responsible for the majority of referrals (Blagg, 1997; Cunneen, 1997; Moore, 2011; Noetic Solutions, 2010; Pearce, 2021; Richards, 2010a; Stewart & Smith, 2004; Trimboli, 2000; Youth Justice Coalition, 2011). As a result, most young people appear in court before being offered a referral to YJC, thereby compromising the Act's diversionary goals. Police reticence to refer youth to YJC warrants further investigation, yet this issue has not been subjected to rigorous scrutiny.

Concerns about the inconsistent use of YJC as a diversionary tool across Australian jurisdictions have been noted in the literature prior to this research. For example, in 2007–2008, NSW police referred 2198 youth conferences—just 3% of juveniles apprehended (BOCSAR, 2007), the lowest rate compared to 6% in Queensland, 17% in South Australia and 25% in the Northern Territory (Richards, 2010a). Moreover, a review of the YOA conducted by Noetic Solutions (2010) found that diversionary options are applied inconsistently across NSW, with some LACs significantly under-utilising them.

A 2004 study by Cunneen et al. (2006) examining the over-representation of First Nations youth in the criminal justice system found that they were significantly less likely to be diverted to a YJC by police. Specifically, Indigenous young people were more than twice as likely to be proceeded against by way of charge (to court) compared to their non-Indigenous counterparts (46% versus 21%). While the proportion of formal interventions involving YJC for Indigenous youth remained relatively stable over a four-year period—declining slightly from 3.4% to 2.9%—a similar downward trend was observed among non-Indigenous youth, whose conferencing rates fell from 4% to 2.4% (Cunneen et al., 2006, p. 21). The empirical data (for this study) confirms persistent under-utilisation of diversion for First Nations young people since the YOA's enactment. These findings, detailed in later chapters, highlight the need for better understanding of police decision-making and attitudes towards alternative justice measures.

Alpert et al. (2005) identify several intersecting factors that influence police decision-making, including the personal attitudes, values and beliefs that officers bring to their roles. Police responses are also shaped by the constraints of laws and policies, which are often dictated, or perhaps mediated, by the cultural and practical contingencies of their institutional and operational environments. The significance of police culture(s) in shaping how officers perceive their roles and perform their duties has been widely acknowledged in the literature (Banton, 1964; Dixon, 1997; Manning, 1989; Reiner, 2010; Skolnick, 1996; Van Maanen, 1973). Reiner (2010, p. 87) describes police culture 'as a patterned set of understandings that helps officers cope with and adjust to the pressures and tensions confronting the police.' Key features include a sense of mission, a thirst for action, cynicism, pessimism, suspicion, isolation, solidarity, conservatism, machismo, racial prejudice and pragmatism.

Research has highlighted an exaggerated sense of mission in policing. As Reiner (2010, p. 89) notes, 'policing is conceived as the preservation of a valued way of life, and the protection of the weak against the predatory.' This perception places excessive pressure on police officers to align their operational strategies with their institutionally valued crime-fighting roles (Ericson, 2007; Manning, 1978/2005). A related concern is how police performance is assessed. Traditional measures of effectiveness rely heavily on statistical indicators focused on crime fighting (Fleming & O'Reilly, 2008). Research suggests that 'in Australia while a demonstrated commitment to community policing is useful when applying for a promotion, such activity is not considered a priority' (Fleming & O'Reilly, 2008, p. 219). Instead, promotions are more likely based on reactive work that can be statistically measured and has previously yielded results for management (Fleming & O'Reilly, 2008). This emphasis has contributed to the downgrading of contemporary policing roles such as community policing, which are often perceived as low-status and unrewarded (Manning, 1978/2005).

In relation to suspicion, authority, isolation and solidarity, police culture has been associated with the application of derogatory labels and stereotypes to suspects, thereby reproducing discriminatory practices based on perceived threat levels (Reiner, 2010). This fosters an 'us versus them' mentality leading to the dismissal of certain groups, which are effectively treated as police property (Choongh, 1997). Although differential enforcement based on class, ethnicity and gender persists (Aly, 2007; Chan, 1997; Choongh, 1997), these practices are not uniformly applied across all individuals or locations (Walklate, 2000). As Chan (1996, p. 112) argues, it is ultimately 'up to individuals to accommodate or resist' prevailing police culture.

While commonly identified features of police culture have been extensively documented, this does not imply that police culture is monolithic, static or impervious to changes within broader social, political and cultural environments (Reiner, 2010). Rather, certain characteristics become dominant due to the ongoing demands of coercion and control inherent in policing (Loftus, 2010; Millie, 2013). Research consistently shows that the nature of police work tends to attract recruits who are politically, morally and socially conservative—traits that reinforce a broader culture of conservatism (Reiner, 2010). This conservatism is often associated with resistance to change, intolerance, reluctance and a strong belief in traditional methods (Reiner, 2010). As diversionary practices and the application of the YOA do not align with the highly valued traditional crime-fighting role, some officers may devalue these approaches. This can intensify tensions between individual attitudes and institutional duties, resulting in varied responses to diversion depending on officers' ideological orientations.

Moreover, research has identified the existence of subcultures within police organisations, shaped by rank and role (Chan, 1996; Chan et al., 2003; Ericson, 1981;

Fielding, 1995; Hobbs, 1998; Ianni & Ianni, 1983; Young, 1991). Culture variation has also been observed between police stations within the same locality (Foster, 1989). As Chan (1996) and Chan et al. (2003) note, officers' construction of cultural attitudes, working rules and accepted behaviours is influenced by individual experiences, role orientations, interpersonal relationships and the broader organisational and political climate. These findings suggest that police culture(s) likely play a direct role in shaping the use of diversionary practices. The previously noted disparities in the application of diversion across LACs may be directly linked to variations in police culture, resulting in different attitudes towards diversionary practices.

Attitudes towards diversion significantly play a role in shaping police decision-making. Existing literature indicates that several factors influence punitive attitudes among police officers when dealing with young offenders. These include rank, mental health challenges and coping styles (Shafiq et al., 2016). For example, Parker et al. (2004) found that higher-ranking Australian police officers were more likely to support punitive policing approaches and less likely to endorse diversionary practices for dealing with young offenders. Similarly, Shafiq et al. (2016), in a study of UK police officers, identified rank as a significant international predictor of punitive attitudes towards young offenders, with higher-ranking officers (Police Constables: PCs) displaying greater punitiveness.

Officers' varying contact levels with young offenders affect their attitudes. Operational officers like PCs, having frequent interactions, may develop negative perceptions and reduced diversion support, particularly without training on youth–adult developmental differences (Rowe, 2008; Shafiq et al., 2016). Targeted training for higher-ranking officers could improve young offender management (Shafiq et al., 2016).

Moreover, mental health and coping styles significantly impact officers' attitudes and actions towards youth (Shafiq et al., 2016). The high-stress nature of policing adversely affects officer well-being (Patterson et al., 2012; Ranta & Sud, 2008). Officers facing mental health challenges tend to favour custodial responses, while those in better psychological health are more supportive of rehabilitative alternatives (Lazarus & Folkman, 1984; Lumb & Breazeale, 2002; Shafiq et al., 2016). Furthermore, officers who use problem-focused coping strategies and seek instrumental support tend to hold less punitive attitudes towards young offenders, while those relying on defensive styles and emotional detachment are more likely to adopt punitive approaches (Copley et al., 2014; Green et al., 2020).

Additionally, officers' perceptions of diversion itself influence decision-making. When officers lack confidence in diversion as a rehabilitative tool, they may view it as ineffective or futile—a perception often reinforced by limited knowledge of diversionary programs (Green et al., 2020). Thus, enhancing officers' understanding of these programs and their therapeutic potential may help shift attitudes. As Shafiq et al. (2016, p. 83) note, 'improved knowledge of adolescent development and typical youth behaviour, as well as exposure to youth in non-law enforcement situations can result in police officers demonstrating more empathic attitudes towards young offenders.' Similarly, officers with a strong understanding of the YOA and firsthand experience with YJC attendance tend to hold more positive views of diversion under the Act (DAGJ, 2011). Foley's (2004) work found that diversion training positively influenced police attitudes in NSW. Stewart and Smith's (2004) research on 184 Queensland officers showed a strong correlation between officers' understanding of conferencing and their likelihood of making referrals. Similarly, Shubert's (1981) work illustrated that effective training helps officers understand youth offending complexities and the purpose of diversion.

A major concern regarding the central role of the police in youth diversion under the YOA is the expansion of their discretionary powers without corresponding accountability measures (Blagg, 1997; Cunneen, 1997). This raises concerns regarding potential misuse of discretion and 'net-widening,' a concept introduced by Cohen (1985) to describe unintended entanglement of more offenders into a web of social control (see also Christie, 2009; Polk et al., 2003). Net-widening occurs when young people are referred to YJC or are given a caution for behaviours that previously would not have warranted formal intervention. While diversion is intended to minimise state involvement—rather than expanding it, empirical data suggests that it can paradoxically increase it by drawing more youth *into* new intervention programs and formal processes (Cohen, 1985; Polk et al., 2003).

Few Australian studies have examined whether the YOA leads to net-widening. Prichard's (2010) research on Tasmanian youth who interacted with the criminal justice system between 1991 and 2002 found no evidence of net-widening due to diversion practices. In contrast, People and Trimboli's (2007) evaluation of the NSW Community Conferencing for Young Adults pilot identified net-widening effects. Although specific studies on net-widening through YJCs, in NSW are lacking, the concern is taken seriously. Scholars have warned that YJCs referrals might be overused in cases where 'true diversions'—such as warnings or cautions—would be more appropriate (see Bargen, 1996; Blagg & Wilkie, 1995). Richards (2010a, p. 7) similarly observed that 'restorative justice measures are used to respond to juveniles who may—in the absence of restorative options—have been given a warning or caution.' While older juveniles (15–17 years) typically comprise the majority of police contacts, Richards found that a disproportionate number of police referrals to YJCs involved younger children aged 10–14. This suggests that YJCs may be disproportionally used for younger juveniles, raising further concerns about the appropriate use of diversion.

Moreover, diversionary interventions operate along gendered, racial and class lines. Despite female offenders being a minority, Richards (2010, p. 6) found equal male–female juvenile referral rates, 'suggesting that restorative measures may be having a net-widening impact on female offenders.' This is significant given that women are the fastest-growing prison demographic in Australia (AIHW, 2020). Net-widening is particularly concerning for young women due to entrenched patriarchal assumptions (Fox et al., 2006). Otto (1994, p. 7) argues that the 'new juvenile justice system, rather than reducing control over young women's identities and lives, has potential to reinforce young women's subordination.'

Police-initiated YJC referrals and officer involvement (in the process) should be critically assessed for their impact on young women's participation, given the persistence of gendered disadvantages in these settings (Bargen, 2005). Gendered social and political contexts contribute to procedural imbalances between victims and offenders, particularly in informal justice settings like YJCs, where they can limit female participation (Field, 2004). While conferencing aims to empower offenders, practices such as shaming may have the opposite effect on young women, often resulting in intimidation rather than promoting accountability (Polk, 1994). This is especially concerning given the high rates of violence and abuse experienced by female offenders (AIHW, 2009; Clark & Fileborn, 2011; Forsythe & Adams, 2009).

Additional concerns relate to the bifurcated treatment of first-time and repeat offenders. In Australia, this approach disproportionately affects First Nations youth, who are more likely to have prior convictions or be *known to police* (Luke & Cunneen, 1995). Systemic racial bias contributes to higher arrest rates and longer criminal records for First Nations young people. Numerous studies have documented discrepancies in diversion rates, with First Nations youth consistently less likely to receive cautions or be referred to YJCs despite their over-representation across all jurisdictions (Chan et al., 2004; Cunneen, 2008a; Cunneen et al., 2006; DAGJ, 2011; Loh & Ferrante, 2003; Ringland & Smith, 2013; Wundersitz & Hunter, 2005). This pattern persists even when controlling for the effect of age, sex, offence type and offending history (Snowball, 2008a, 2008b).

Similarly, concerns exist about lower diversion rates for non-English-speaking minorities (Strang, 2001), though limited statistical data prevents definitive conclusions. While police discretionary power plays a key role in referring First Nations and minority ethnic youth to YJCs, it can be overridden by judicial authority under Section 40 of the YOA, which allows courts to refer young offenders who have 'fallen through the net.' Nonetheless, balancing flexibility with clearer and firmer policy guidelines remains essential to address potential bias in police discretion.

The YOA provides guidance on decision-making by identifying factors such as the seriousness of the alleged offence, level of violence involved, degree of harm caused, and the youth's offending history (YOA, s. 37, pt. 3). Police and magistrates, as 'gatekeepers' are specifically permitted to consider 'the number and nature of any offences committed by the child and the number of times the child has been dealt with under this Act' (YOA, s. 20, pt. 3 (s.37; s.40); pt. 5). However, the NSW Law Reform Commission (2005, p. 52) notes that this provision contradicts Section 15, part 3 of the *Children (Criminal Proceedings) Act 1987* (NSW), which 'prohibits the admission of any evidence that a person has previously been dealt with under the YOA in relation to any subsequent offence.' Although the legislation lists 'prior offending history' last (in order of criteria to consider)—after seriousness, harm and violence—it is often prioritised in practice (NSWLRC, 2005).

Research on police attitudes towards youth diversion confirms that offence seriousness, prior offending and youth's demeanour are key factors in diversionary decision-making (Carrington, 1998; Doob & Cesaroni, 2004; Doob & Chan, 1982; Marinos & Innocente, 2008), with prior offending playing a dominant role. Carrington and Schulenberg's (2004) study in Ontario found an inverse correlation between prior police contact and diversion likelihood. Similarly, Marinos and Innocente (2008) found that past records significantly influenced decisions against diversion. In NSW, Green et al. (2020, p. 9) reported that police officers 'suggested being able to readily identify those young people described as "recidivists" noting that they are less likely to dedicate time and effort to assist them,' highlighting the strong influence of recidivism on decision-making.

Under Section 37, part 3(e) of the YOA, specialist youth police officers may consider 'any other matter the official thinks appropriate in the circumstances.' This broad discretionary clause is intended to allow police and magistrates to base decisions on contextual or mitigating factors. However, in practice, it can provide carte blanche to consider *any matter* that *they deem* appropriate. As De Lint (1998) argues, the significance of this flexibility should not be underestimated. Police decisions—from initial contact to diversion determinations—can influence subsequent judicial outcomes for a young person, including sentencing (Cunneen, 2001; Luke & Cunneen, 1995; NSWLRC, 2005). Thus, discretionary decision-making by individual police officers coalesces into patterns that disproportionately affect minority groups, including First Nations youth (Cunneen & White, 2007), Lebanese, Indo-Chinese youths (Collins et al., 2000) and Pacifica youth (Cunneen, 1995; Ravulo, 2016). Punitive decisions at this early stage can escalate future interventions (Cunneen, 2001). Nonetheless, when police choose not to divert a young person and proceed with charges, magistrates retain discretionary authority to consider diversion under the YOA.

Children's Courts as gatekeepers to YJC: limited research on judicial perceptions of restorative justice

In NSW, the Children's Court is a specialist, independent division of the Local Court that adjudicates both criminal, and care and protection matters involving children (Fernandez et al., 2013, 2014). The Court is headed by a President who concurrently serves as a District Court Judge. Fifteen specialist magistrates are appointed for terms of up to five years and are permanently based in specialist Children's Courts, located in urban areas—namely Parramatta, Surry Hills, Broadmeadow and Woy Woy[1]. Additionally, specialist Children's magistrates also deal with Children's Court cases at shared Local Court facilities—also urban areas—in Campbelltown, Port Kembla, Sutherland, Nowra and Wyong (NSWDCJ, 2023).

Due to significant geographical distances between rural and urban areas in NSW, Local Court magistrates occasionally preside over Children's Court matters where specialist magistrates are unavailable (Fernandez et al., 2014). To address this, a rural circuit for specialist magistrates was established in 2010 to assist with criminal and care and protection matters in regional areas (NSWDCJ, 2023). During the period of data collection for this study, the Children's Court operated across four country care circuits—Northern Rivers, Mid-North Coast, Western Circuit, and the Riverina (Johnstone, 2014)—which later expanded to include New England, Central Coast and Hunter circuits (NSWDCJ, 2025). The Court's criminal jurisdiction is primarily governed by the *Children (Criminal Proceedings)*

Act 1987, the YOA and the *Bail Act 1978*. Although the YOA was initially envisioned to result in most referrals to YJCs coming from police, magistrates have become the primary source of referrals (Moore, 2011; Richards, 2010a; Taussig, 2012).

Criminal justice policies and sentencing decisions are shaped by broader political and social contexts (Steffensmeier et al., 1998), while individual perceptions of jurors and judges can influence determinations of guilt (Kalven & Zeisel, 1966; Smith & Damphousse, 1998). Whether diversion decisions are influenced by distinct factors compared to sentencing remains underexplored. Sentencing research highlights the importance of understanding how legal practitioners' perceptions inform their actions (Mears, 2000; Rogers & Erez, 1999). It is likely that magistrates' perceptions of restorative justice, youth conferencing and their underlying philosophies similarly shape diversionary decision-making. However, there is limited literature examining magisterial views regarding restorative justice and youth justice conferencing.

Research indicates cautious support for restorative justice amongst magistrates (Richards et al., 2017). For instance, US studies report general support but raise concerns about its value for victims and offenders, potential erosion of judicial authority, fairness, protection of young people's rights and equity across cases (Bazemore, 1998; Bazemore & Leip, 2000). Canadian research involving 12 Toronto youth court judges found general but cautious support, particularly in its application to Indigenous youth (Stephens, 2007). In contrast, a study of 69 South African magistrates and prosecutors found broad support for restorative justice, particularly among those working with young people. However, 16% believed it was more appropriate for adults (Naudé & Prinsloo, 2005).

Additionally, some studies highlighted concerns about procedural limitations: Canadian judges (in the study aforementioned) cited limited resources, insufficient funding and a lack of accessible community service information as key barriers to supporting restorative alternatives (Stephens, 2007). While in Naudé and Prinsloo's (2005) study, two-thirds of South African respondents viewed restorative justice as potentially ineffective due to inadequate community resources. The findings also highlighted a need for training on the objectives and effectiveness of restorative justice, as widespread misconceptions led to reluctance in applying it to serious offences, sexual offences and repeat offenders. Bazemore and Leip's (2000) found that some US judges perceived a strong focus on offender rehabilitation as conflicting with victim involvement. Additionally, Bazemore (1998) observed that practices such as community service and restitution were rated most positively, even though they are not the most central components of restorative justice, which places greater emphasis on dialogue, accountability, and repairing harm through inclusive processes.

At a national level, judicial perspectives on restorative justice have been explored through the Australian Children's Courts study (Sheehan & Borowski, 2013). Findings from NSW, Victoria, Queensland, Western Australia, South Australia and the ACT indicate measured support for restorative justice. In Victoria, interviews with

20 magistrates revealed unanimous support for a 'therapeutic jurisprudence-informed problem-solving court' (Borowski & Sheehan, 2013, p. 141). In the ACT, restorative justice was viewed as less formal and more conducive to open communication between young people, families and the court (Camilleri et al., 2013). In Western Australia, magistrates and other stakeholders supported diversion and early intervention but noted their concerns regarding resource limitations, particularly affecting First Nations youth (Spiranovic et al., 2015). In South Australia, stakeholders raised concerns about resource scarcity and insufficient inter-agency collaboration (King et al., 2013).

The study in NSW revealed overwhelming support for restorative justice, particularly for YJCs. Respondents value restorative justice's capacity to foster empathy, promote accountability and encourage behavioural responsibility (Richards et al., 2017). However, as Richards et al. (2017) note, this strong support has not translated into high referral rates, especially among First Nations youth. Concerns included the under-utilisation of YJCs, inconsistent application across NSW and insufficient resources. The study also recommended improving education and training to address gaps in the understanding of restorative justice measures.

Queensland studies report mixed findings but reflect similar themes. Tilbury and Mazerolle (2013) found that while YJCs were viewed positively, they were not seen as ideal. Concerns included inequity, comprehension difficulties for young people and outcomes that were sometimes harsher than court sanctions. The study recommended judicial education on relevant legislation, child development psychology and the principle of detention as a last resort.

As existing research suggests, decisions by legal actors—including the police—are shaped by both micro-institutionalised and macro-political forces. These dynamics are further explored in the analysis-focused chapters of this book, drawing on interviews with key decision-makers conducted as part of the current study. The following section offers a brief overview of three international models of youth conferencing, highlighting the broader relevance of the Australian case study within a global context.

A brief glimpse at three international examples of youth conferencing

This section offers a brief glimpse into three international examples of youth conferencing, highlighting how restorative justice principles are adapted across different jurisdictions. Rather than providing a comprehensive overview, these snapshots illustrate the varied yet fundamentally similar ways in which restorative justice conferencing is employed globally. Each example shares core elements with Australia's youth justice conferring model—some more than others—such as diverting young people from formal justice systems, encouraging community involvement and promoting responsibility and accountability.

Aotearoa New Zealand—family group conferences

Aotearoa New Zealand has been at the forefront of restorative justice innovation, particularly in the youth justice context. Under the *Oranga Tamariki*

Act 1989 (formally known as the *Children, Young Persons and Their Families Act 1989* [CYPF]), police powers to arrest are strictly limited. Instead, responses include warnings, alternative action (referral to a Youth Aid Officer that can arrange alternative action, such as reparation/community work) and Family Group Conferences (FGC). Due to the stringent limits on police arrest, approximately 80% of young people in New Zealand are diverted rather than charged (Cleland, 2016; Cleland & Quince, 2014; Justice, 2010)—with the majority of these cases dealt through diversionary mechanisms such as informal and formal police cautions, or referrals to Youth Aid Officer for an alternative action. Only a smaller percentage of the diversions—of the most serious nature—will proceed to an FGC.

When a young person is arrested and brought before the Youth Court, the court is required to refer the case to an FGC before sentencing can occur (Maxwell & Morris, 2006). FGC is central as a decision-making forum for cases involving young people, including those charged with serious offences or young people with significant needs (Cleland, 2016).

The Aotearoa New Zealand's FGCs model contrasts with Australia's YJC (particularly in NSW) in several key areas, including facilitation, legal mandate, cultural integration and eligibility criteria (Trimboli, 2000). In Aotearoa New Zealand, FGCs are a legislated and mandatory component of the youth justice process, governed by the *Oranga Tamariki Act 1989* (formerly the *Children, Young Persons and Their Families Act 1989*). The Act applies nationally and requires that an FGC be convened for most youth offences before court proceedings can occur. These conferences are facilitated by trained coordinators from the Ministry of Social Development, with police participating as stakeholders rather than leading the process. The model is deeply rooted in Māori cultural values and emphasises collective decision-making and community healing (Cleland & Quince, 2014; Trimboli, 2000).

Moreover, Aotearoa New Zealand's FGCs do not require a formal admission of guilt prior to participation, allowing for greater flexibility and inclusivity. Australia's YJC, however, mandates that the young person admits to the offence before being eligible for referral—an issue previously noted as undermining diversion efforts. Offence eligibility also differs: FGCs in Aotearoa New Zealand are used for a broad range of offences, including serious ones, whereas YJCs in Australia are generally limited to the less serious offences and subject to police or judicial discretion. While both models share restorative principles—such as diversion from formal court processes, community involvement and a focus on repairing harm—Aotearoa New Zealand's approach is more structurally embedded, culturally responsive and broadly accessible.

Nonetheless, Aotearoa New Zealand's FGC model has faced criticism for filtering offenders before they get to the Youth Court and failing to ensure equitable access (Cleland & Quince, 2014). Further, evidence has shown that young Māori offenders are less likely to receive the benefit of discretion not to prosecute (Cleland & Quince, 2014), mirroring concerns raised in Australia regarding the under-representation of First Nations youth in diversionary processes. This suggests that, while structurally different, both models are susceptible to systemic biases that can undermine their restorative potential and perpetuate existing inequalities.

Northern Ireland—youth conferencing service

Northern Ireland's approach to youth justice underwent a significant transformation in 2003 with the creation of the Youth Justice Agency (YJA), which was tasked with implementing a more restorative and community-focused system. This reform introduced a suite of new sentencing options—including youth conference orders, reparation and community responsibility orders for children under 14—marking a shift away from traditional punitive models. Unlike other UK jurisdictions where restorative practices have been inconsistently applied and reliant on short-term funding, Northern Ireland has embedded these principles across its justice system (Haydon, 2009).

Police, prosecutors and courts were each granted powers to divert young people from formal prosecution through mechanisms such as informal warnings, restorative cautions and youth conferencing. These conferences, led by trained coordinators, aim to bring together the young person, the victim (when possible) and relevant professionals to develop a tailored plan addressing the harm caused. If approved by the Public Prosecution Service or the court, the plan is implemented under the YJA supervision. Despite early hurdles, youth conferencing services expanded across the region. A strategic framework introduced in 2006 aligned the youth justice system with the UNCRC, though critics argue that key recommendations—such as raising the MACR and reducing the use of custody for very young children—were not adequately addressed.

The conferencing model in Northern Ireland has shown promising outcomes: victim participation and satisfaction rates are high (Campbell et al., 2005), and the use of custodial sentences has declined as conferencing has expanded (Jacobson and Gibbs, 2009). Studies indicate that some young people find the process helpful, allowing them to reflect on their actions and make positive changes in their lives (Maruna et al., 2007). In contrast, other young offenders report negative experiences as they found conferences to be frustrating, demeaning and shaming (Maruna et al. 2007). However, Haydon (2007) notes young people feeling excluded (and marginalised) from decision-making and describes the process as punitive and disempowering.

Furthermore, when conference plans are rejected by the Public Prosecution Service or the courts, the young person is typically subjected to prosecution or an alternative sentence (Jacobson & Gibbs, 2009)—an outcome that can erode trust in the process and undermine its restorative intent (Maruna et al., 2007). Despite these concerns, the YJA (2009) claims that youth conferencing in Northern Ireland represents one of the most comprehensive and institutionalised restorative justice models in Europe, balancing the needs of victims, communities and young offenders within a structured, dialogic framework. However, this brief overview also reveals underlying tensions and inconsistencies that may be better understood when viewed through the same critical lens applied to the NSW case study explored in this book, especially in relation to the risk-based technologies and governance strategies discussed in Chapter 3.

Canada—Section 19 conferencing

In Canada, youth justice conferences—authorised under Section 19 of the *Youth Criminal Justice Act* (YCJA)—are structured yet informal gatherings of professionals, community members, and often the young person and their family. These conferences aim to support decision-making at various stages of the justice process, from pre-charge diversion to sentencing and reintegration planning. Rooted in restorative justice principles, they seek to humanise the justice process by fostering dialogue, accountability and tailored support (Giberson et al., 2023).

In theory, this model offers a compelling alternative to adversarial court proceedings. It emphasises youth voice, inter-agency collaboration and holistic responses that reflect the young person's needs and circumstances. In practice, however, implementation across Canada has been inconsistent and fragmented, with limited data on usage, processes and outcomes. To address this gap, the Department of Justice Canada conducted a national survey in 2022, gathering insights from all 13 provinces and territories.

The findings as reported by Paquin-Marseille and Higgison (2022) revealed that Section 19 conferences are used in 11 jurisdictions, with Quebec and Yukon relying on alternative mechanisms. Conferences are convened at various stages of the justice process and serve multiple purposes, including sentencing advice, bail conditions and restorative justice. While most jurisdictions have developed policies or guidelines, practices vary significantly.

Participants typically include the young person, their families, probation officers, social workers, school representatives and Indigenous Elders. Judges, police, Crown prosecutors and defence counsel may also be involved. This diversity helps ensure decisions are informed by multiple perspectives and tailored to the youth's needs. Reported benefits include increased youth engagement, enhanced collaboration among justice and social service professionals and culturally responsive approaches. Conferences are particularly effective in addressing complex needs such as those related to mental health, Fetal Alcohol Spectrum Disorder (FASD) and crossover youth. Some jurisdictions also suggest they may contribute to reduced recidivism.

Nonetheless, several challenges persist. These include logistical difficulties, lack of dedicated coordinators, limited community resources and low participation from families or victims. Under-utilisation may also stem from limited awareness or training among justice professionals and systemic challenges. Finally, only a few jurisdictions collect consistent data on Section 19 conferences, and even fewer have conducted formal evaluations, highlighting a critical gap in assessing their impact and informing future practice.

This brief overview of recent findings by the Department of Justice in Canada indicates that, although Section 19 conferences operate within a more complex and decentralised framework compared to models in Aotearoa New Zealand, Northern Ireland or NSW, (Australia), there are clear commonalities in both the challenges faced—such as logistical barriers and limited resources—and the benefits realised, particularly in fostering collaboration, youth engagement and culturally responsive justice practices across jurisdictions.

Conclusion

The historical trajectory of juvenile justice policies has oscillated between welfare-oriented and justice-focused models. In Australia, this pendulum swing is evident as policy has alternately focused on children's 'needs' versus their 'deeds.' The shift to the justice model in the 1980s marked a legislative distinction between criminal and care jurisdictions within the Children's Court, representing a move from addressing needs to focusing on deeds. This transition created tension, as the justice model failed to recognise that children's offending often arises from welfare issues rather than criminogenic factors.

Restorative justice approaches emerged in the 1990s, emphasising diversion and attempting to redress the tensions between punitive and welfare responses to youth offending. While there were *ideal* expectations for the YOA in NSW to provide an inclusive and re-integrative form of justice that diverts young people from the formal criminal justice system, these aspirations have largely remained unfulfilled. Consequently, tensions between welfare and justice paradigms continue to permeate restorative diversionary alternatives such as YJCs. These ongoing tensions are evident within the structure of the YOA, although there is insufficient evidence regarding how they influence decision-making by key actors involved in diversionary practices.

This chapter suggests an exclusion/inclusion dichotomy in youth governance, with the most disadvantaged populations—particularly First Nations youth—being disproportionally excluded from diversion. The emergence of restorative justice and diversion has coincided with Australia's shift towards neoliberal governance, characterised by a heightened focus on individual responsibility, accountability and risk management within the justice system's response to offending. The next chapter examines how this neoliberal emphasis on risk governance impacts Australian youth justice and its relationship to diversion.

Note

1 At the time of the current study, Surry Hills Children's Court did not exist; instead, Glebe Children's Court was operational.

References

Alpert, G. P., MacDonald, J. M., & Dunhman, R. (2005). Police suspicion and discretionary decision-making during citizen stops. *Criminology*, *43*(2), 407–434.

Aly, A. (2007). Australian Muslim responses to the discourse on terrorism in the Australian popular media. *Australian Journal of Social Issues*, *42*, 27–40.

Attorney-General's Department. (2010). *National youth policing model*. Australian Government.

Australasian Juvenile Justice Administrators. (2009). *Juvenile justice standards 2009*.

Australasian Juvenile Justice Administrators (AJJA). (2014). *Principles of youth justice in Australia*. https://www.ayja.org.au/documents/principles-of-youth-justice-in-australia/

Australian Institute of Health and Welfare. (2009). *The health of Australia's prisoners*. Australian Government.

Australian Institute of Health and Welfare. (2011). *The health of Australia's prisoners 2010*. (Cat. no. PHE 149). Australian Government. https://www.aihw.gov.au/reports/prisoners/health-australias-prisoners-2009

Australian Institute of Health and Welfare. (2020). *The health and welfare of women in Australia's prisons*. https://www.aihw.gov.au/reports/prisoners/health-and-welfare-of-women-in-prison/summary

Australian Institute of Health and Welfare. (2024). *Youth justice in Australia 2022–23*. https://www.aihw.gov.au/reports/youth-justice/youth-justice-in-australia-annual-report-2022-23

Bail Act 1978 (NSW).

Banton, M. (1964). *The policeman in the community*. Tavistock.

Bargen, J. (1996). Kids, cops, courts, conferencing and children's rights: A note on perspectives. *Australian Journal of Human Rights, 2*, 209–228.

Bargen, J. (2005, March 3–5). *Regulating police discretion: An assessment of the impact of the NSW Young Offenders Act 1997 Youth Justice Conferencing* [Conference Paper]. "Building a Global Alliance for Restorative Practices and Family Empowerment, Part 3". The International Institute for Restorative Practices Sixth International Conference on Conferencing, Circles and other Restorative Practices, Penrith, NSW, Australia.

Bazemore, G. (1998). Crime victims and restorative justice in juvenile courts: Judges as obstacle or leader?. *Western Criminology Review, 1*(1), 1–36.

Bazemore, G., & Leip, L. (2000). Victim participation in the new juvenile court: Tracking judicial attitudes toward restorative justice reforms. *The Justice System Journal, 21*(2), 199–226.

Bazemore, G., & Schiff, M. (Eds.). (2001). *Restorative and community justice: Repairing harm and transforming communities*. Anderson Publishing.

Becker, H. (1963). *Outsiders: studies in the sociology of deviance*. Free Press.

Bernard, T. (1992). *The cycle of juvenile justice*. Oxford University Press.

Bernburg, J. C., & Krohn, M. D. (2003). Labelling, life, chances, and adult crime: The direct and indirect effects of official intervention in adolescence on crime in early adulthood. *Criminology, 41*(4), 1287–1318.

Blackmore, R. (1989). *The Children's Court and community welfare in NSW*. Longman Cheshire.

Blackmore, R. (1998). State-intervention with children – Two centuries of history. *Australian Journal of Forensic Sciences, 30*(1), 5–17.

Blagg, H. (1997). A just measure of shame? Aboriginal youth and conferencing in Australia. *British Journal of Criminology, 37*(4), 481–501.

Blagg, H., Morgan, N., Cunneen, C., & Ferrante, A. (2005). *Systemic racism as a factor in the over-representation of Aboriginal people in the Victorian criminal justice system*. Equal Opportunity Commission. https://tr.uow.edu.au/uow/file/64419d5f-d183-49c2-90d9-d81c8dc44f17/1/2005-blagg-1-210.pdf

Blagg, H., & Wilkie, M. (1995). *Young people and police powers*. Australian Youth Foundation Sydney.

Borowski, A., & Sheehan, R. (2013). The Children's Court of Victoria. In R. Sheehan & A. Borowski (Eds.), *Australia's Children's Courts today and tomorrow* (pp. 123–142). Springer.

Braithwaite, J. (1989). *Crime, shame and reintegration*. Cambridge University Press.

Braithwaite, J. (1993). Juvenile offending: New theory and practice. In L. Atkinson & S. Gerull (Eds.), *National conference on juvenile justice*. Australian Institute of Criminology.

Braithwaite, J., & Mugford, S. (1994). Conditions of successful reintegration ceremonies: Dealing with juvenile offenders. *British Journal of Criminology, 34*(2), 139–171.

Camilleri, P., Thomson, L., & McArthur, M. (2013). Needs or deeds? Child protection and youth justice in the Australian Capital Territory. *Journal of Social Welfare & Family Law, 35*, 193–206.

Campbell, C., Devlin, R., O'Mahony, D., Doak, J., Jackson, J., Corrigan, T., & McEvoy, K. (2005). *Evaluation of the Northern Ireland youth conference service*. Statistics and Research Branch of the Northern Ireland Office.

Carrington, K. (1993). *Offending girls: Sex, youth and justice*. Allen and Unwin.

Carrington, K. (2011). Punitiveness and the criminalisation of the other: State wards, unlawful non-citizens and Indigenous youth. *Somatechnics, 1*(1), 30–47.

Carrington, K., & Pereira, M. (2009). *Offending youth: Sex, crime and justice*. Federation Press.
Carrington, P. J. (1998). *Factors affecting police diversion of young offenders: A statistical analysis*. Solicitor General Canada.
Carrington, P. J., & Schulenberg, J. L. (2004). *Prior police contacts and police discretion with apprehended youth*. Canadian Centre for Justice Statistics.
Cashmore, J. (2013). Juvenile justice: Australian court responses situated in the international context. In R. Sheehan & A. Borowski (Eds.), *Australia's Children's Courts today and tomorrow* (pp. 197–207). Springer.
Chan, J. (1996). Changing police culture. *British Journal of Criminology*, *36*(1), 109–134.
Chan, J. (1997). *Changing police culture: Policing in a multicultural society*. Cambridge University Press.
Chan, J., Bargen, J., Luke, G., & Clancey, G. (2004). Regulating police discretion: An assessment of the impact of the NSW *Young Offenders Act* 1997. *Criminal Law Journal*, *28*(2), 74–92.
Chan, J., Devery, C., & Doran, S. (2003). *Fair cop: Learning the art of policing*. University of Toronto Press.
Chen, S., Matruglio, T., Weatherburn, D., & Hua, J. (2005). The transition from juvenile to adult criminal careers. *Crime and Justice Bulletin*, *86*, 1–12.
Child Welfare Act 1923. (NSW).
Choongh, S. (1997). *Policing as social discipline*. Oxford University Press.
Christie, N. (2009). Restorative justice: Five dangers ahead. In P. Knepper, J. Doak, & J. Shapland (Eds.), *Urban crime prevention, surveillance and restorative justice: Effects of social technologies* (pp. 230–239). CRC Press.
Clark, H., & Fileborn, B. (2011). *Responding to women's experiences of sexual assault in institutional and care settings* (ACSSA Wrap No. 10). Australian Institute of Family Studies. https://apo.org.au/node/27150
Cleland, A. (2016). Will New Zealand's youth justice system take the next step? In A. Cleland & T. Liefaard (Eds.), *The United Nations Convention on the Rights of the Child: Taking stock after 25 years and looking ahead* (pp. 316–340). Brill.
Cleland, A., & Quince, K. (2014). *Youth justice in Aotearoa New Zealand: Law, policy and critique*. Butterworths.
Cohen, S. (1985). *Visions of social control: Crime, punishment and classification*. Polity Press.
Collins, J., Noble, G., Poynting, S., & Taber, P. (2000). *Kebaks, kids, cops and crime: Youth, ethnicity and crime*. Pluto Press.
Copley, J., Johnson, D., & Bain, S. (2014). Staff attitudes towards young people in looked after accommodation. *Journal of Forensic Practice*, *16*(4), 257–267.
Coppins, V., Casey, S., & Campbell, A. (2011). The child's best interest: A review of Australian juvenile justice legislation. *The Open Criminology Journal*, *4*, 23–31.
Crawford, J. (2005). *Establishment of the Children's Court – Then and 100 years on*. Lawlink.
Cressey, D. R., & McDermott, R. A. (1974). *Diversion from the juvenile justice system*. U S Government Printing Office.
Criminal Procedure Act 1986 (NSW).
Crofts, T. (2015). A brighter tomorrow: Raise the age of criminal responsibility. *Current Issues in Criminal Justice*, *27*(1), 123–131.
Cunneen, C. (1995). Ethnic minority youth and juvenile justice: Beyond the stereotype of ethnic gangs. *Current Issues in Criminal Justice*, *6*(3), 387–394.
Cunneen, C. (1997). Community conferencing and the fiction of Indigenous control. *The Australian and New Zealand Journal of Criminology*, *30*, 292–311.
Cunneen, C. (2001). *Conflict, politics and crime: Aboriginal communities and the police*. Allen & Urwin.

Cunneen, C. (2008a). Understanding restorative justice through the lens of critical criminology. In T. Anthony & C. Cunneen (Eds.), *The critical criminology companion* (pp. 290–302). Hawkins Press.

Cunneen, C. (2008b). Changing neo-colonial impacts of juvenile justice. *Current Issues in Criminal Justice, 20*(1), 43–58.

Cunneen, C. (2010). The limitations of restorative justice. In C. Cunneen & C. Hoyle (Eds.), *Debating restorative justice* (pp. 101–188). Hart Publishing.

Cunneen, C. (2011). State crime, the colonial question and Indigenous peoples. In A. Smuelers & R. Haveman (Eds.), *Supranational criminology: Towards a criminology of international crimes* (pp. 159–180). Intersentia Press.

Cunneen, C. (2012). Restorative justice, globalization and the logic of empire. In J. McCulloch & S. Pickering (Eds.), *Borders and crime pre-crime, mobility and serious harm in an age of globalization* (pp. 147–162). Palgrave.

Cunneen, C. (2020). *Arguments for raising the minimum age of criminal responsibility*. Jumbunna Institute for Indigenous Education and Research, University of Technology.

Cunneen, C., & Goldson, B. (2015). Restorative justice? A critical analysis. In B. Goldson & J. Muncie (Eds.), *Youth crime and justice* (2 ed., pp. 137–156). Sage.

Cunneen, C., & Libesman, T. (2000). Postcolonial trauma: The contemporary removal of Indigenous children and young people from their families in Australia. *Australian Journal of Social Issues, 35*(2), 99–115.

Cunneen, C., Luke, G., & Ralph, N. (2006). *Evaluation of the Aboriginal over-representation strategy report to the NSW Department of Juvenile Justice Sydney*. Institute of Criminology University of Sydney Law School.

Cunneen, C., & White, R. (1996). *Juvenile justice: An Australian perspective*. Oxford University Press.

Cunneen, C., & White, R. (2007). *Juvenile justice: Youth and crime in Australia* (3 ed.). Oxford University Press.

Cunningham, H. (1991). *Children of the poor*. Blackwell.

Cunningham, H. (1995). *Children and childhood in western society since 1500*. Longman.

Cunningham, H. (2020). *Children and childhood in western society since 1500* (3 ed.). Routledge.

Daly, K. (1999, October 16). *What is the future of the Youth Court? Reflecting on the relationship of informal and formal justice?* [Paper presentation]. The Australian and New Zealand Youth Court Judges and Magistrates Conference, Adelaide, South Australia.

Daly, K., & Hayes, H. (2001). *Restorative justice and conferencing in Australia* (Trends and Issues in Crime and Criminal Justice, No. 186, 1–6). Australian Institute of Criminology.

Day, A. (2011). Current directions in youth justice and young offender programming. *The Open Criminology Journal, 4*, 10–12.

De Lint, W. (1998). Regulating autonomy: Police discretion as a problem for training. *Canadian Journal of Criminology 40*(3), 277–304.

DeLisi, M., Hochstetler, A., Jones-Johnson, G., Caudill, J., & Marquart, J. (2011). The road to murder: the enduring criminogenic effects of juvenile confinement among a sample of adult career criminals. *Youth Violence and Juvenile Justice, 9*, 207–721.

Department of Attorney General and Justice (NSW). (2011). *Review of the Young Offenders Act 1997 and the Children (Criminal Proceedings) Act 1987: Consultation Paper*. NSW Government. https://dcj.nsw.gov.au/content/dam/dcj/dcj-website/documents/about-us/engage-with-us/public-consultations/unsorted/consultation_paper_-_yoa_and_ccpa_review.doc

Destitute Children Act 1866 (30Vic No11).

Dickey, B. (1987). *No charity there: A short history of social welfare in Australia*. Allen and Unwin.

Dixon, D. (1997). *Law in policing: Legal regulation and police practices*. Clarendon Press.

Donzelot, J. (1979). *The policing of families*. Pantheon Books.

Doob, A. N., & Cesaroni, C. (2004). *Responding to youth crime in Canada*. University of Toronto Press.

Doob, A. N., & Chan, J. (1982). Factors affecting police decisions to take juveniles to court. *Canadian Journal of Criminology and Criminal Justice*, *34*(1), 35–50.

Dwyer, A. (2011). 'It's not like we're going to jump them': How transgressing heteronormativity shapes police interactions with LGBT young people. *Youth Justice*, *11*(1), 203–220.

Ericson, M., & Vinson, T. (2010). *Young people on remand in Victoria: Balancing individual and community interest*. Jesuit Social Services.

Ericson, R. V. (1981). *Making crime: A study of detective work*. Butterworth.

Ericson, R. V. (2007). Rules in policing: Five perspectives. *Theoretical criminology*, *11*(3), 367–401.

Farrington, D. P. (1977). The effects of public labeling. *British Journal of Criminology*, *17*, 112–125.

Feeley, M., & Simon, J. (1994). Actuarial justice: The emerging new criminal law. In D. Nelken (Ed.), *The futures of criminology* (pp. 173–201). Sage.

Fernandez, E., Bolitho, J., Hansen, P., & Hudson, M. (2013). The Children's Court in New South Wales. In R. Sheehan & A. Borowski (Eds.), *Australia's Children's Court today and tomorrow* (pp. 27–44). Springer.

Fernandez, E., Bolitho, J., Hansen, P., Hudson, M., & Kendall, S. (2014). *A study of the Children's Court of New South Wales. Part of a national assessment of Australia's Children's Courts*. University of New South Wales Australia. https://childrenscourt.nsw.gov.au/documents/other/chcourt%20assessment.pdf

Field, R. (2004). Victim-offender conferencing: Issues of power imbalance for women juvenile participants. *Murdoch University Law Review*, *11*(1), 1–20.

Fielding, N. (1995). *Community policing*. Oxford University Press.

Finkelhor, D., & Hashima, P. (2001). The victimization of children and youth: A comprehensive overview. In S. O. White (Ed.), *Handbook of youth and justice* (pp. 49–78). Kluwer Academic/Plenum.

Fleming, J., & O'Reilly, J. (2008). The 'small-scale initiative': The rhetoric and the reality of community policing in Australia. *Policing*, *1*(2), 214–222.

Foley, T. (2004). *"Changed my mode of thinking..." police attitudes to the use of discretionary options for juvenile drug offenders*. Report to NSW Police, Australian National University.

Forsythe, L., & Adams, K. (2009). *Mental health, abuse, drug use and crime: Does gender matter?* (Trends & Issues in Crime and Criminal Justice, no. 384). Australian Institute of Criminology.

Foster, J. A. (1989). Two stations: An ethnography study of policing in the inner city. In D. Downes (Ed.), *Crime and the city* (pp. 128–153). Macmillan.

Fox, D., Dhami, M. K., & Mantle, G. (2006). Restorative final warnings: Policy and practice issues. *The Journal of Criminal Justice*, *45*(2), 129–140.

Garfinkel, H. (1956). Conditions of successful degradation ceremonies. *American Journal of Sociology*, *61*, 420–424.

Garland, D. (1985). *Punishment and welfare*. Gower.

Garland, D. (1996). The limits of the sovereign state. *British Journal of Criminology*, *36*(4), 445–471.

Gatti, U., Tremblay, R. E., & Vitaro, F. (2009). Latrogenic effect of juvenile justice. *Journal of Child Psychology and Psychiatry*, *50*, 991–998.

Giberson, E. M., Tracy, B., Kabbash, L., Ronis, S. T., Campbell, M. A., Gryshchuk, L. (2023). Section 19 conferencing in the Canadian youth criminal system. *Canadian Journal of Criminology and Criminal Justice*, *63* (2), pp. 97–118.

Goffman, E. (1963). *Stigma: Notes on the management of spoiled identity*. Prentice-Hall.

Golder, H. (1991). *High and responsible office- a history of the NSW magistracy*. Sydney University Press.

Goldson, B. (2004). Victims or threats? Children, care and control. In J. Fink (Ed.), *Care: personal lives and social policy* (pp. 77–109). The Policy Press in association with The Open University.

Goldson, B. (2013). "Unsafe, unjust and harmful to wider society": Grounds for raising the minimum age of criminal responsibility in England and Wales. *Youth Justice: An International Journal 13*(2), 111–130.

Goodall, H. (1990). Saving the children gender and the colonisation of Aboriginal Children in NSW, 1788 to 1990. *Aboriginal Law Bulletin 9, 1*(44), 6–9.

Green, R., Gray, R. M., Bryant, J., Rance, J., & MacLean, S. (2020). Police decision-making with young offenders: Examining barriers to the use of diversion options. *Australian & New Zealand Journal of Criminology, 53*(1), 137–154.

Hay, D., Payne, A., & Chadwick, A. (2004). Peer relations in childhood. *Journal of Child Psychology and Psychiatry, 45*(1), 84–108.

Haydon, D. (2007). *Developing a framework to inform youth justice policy and practice in Northern Ireland: Background paper, include youth, Belfast.*

Haydon, D. (2009). *Developing a manifesto for youth justice in Northern Ireland: Background paper, include youth, Belfast.*

Hendrick, H. (2003). *Child welfare: Historical dimensions, contemporary debate*. The Policy Press.

Hendrick, H. (2015). Histories of youth crime and justice. In B. Goldson & J. Muncie (Eds.), *Youth, crime and justice* (2 ed., pp. 3–16). Sage Publications Ltd.

Hennessy, N. (1999). *Review of gatekeeping role in Young Offenders Act 1997 (NSW): Report to Youth Justice Advisory Committee*. Sydney.

Hobbs, D. (1998). *Doing the business: Entrepreneur-ship, the working class and detectives in the East End of London* (2 ed.). Oxford University Press.

Holman, B., & Zeidenberg, J. (2006). *The dangers of detention: The impact of incarcerating youth in detention and other secure facilities*. Justice Policy Institute.

Hua, J., Baker, J., & Poynton, S. (2006). *Generation Y and crime: A longitudinal study of contact with NSW criminal courts before the age of 21* (Bulletin No. 96). NSW Bureau of Crime Statistics and Research.

Huizinga, D., Kimberly, H., Ehret, B., & Elliott, A. (2004). *The effect of juvenile justice system processing on subsequent delinquent and criminal behavior: A cross-national study.* NCJRS.

Ianni, E. R., & Ianni, R. (1983). Street cops and management cops: The two cultures of policing. In M. Punch (Ed.), *Control in the police organisation.* MIT Press.

Jacobson, J., & Gibbs, P. (2009). *Making amends: Restorative youth justice in Northern Ireland.* The Prison Reform Trust.

Johnstone, P. (2014, March 25). *Emerging developments in juvenile justice.* The 5th Annual Juvenile Justice Summit, Melbourne. https://childrenscourt.nsw.gov.au/documents/other/paper%20for%20jj%20summit%2020.3.14.pdf

Jordan, L., & Farrell, J. (2013). Juvenile justice diversion in Victoria: A blank canvas? *Current Issues in Criminal Justice, 24*(3), 419–437.

Juvenile Offender Act 1850. (14Vic No11).

Kalven, H., & Zeisel, H. (1966). *The American jury*. Little Brown.

Kelly, L., & Armitage, V. (2015). Diverse diversions: Youth justice reform, localized practices, and a 'new interventionist diversion'?. *Youth Justice, 15*(2), 117–133.

King, D., Day, A., & Delfabbro, P. (2013). The Children's Court of South Australia. In R. Sheehan & A. Borowski (Eds.), *Australia's Children's Courts today and tomorrow* (pp. 165–186). Springer.

Kirby, M. (1999). Domestic implementation of international human rights norms. *Australian Journal of Human Rights, 5*(2), 109.

Lazarus, R. S., & Folkman, S. (1984). *Stress, appraisal and coping*. Springer.

Legal Aid NSW. (2012). *Children and young persons (care and protection) regulation 2000 statutory review* [Discussion Paper] (Submission to Family and Community Services).

Lemert, E. (1969). Primary and secondary deviation. In D. R. Cressey & D. A. Ward (Eds.), *Delinquency, crime and social process*. Harper and Row.

Loftus, B. (2010). Police occupational culture: Classic themes, altered times. *Policing and Society*, *20*(1), 1–20.

Loh, N., & Ferrante, A. (2003). *Aboriginal involvement in the Western Australian criminal justice system: a statistical review, 2001*. Perth: Crime and Research Centre.

Luke, G., & Cunneen, C. (1995). *Aboriginal over-representation and discretionary decisions in the NSW juvenile justice system*. NSW Juvenile Justices Advisory Council.

Lumb, R., & Breazeale, R. (2002). Police officer attitudes and community policing implementation: Developing strategies for durable organizational change. *Policing and Society*, *13*(1).

Manning, P. K. (1978/2005). The police: Mandate, strategies and appearances. In T. Newburn (Ed.), *Policing key readings* (pp. 154–172). Willan.

Manning, P. K. (1989). Occupational culture. In W. G. Bayley (Ed.), *The encyclopedia of police science* (pp. 360–363). Garfield.

Marien, M. C. (2012b, March 29). *Juvenile justice: What is effective and what needs reform* [Paper presentation]. Legal Studies State Conference Rosehill.

Marinos, V., & Innocente, N. (2008). Factors influencing police attitudes towards extrajudicial measures under the *Youth Criminal Justice Act*. *Canadian Journal of Criminology and Criminal Justice*, *50*(4), 469–489.

Marshall, T. F. (1996). The evolution of restorative justice in Britain. *European Journal on Criminal Policy and Research*, *4*, 21–43.

Maruna, S., Wright, S., Brown, J., van Marle, F., Devlin, R., & Liddle, M. (2007). *Youth conferencing as shame management: Results of a long-term follow-up study*. 10.13140/RG.2.2.33382.78408.

Matza, D. (1964). *Delinquency and drift*. Wiley.

Matza, D. (1969). *On becoming deviant*. Prentice Hall.

Maxwell, G., & Morris, A. (2006). Youth justice in New Zealand: restorative justice in practice? *Journal of Social Issues*, *62*(2), 239–258.

May, M. (1973). Innocence and experience: The evolution of the concept of juvenile delinquency in the mid nineteenth-century. *Victorian Studies*, *17*(1), 7–29.

McAra, L., & McVie, S. (2007). Youth justice? The impact of system contact on patterns of desistance from offending. *European Journal of Criminology*, *4*, 315–345.

McAra, L., & McVie, S. (2010). Youth crime and justice: Key messages from the Edinburgh study of youth transitions and crime. *Criminology and Criminal Justice*, *10*(2), 179–209.

McFarlane, K. (2015). *Care-criminalisation: The involvement of children in out of home care in the NSW criminal justice system* [Thesis, Law and Justice UNSW Faculty]. https://unsworks.unsw.edu.au/bitstreams/0b50666b-fb42-4717-bcaf-aaee30fc512f/download

Mears, D. P. (2000). Assessing the effectiveness of juvenile justice reforms: A closer look at the criteria and the impacts on diverse stakeholders. *Law and Policy*, *22*(20), 175–201.

Millie, A. (2013). The policing task and the expansion (and contraction) of British policing. *Criminology and Criminal Justice*, *13*(2), 143–160.

Moore, E. (2011). *The use of police cautions and youth justice conferences in NSW in 2010* (Criminal Justice and Statistics Bureau Brief 74). NSW Bureau of Crime Statistics and Research.

Muncie, J. (2004). Youth justice: Responsibilisation and rights. In J. Roche, S. Tucker, R. Thomson, & R. Flynn (Eds.), *Youth in society* (pp. 131–144). The Open University.

Muncie, J. (2006). Governing young people: Coherence and contradiction in contemporary youth justice. *Critical Social Policy*, *26*(4), 770–793.

Muncie, J. (2008). The 'punitive turn' in juvenile justice: Cultures of control and rights compliance in Western Europe and the USA. *Youth Justice*, *8*, 107–121.

Naffine, N., & Wundersitz, J. (1994). Trends in juvenile justice. In D. Chappell & P. Wilson (Eds.), *The Australian criminal justice system in the mid 1990s* (pp. 235–250). Butterworths.

Naffine, N., Wundersitz, J., & Gale, F. (1991). Reforming the law: Idealism versus pragmatism. *Adelaide Law Review, 13*(1), 1–22.

National Inquiry into the Separation of Aboriginal and Torres Strait Islander Children from Their Families (NISATSIC). (1997). *Bringing them home: Report of the national inquiry into the separation of Aboriginal and Torres Strait Islander children and their families.* Human Rights and Equal Opportunity Commission.

Naudé, B., & Prinsloo, J. (2005). Magistrates' and prosecutors' views of restorative justice. In T. Maepa (Ed.), *Beyond retribution: Prospects for restorative justice in South Africa* (pp. 53–65). Institute for Security Studies.

Neglected Children's and Juvenile Offenders Act 1905. (NSW).

Nejelski, P. (1976). Diversion: The promise and the danger. *Crime and Delinquency, 22*, 393–410.

New South Wales Law Reform Commission. (2005). *Young Offenders* (Report no 104). NSW Law Reform Commission. https://lawreform.nsw.gov.au/documents/Publications/Reports/Report-104.pdf

Noetic Solutions. (2010). *A strategic review of the New South Wales juvenile justice system: Report for the Minister for Juvenile Justice.* New South Wales Department of Human Services.

NSW Bureau of Crime Statistics and Research (BOCSAR). (2007). *New South Wales Regional Statistics 2007.* (Catalogue no 1368.1). ABS. http://www.abs.gov.au/AUSSTATS/abs@.nsf/7d12b0f6763c78caca257061001cc588/dfd6faea24f68ad6ca257235001cd238!OpenDocument

NSW Department of Communities and Justice. (2023). *Court structure.* Children's Court New South Wales. https://childrenscourt.nsw.gov.au/about-the-court/court-structure.html#Children's1

NSW Department of Communities and Justice. (2025). *General court listings.* Children's Court New South Wales. https://childrenscourt.nsw.gov.au/listings/general-court-listings.html

NSW Parliamentary Debates, Legislative Council. (2002, August 27). *Parliamentary Debates*, p. 4227.

O'Brien, A. (1998). *Poverty's prison: The poor in New South Wales, 1880–1918.* Melbourne University Press.

O'Connor, I. (1997). Models of juvenile justice. In A. Borowski & O. O'Connor (Eds.), *Juvenile crime, justice and corrections* (pp. 229–253). Longman.

Otto, D. (1994). Amnesty International's concerns in Southeast Asia. In D. Kingsbury & G. Barton (Eds.), *Difference and tolerance: Human rights issues in Southeast Asia* (pp. 66–79). Deakin University Press.

Parker, A., Mohr, P., & Wilson, C. (2004). Attitudinal and personality predictors of diversionary behaviour by police. *Policing: An International Journal of Police Strategies & Management, 27*(1), 9–21.

Paternoster, R., & Iovanni, L. A. (1989). The labelling perspective and delinquency: An elaboration of the theory and assessment of the evidence. *Justice Quarterly, 6*(3), 359–394.

Patterson, G., Chung, I., & Swan, P. (2012). The effects of stress management interventions among police officers and recruits. *Campbell Systematic Reviews, 8*(1), 1–54.

Paquin-Marseille, L., & Higgison, K. (2022). *Section 19 of the Youth Criminal Justice Act: A look at the use of conferences across Canada.* Department of Justice Canada. https://www.justice.gc.ca/eng/rp-pr/jr/19/docs/rsd-2022-youth_justice_section-19-conferences-eng.pdf

Pearce, E. (2021). Why 'admission of guilt' is not working in youth diversionary schemes in NSW – Exploratory findings from interviews with police officers. *Current Issues in Criminal Justice, 33*(3), 285–299.

People, J., & Trimboli, L. (2007). *Evaluation of the NSW community conferencing for young adults pilot program.* NSW Bureau of Crime Statistics and Research.

Phoenix, J., & Kelly, L. (2013). 'You have to do it for yourself': Responsibilisation in young people's situated knowledge of youth justice practice. *British Journal of Criminology, 53*, 419–437.
Picton, C., & Boss, P. (1981). *Child welfare in Australia*. Harcourt Brace Jovanich Group.
Polk, K. (1993). The search for alternatives to coercive justice. In F. Gale, N. Naffine, & J. Wundersitz (Eds.), *Juvenile justice: Debating the issues* (pp. 106–115). Allen & Unwin.
Polk, K. (1994). Family conferencing: Theoretical and evaluative concerns. In C. Alder & J. Wundersitz (Eds.), *Family conferencing and juvenile justice: The way forward or misplaced optimism?* (pp. 15–44). Australian Institute of Criminology.
Polk, K., Alder, C., Muller, D., & Rechtman, K. (2003). *Early intervention: Diversion and youth conferencing, A national profile and review of current approaches to diverting juveniles from the criminal justice system*. Australian Government Attorney-General's Department.
Pratt, J. (1986). Diversion from the Juvenile Court: A history of inflation and a critique of progress. *British Journal of Criminology, 26*(3), 212–233.
Pratt, J. (1993). Welfare and justice: Incompatible philosophies. In F. Gale, N. Naffine, & J. Wundersitz (Eds.), *Juvenile justice: Debating the issues* (pp. 38–51). Allen and Unwin.
Prenzler, T., & Hayes, H. (1999). Victim-offender mediation and the gatekeeping role of police. *International Journal of Police Science and Management, 2*(1), 17–32.
Prichard, J. (2010). Net-widening and the diversion of young people from Court: A longitudinal analysis with implications for restorative justice. *Australian & New Zealand Journal of Criminology, 43*(1), 112–129.
Ranta, R. S., & Sud, A. (2008). Management of stress and burnout of police personnel. *Journal of the Indian Academy of Applied Psychology, 341*(1), 29–39.
Ravulo, J. (2016). Pacific Youth Offending within an Australian Context. *Youth Justice, 16*(1), 34–48.
Reformatory School Act 1866. (30Vic No IV).
Reiner, R. (2010). *The politics of the police* (4 ed.). Oxford University Press.
Richards, K. (2010a). Police-referred restorative justice for juveniles in Australia. *Current Issues in Criminal Justice, 398*, 1–8.
Richards, K. (2010b). Restorative justice and "Empowerment": Producing and governing active subjects through "Empowering" practices. *Critical Criminology, 19*(2), 91–105.
Richards, K. (2011a). *Trends in juvenile detention in Australia* (Trends and Issues in Crime and Criminal Justice, No. 416). Australian Institute of Criminology.
Richards, K. (2011b). *What makes juvenile offenders different from adult offenders?* (Trends and Issues in Crime and Criminal Justice, No. 409). Australian Institute of Criminology.
Richards, K. (2014). Blurred lines: Reconsidering the concept of 'diversion' in youth justice systems in Australia. *An International Journal, 14*(2), 122–139.
Richards, K., Bartels, L., & Bolitho, J. (2017). Children's Court magistrates' views of restorative justice and therapeutic jurisprudence measures for young offenders. *Youth Justice, 17*(1), 22–40.
Richards, K., & Lee, M. (2013). Beyond the 'three dogmas of juvenile justice': A response to Weatherburn, McGrath and Bartels. *University of New South Wales Law Journal, 36*(3), 839–862.
Richards, K., & Renshaw, L. (2013). *Bail and remand for young people in Australia: A national research project* (AIC reports: Research and Public Series 125). Australian Institute of Criminology.
Ringland, C., & Smith, N. (2013). *Police use of court alternatives for young persons in NSW* (Contemporary Issues in Crime and Criminal Justice, no. 167). NSW Bureau of Crime Statistics and Research.

Rogers, L. J., & Erez, E. (1999). The contextuality of objectivity in sentencing among legal professionals in South Australia. *International Journal of the Sociology of Law, 27*(3), 267–286.

Rose, D. (2006). Poverty and crime. In K. Serr (Ed.), *Thinking about poverty* (pp. 107–117). The Federation Press.

Rowe, M. (2008). *Introduction to policing.* Sage.

Schubert, F. A. (1981). Police policy and rulemaking: The need for definition. *Journal of Police Science and Administration, 9*(3), 261–271.

Schur, E. M. (1973). *Radical nonintervention.* Prentice Hall.

Scott, D., & Swain, S. (2002). *Confronting cruelty: Historical perspectives on child protection in Australia.* Melbourne University Press.

Seymour, J. (1997). Children's Courts in Australia: Their current role and functions. In A. Borovski & I. O'Connor (Eds.), *Juvenile crime, justice and corrections* (pp. 292–306). Longman.

Seymour, J. (1998). *Dealing with juvenile offenders.* Law Book Company.

Shafiq, N., Ohlsson, I., & Mathias, P. (2016). Predictors of punitive attitudes among police officers. *Journal of Forensic Practice, 18*(1), 76–86.

Sheehan, R. (2001). *Magistrates' decision-making in child protection cases.* Ashgate.

Sheehan, R., & Borowski, A. (Eds.) (2013). *Australia's Children's Courts today and tomorrow.* Springer.

Skardhamar, T. (2009). Reconsidering the theory of adolescent-limited and life-course persistent anti-social behaviour. *British Journal of Criminology, 49,* 863–878.

Skolnick, J. (1996). *Justice without trial: Law enforcement in democratic society.* Macmillan College Division.

Smith, B. L., & Damphousse, K. R. (1998). Terrorism, politics, and punishment: A test of structural-contextual theory and the "liberation hypothesis". *Criminology, 36,* 67–92.

Snowball, L. (2008a). *Diversion of Indigenous juvenile offenders* (Trends and Issues in Crime and Criminal Justice, no 355). Australian Institute of Criminology.

Snowball, L. (2008b). *Juvenile diversion of Indigenous offenders: A study examining juvenile offenders in Western Australia, South Australia and New South Wales* (Trends and Issues in Crime and Criminal Justice, no. 355). Australian Institute of Criminology.

Spiranovic, C., Clare, J., Bartels, L., Clare, M., & Clare, B. (2015). Aboriginal young people in the Children's Court of Western Australia: Findings from the national assessment of Australian Children's Courts. *University of Western Australia Law Review, 38*(2), 86–116.

Steffensmeier, D., Ulmer, J., & Kramer, J. (1998). The interaction of race, gender and age in criminal sentencing: The punishment cost of being young, black and male. *Criminology, 36,* 763–798.

Steinberg, L. (2005). Cognitive and affective development in adolescence. *Trends in Cognitive Sciences, 9*(2), 69–74.

Stephens, M. (2007). Lessons from the front line in Canada's restorative justice experiment: The experience of sentencing judges. *Queen's Law Journal, 33,* 19–78.

Stephenson, M. (2007). *Young people and offending: Education, youth justice and exclusion.* Willian.

Stewart, A. L., & Smith, F. (2004). Youth justice conferencing and police referrals: The gatekeeping role of police in Queensland, Australia. *Journal of Criminal Justice, 32,* 345–357.

Strang, H. (2001). *Restorative justice programs in Australia: A report to the Criminology Research Council.* Australian Institute of Criminology.

Straton, J. (1992). *The young ones: Working class culture, consumption and the category of youth.* Black Swan Press.

Sullivan, R. (1993). *Children in the Children's Court: Youth experiences of New South Wales Children's Courts.* National Children's and Youth Law Centre.

Swain, S. (2014). *History of inquiries reviewing institutions providing care for children.* Royal Commission into Institutional Responses to Child Sexual Abuse.

Sykes, G., & Matza, D. (1957). Techniques of neutralization: A theory of delinquency. *American Sociological Review*, *22*(6), 644–670.

Taussig, I. (2012). *Youth justice conferences: Participant profile and conference characteristics* (Crime and Justice Statistics Bureau Brief No. 73). NSW Bureau of Crime Statistics and Research.

Tilbury, C., & Mazerolle, P. (2013). The Children's Court in Queensland: Where to from here? In R. Sheehan & A. Borovski (Eds.), *Australia's Children's Courts today and tomorrow* (pp. 65–83). Springer.

Trimboli, L. (2000). *An evaluation of the NSW Youth Justice Conferencing Scheme*. NSW Bureau of Crime Statistics and Research.

United Nations. (November 20, 1989). *United Nations Convention on the Rights of the Child* (UNCRC). https://www.unicef.org.au/united-nations-convention-on-the-rights-of-the-child

United Nations Committee on the Rights of the Child. (2007). *General Comment No. 10 on Children's Rights Juvenile Justice*. https://www.refworld.org/legal/general/crc/2007/en/43085

United Nations General Assembly. (1985). *United Nations Standard Minimum Rules for the Administration of Juvenile Justice ("The Beijing Rules"): resolution/adopted by the General Assembly* (A/RES/40/33). http://www.refworld.org/docid/3b00f2203c.html

Van Maanen, J. (1973). Observations on the making of policemen. *Human Organisation*, *32*(4), 407–418.

Waegel, W. B. (1989). *Delinquency and juvenile control: A sociological perspective*. (Vol. 39). Prentice Hall.

Walklate, S. (2000). Reflections on "New Labour" or "Back to the Future"?. *Criminal Justice Matters*, *38*, 7–8.

Weatherburn, D., McGrath, A., & Bartels, L. (2012). Three dogmas of juvenile justice. *University of New South Wales Journal*, *35*(3), 781–809.

Windshuttle, E. (1980). Discipline, domestic training and social control: The female school of industry, Sydney, 1826–1847. *Labour History*, *39*, 1–14.

Wundersitz, J. (1997). Pre-court diversion: The Australian experience. In A. Borovski & I. O'Connor (Eds.), *Juvenile crime, justice and corrections* (pp. 270–291). Addison-Wesley Longman Australia Pty Ltd.

Wundersitz, J. (2000). Juvenile justice in Australia: Towards the new millennium. In D. Chappell & P. Wilson (Eds.), *Crime and the criminal justice system in Australia: 2000 and beyond* (5 ed., pp. 102–118). Butterworths.

Wundersitz, J., & Hunter, N. (2005). *Juvenile justice in South Australia: Where are we now?* (Information Bulletin no. 40). Adelaide Office of Crime Statistics and Research Attorney General's Department.

Young, M. (1991). *An inside job: Policing and police culture in Britain*. Clarendon.

Young Offenders Act 1997 (NSW).

Youth Justice Agency (YJA). (2009). *Youth justice agency annual report and accounts 2008–9*. The Stationery Office.

Youth Justice Coalition. (2011). *Review of the Young Offenders Act and the Children Criminal Proceedings Act: Submission to the Department of Attorney and General Justice*. Youth Justice Coalition.

Zehr, H. (1997). Restorative justice: The concept. *Corrections Today*, *59*(7), 68–70.

Zehr, H. (2015). *Changing lenses, restorative justice for our times* (25th Anniversary ed.). Herald Press. http://www.abs.gov.au/AUSSTATS/abs@.nsf/7d12b0f6763c78caca257061001cc588/dfd6faea24f68ad6ca257235001cd238

3 Risk, Neoliberalism and Young Offenders

Introduction

Youth justice governance, particularly in regions like the UK, Australasia, and North America, is often caught between preventative and punitive paradigms. This tension is exemplified by the preoccupation with 'risk' management within youth governance. Risk is prolific in contemporary youth governance, and its influence is often linked to crime prevention. Actuarial risk assessment tools such as the Youth Level of Service/Case Management Inventory Australian Adaptation (YLS/CMI-AA) are designed to categorise young people according to risk levels, thereby informing the selection of interventions deemed appropriate based on calculated risk factors. However, the application of risk management principles to youth governance has been criticised for promoting a reductionist approach that prioritises the management of aggregated risk over the provision of individualised responses to youth offending (Case & Haines, 2015). This shift, as Feeley and Simon (1992) argue, reflects a broader trend toward governing populations rather than addressing specific needs of individual young people.

The concept of risk is both a product of and a tool reinforcing neoliberal agendas. As discussed in this chapter—which provides a theoretical framework, risk discourses and practices enable the mobilisation of rational choice theory and individual responsibility—core tenets of neoliberal governmentality. Neoliberalism's reliance on market principles to govern behaviour, coupled with its emphasis on reducing the role of the state, positions individuals as rational agents solely responsible for their actions, while simultaneously absolving the state of its responsibilities. Governance, in this context, operates at a molecular level (Rose, 1999), with individuals expected to align their choices with societal norms and avoid risk; failure to do so results in exclusion and marginalisation. Neoliberal discourse also revives historical distinctions between the *deserving* and *undeserving*, reinforcing social hierarchies based on perceived merit. Within this framework, the construction of young people as inherently *risky* has profound implications for how they are governed—manifesting in punitive measures, heightened concern with anti-social behaviour, and 'tough on crime' approaches justified by deterrence, retribution and community protection.

DOI: 10.4324/9781003470366-3

Despite the implementation of complex governance technologies, efforts to promote individual-level reform have not disappeared. Under the YOA, there is an idealised platform for restorative justice approaches at the individual level. However, the legislation's principles and objectives span restoration and prevention, as much as punishment. Diversionary paths are often reserved for those deemed *less risky*, while traditional punitive measures are applied to those classified as *risky and high-risk*—typically the most disadvantaged and in-need individuals. This bifurcation highlights how diversionary decision-making can further segment youth justice systems.

This chapter situates neoliberal and risk-oriented approaches within the context of the YOA in NSW, examining how risk management ideologies may channel specific groups into the traditional criminal justice system rather than diverting them away through the legislative alternatives. This failure to divert manifests in context-specific ways within institutions such as the NSW Police Force and the NSW Children's Court, both of which are central to this book's analysis.

Risk and modern youth justice governance

Extensive work in the social sciences has featured risk prominently as a central theme (Beck, 1992; Cohen, 1985; Douglas, 1992; Feeley & Simon, 1992; Garland, 1996, 2001; Giddens, 1990, 1991; Rose, 1999). The English publication of Ulrich Beck's *Risk Society: Toward a New Modernity* in 1992 heralded a major shift in risk analyses, arguing that modern Western societies are defined by pervasive anxiety over ubiquitous risks and a growing distrust in modern institutional capacities to manage them. Similarly, Giddens (1991, p. 124) contends that 'in conditions of modernity, for lay actors as well as for specific fields, thinking in terms of risk and risk assessment is a more or less ever-present exercise, of a partly imponderable character.' As discussed later in this chapter, these pervasive perceptions of risk and the corresponding institutional mistrust have shaped criminal justice policies and practices, including those in youth justice governance.

Chan and Rigakos (2002) note that Beck (1992) and Giddens (1990, 1991) adopt an ontological perspective on risk, viewing the contemporary preoccupation with risk management as a reaction to an increasingly uncertain world. As individuals and institutions navigate the complexities of (post)modernity and industrialisation, science is both a source of reassurance and a generator of new risks. Such articulations of risk cultivate insecurities while focusing on 'scapegoats' (Ericson & Haggerty, 1997, p. 86) and relying on new expertise and knowledge to provide feasible solutions (Schehr, 2005). Consequently, an ever-expanding array of technological solutions is introduced to manage risks. However, risks also emanate from new technologies, thus making the cycle of risk management endless and self-perpetuating (Beck, 1992). In Beck's thesis, risk is conceptualised in terms of global hazards—such as global warming, emerging pandemics, a comet striking earth, or geopolitical conflict—challenges that transcend boundaries.

In the context of youth offending, the concept of risk differs significantly from that associated with global hazards. Nevertheless, risk theory offers valuable insights into youth governance, particularly amid contemporary political shifts marked by oscillations between 'law and order' politics and an over-playing of risk. In such a risk-driven climate—characterised by economic rationalism, neoliberalism and a focus on cost-effective offender management—traditional conceptions of crime control are increasingly being replaced by a range of contemporary practices, whereby social control is achieved by newly responsibilised individuals and non-state agencies (Garland, 2001; O'Malley, 2001).

Understanding the intersections of risk, crime and crime control requires attention to institutional or 'governmentality' perspectives, which conceptualise risk as '...ways of thinking and acting, involving calculations about probable futures in the present followed by interventions into the present in order to control that potential future' (Rose, 2001, p. 7). Adopting a Foucauldian approach, some risk theorists examine the roles of institutions in adapting surveillance technologies as a mode of discipline (Barry et al., 1996; Burchell et al., 1991). These scholars emphasise that welfare ideals are increasingly framed in actuarial terms, thereby becoming integral to the risk society (O'Malley, 1992; Simon, 1987). The increased emphasis on individual responsibility repositions offenders not as victims of structural and social inequalities but as rational actors accountable for their choices and actions. Thus, sentencing and corrections have moved away from therapeutic aims toward retributive, cost-driven sanctions that deprioritise offenders' needs and rehabilitation (O'Malley, 1992).

Several criticisms have been levelled against criminological theories of risk. For instance, O'Malley (2001) highlights that class, race and gender rarely surface within this theoretical framework. However, he argues that this type of governance is just as much about constructions of risks and the empirical mapping of rationalities and techniques as it is about ostracising classes of people (O'Malley, 2001). Similarly, Chan and Rigakos (2002) contend that risk theory is often formulated within narrow conceptions that treat risk 'as a neutral concept and risk assessment as intended apolitical actuarial practice of late modernity' (p. 743). This approach effectively sidelines the politics of gender, class and race, despite these factors being deeply embedded in risk formulations. For instance, the negotiation of risk-taking and risk avoidance reveals that understandings of risk are inherently gendered rather than universalised. Men and women encounter different types of risks, yet women's risk experiences have been inadequately recognised because *risky behaviour* is predominantly conceptualised through a masculine lens (Chan & Rigakos, 2002). Thus, women face heightened scrutiny for undertaking behaviours perceived as risky, which deviate from traditional feminine gender norms (Jewkes, 2004).

Indeed, numerous criticisms have been raised regarding various theoretical perspectives on risk. For example, governmentality approaches have been critiqued for their emphasis on instrumental rationalities, which tend to underplay the expressive elements of contemporary penality—namely, the punitive sentiment that has become central to punitive justice and penal policy (Garland, 1997). Additionally, criticisms of risk society theory generally cluster around four main areas: the contention that the distinction between traditional and late modernity is overstated; the flawed assumption that risks are under-regulated and have weakened social control; the overstatement that the dissolution of traditional bonds intensifies risks; and the inaccurate diagnosis that risks are proliferating (Kemshall, 2003).

While an exhaustive analysis of the extensive criticisms and diverse perspectives on risk theories is beyond the scope of this book, it is important to note the significant overlap in conceptualising the risk society as a plethora of progressive dangers that shape institutionalised practices and individual identities (Castel, 1991; Ericson & Haggerty, 1997). Individuals are 'panoptically sorted' (Gandy, 1993, 2021) and actuarially encoded by a headless monster of surveillance with an endless array of tentacles (Foucault, 1991; O'Malley, 1991; Shearing, 1993). Likewise, the governance of children and young people is increasingly subjected to a risk-oriented ethos.

Risk theoretical frameworks are thus crucial for understanding contemporary crime and criminal justice. In this context, risk is conceptualised as an estimate of future dangerousness, making it a central concept within security paradigms (Aradau et al., 2008). This shift has challenged the transformative and rehabilitative logics that once underpinned correctionalism (Kempf-Leonard & Peterson Sparks, 2000). Meanwhile, offender profiling and risk assessment have been widely embraced. The proliferation of the 'what works' paradigm suggests that 'some forms of intervention can be successful in reducing some re-offending for some offenders at sometimes' (Muncie, 2006, p. 779), a notion that has been widely welcomed by policymakers. These stakeholders have focused on a variety of techniques—including preventative detention, incapacitation, increased use of community-based options, and diversionary alternatives for *less serious* offenders—all of which emphasise risk as central to regulating and managing offenders in cost-effective ways within an environment shaped by economic rationalism and broader neoliberal ideologies (Feeley & Simon, 1992, 1994; Priday, 2006).

The increasing prominence of risk-oriented practices is evident throughout the entire criminal justice system. Contemporary debates in criminal justice frequently concentrate on recidivism among so-called hardened criminals, exemplified by heightened concerns surrounding sexual offenders. This focus has precipitated the development of risk-oriented strategies to manage individuals convicted of such offences. Notable examples include sex offender registers and Multi-Agency Protection Panels (MAPPs), which emphasise risk assessment and classification. Additionally, notification systems similar to Megan's Law in the United States (US) allow community members access to information about local offenders (Keyzer & McSherry, 2015).

Moreover, emerging discourses on crime prevention—centred on community engagement and citizens' preventative actions—are omnipresent, from the trend of living in gated communities to the marketing of CCTV, security devices and private security. Traditional objectives of the criminal system, such as punishment and 'just deserts,' have been supplanted by a focus on preventive harm-reduction and cost-effective techniques (Garland, 2001). Concurrently, policing strategies have significantly shifted towards surveillance and proactive targeting of people, a practice known as problem-oriented policing (Tilley, 2008). Disillusionment with the ideal or possibility of reform and rehabilitation is part of this logic. Furthermore, there is a pervasive social discourse on various forms of risk, often associated with young people, crime, health, education failure, unemployment, and other issues. Consequently, certain youth populations are perceived as the very embodiment of risk—risk of 'going bad.'

Over the past three decades, young people have been subjected to a range of interventions predicated on the identification of population-risk factors (Turnbull & Spence, 2011). The dual construction of youth as both 'risk subjects' and 'subjects at risk' has significantly influenced front-line practice and remains a dominant narrative driving contemporary penal policy (Armstrong, 2005; Feeley & Simon, 1994; Goldson, 2000; Kemshall, 2008; Turnbull & Spence, 2011). Such predictions of risk and policies of incapacitation, with an emphasis on actuarialism, share much in common with the development of restorative justice and diversion strategies. As Cunneen and Goldson (2015) assert, 'risk assessment becomes a fundamental technology for dividing child and youth populations between those who benefit from restorative justice practices' (p. 17) and those, who having been refused diversion, 'are channelled into more retributive (read punitive) processes' (p. 18). Discussions on risk are therefore instrumental in contextualising the role of diversion and essential for framing diversionary decision-making processes. However, while risk thinking is integral to these processes, other factors also play a significant role. For instance, punitiveness has persisted over time and plays into risk paradigms. Underlying this punitiveness are various social, structural and institutional prejudices or dispositions towards specific populations. Consequently, although risk is a crucial element shaping practices in criminal justice concerning youth diversion, numerous other nuances also factor into these practices.

In discussing the relationship between restorative justice, risk management and punitivism, it is crucial to emphasise that restorative justice encompasses more than these elements. While restorative justice practices are influenced by technocratic pressures, they also have antecedents that are independent of such forces. Over recent decades, a new sensitive age focusing on the emotionality of the law and the non-rational, even spiritual, has spread around the world (Laster & O'Malley, 1996). Early iterations of restorative justice drew inspiration from religious movements advocating for inclusive, interpersonal, problem-solving approaches as alternatives to traditional adversarial justice systems (Van Ness et al., 2022; Zehr, 2015).

Restorative justice represents a shift toward the emotionalisation of crime (Karstedt, 2002; Sherman, 2003). This is evident in how YJCs reframe justice as a relational process that establishes emotional connections between victims, offenders and communities (Karstedt, 2002). The focus on reintegrative shaming within YJCs exemplifies this shift towards emotionalisation of the law. As Laster and O'Malley (1996) observe, 'the legal order absorbs and reciprocally shapes multiple and contradictory tendencies' (p. 22). Currently, both technocratic approaches and emotional dimensions compete and coexist within the formal structures of the criminal system.

Nevertheless, the shaping of contemporary crime control by risk practices, as described, has partly transformed the criminal justice system. As O'Malley (2006) contends, there are close links between the socio-economic changes associated with a neoliberal ethos and the extensive changes observed in contemporary crime control strategies. He highlights several key developments: first, the rise of predictive rational models, which in turn result in the gradual displacement of more socially oriented approaches to explaining crime causation; second, the progressive prioritisation of deterrence over rehabilitation; and third, the emphasis on individual responsibilisation and cost-effectiveness.

From the risk society to neoliberalism and responsibilisation

Over the past three decades, neoliberalism has significantly influenced contemporary debates in youth justice. Neoliberalism refers to a political-economic ideology that advocates market deregulation, privatisation, reduced state intervention, and the promotion of individual responsibility within social and economic domains (Bauman, 1998). In this global neoliberal framework, power and authority transition from nation-states to multinational corporations that dominate trade and capital mobility. Consequently, individual states experience constraints on their power (Bauman, 1998; Beck, 2006; Bell, 2011; Reiner, 2007). To attract international capital and mitigate job losses and declines in taxable income, globalised nation-states must become competitive by adopting similar economic, social welfare and criminal justice policies (Bauman, 1998). This trend coincides with a reduction in social welfare provisions, impacting the governance of all vulnerable groups, including children and young people (Muncie, 2005).

Along this continuum, in the context of criminal justice, a 'neoliberal penality'—a form of rationality within neoliberalism where the penal sphere is the only legitimate domain for state-imposed order (Harcourt, 2010, p. 77)—promotes criminalisation. As Harcourt (2010) argues, the discourse of neoliberal penality 'facilitates the growth of the carceral sphere' (p. 81). According to Wacquant (2008), this form of neoliberal punitiveness is a deliberate component of a 'political project that aims to subordinate all human activities to the tutelage of the market' (p. 20). He further explains that, as a political project, neoliberal punitiveness is legitimised through zero-tolerance discourses and an expansion of laws and surveillance strategies, bolstered by the extension of crime control agencies.

While neoliberalism cannot be directly linked to specific ideas and practices of individuals within the criminal justice system, it has nevertheless helped to create broader feelings of insecurity and egotism that sustain the punitive sentiment amongst its practitioners (Bell, 2011). Crime becomes a tool for neoliberal governments to exploit public fears and insecurities, thereby serving as a vehicle to secure electoral support (Bell, 2011). Complex issues in criminal justice are often deliberately simplified to garner consensus around tough 'law and order' policies. This leads to an authoritarian consensus involving the government, the media and the public on the need for punitive measures—a stance challenging for the judiciary to oppose. Despite their independence and discretionary powers in sentencing, the majority of the judiciary view themselves as public servants who cannot disregard public opinion, and are therefore willing to align with the authoritarian consensus (Bell, 2011). As Sir Mason (2019) highlights, however, 'judicial independence is the feature of the system which is most prized by the judges themselves' (p. 31). Thus, the judiciary naturally prefers to base their decisions on legal arguments, even if it is contrary to public opinion.

It is important to note that, in the abstract, public perceptions, both in Australia and internationally, often regard sentences as overly lenient and express limited confidence in the criminal justice system's response to crime (Jones et al., 2008; Roberts et al., 2003; Roth, 2014; Warner et al., 2011). However, punitive attitudes tend to diminish when individuals are provided with more detailed information about the cases (Gelb, 2008; Moore, 2012; Warner et al., 2011).

Less is known about public attitudes toward restorative justice. Nevertheless, existing research indicates substantial support for it (Moore, 2012; Pali & Pelikan, 2010; Roberts et al., 2003). Public support for restorative justice is associated with factors such as victim inclusion and reparation, offender gestures of remorse and restoration, particularly with first-time juvenile offenders (Pali & Pelikan, 2010; Roberts et al., 2003), and offences like theft/vandalism and assault (Moore, 2012; Prison Reform Trust, 2011).

However, it must be acknowledged that even with moderate and stable public support for restorative justice, political rhetoric is sometimes dominated by penal populism infused with distinct neoliberal undertones. Risk discourses justify the necessity of the punitive turn. The concept of neoliberalism plays a crucial role in comprehending actuarial justice. Indeed, 'the development and advance of the capital neoliberal state has produced a barrage of institutional processes and practices both to reduce danger and encourage individualised risk management strategies' (Walklate & Mythen, 2011, p. 101).

At a macro level, risk management emphasises structural regulation, whereas at a micro level, it focuses on self-management (O'Malley, 2012; Walklate & Mythen, 2011; Wilkinson, 2009). Neoliberalism shifts away from state and collective responsibilisation (Priday, 2006). Similarly, the risk discourse emphasises individual responsibility and active citizenship, encouraging people to manage their own risks rather than relying on state interventions (Briggs, 2013; Giddens, 1990; Kelly, 2001; Kemshall, 2008; O'Malley, 1992, 2010; Phoenix & Kelly, 2013; Priday, 2006). This creates opportunities to govern at a distance (Burchell, 1996; Rose, 2000; Rose & Miller, 2008). The neoliberal governance of young people is secured through the dominance of risk thinking, policies and practices that individualise politically and socially produced risks, as well as strategies of responsibilisation aimed at transforming and reconstructing the 'young offender into prudential self-governing "young citizens" ready to manage their risk and take responsibility for themselves' (Phoenix & Kelly, 2013, p. 421).

Garland (1997, 2001) describes responsibilisation as a governance strategy whereby non-criminal justice local and community organisations are tasked with delivering social control. Drawing on a key distinction between 'authority' and 'accountability,' he argues that the strategy of responsibilisation serves to absolve the state of responsibility. This is particularly evident in youth justice, where legislative changes have necessitated multi-agency collaboration bringing diverse and disparate agencies together towards a common goal (Phoenix & Kelly, 2013). The *Crime and Disorder Act 1998* in the UK exemplifies this approach by mandating various statutory and voluntary agencies to assume responsibility for crime prevention (Muncie, 2006; Muncie et al., 1995).

Similarly, Bargen's examination of the YOA in NSW highlights 'an unusual mixture of cross government and community co-operation' under the Act, extending crime control responsibilities to the community (2001, p. 7). Garland's concept of responsibilisation suggests that the *working together* strategies enable action addressing the underlying economic, political or social marginalisations (Goldson, 2002, 2005; Goldson & Muncie, 2006). In this sense, responsibilisation is not so much realised in the young person, but is, rather, a reconfiguration of governance through multi-agency relations with central government (Phoenix & Kelly, 2013).

Although Garland's conception of responsibilisation holds significance in the underlying principles and practices of the YOA, perhaps even more pertinent in this context is Rose and Miller's (1992) observation on the shift of discourse towards the notion of the 'responsible citizen of neo-liberal rule' (p. 198). This shift creates opportunities for governing at a distance through mechanisms of inclusion and exclusion (Burchell, 1996; Rose & Miller, 2008). In this model of neoliberal responsibilisation, the state, local agencies and voluntary/community organisations are tasked with three main responsibilities: creating social and political conditions that enable individuals to participate as active agents, categorising and identifying those suitable for the intervention practices, and intervening appropriately to shape conduct (Phoenix & Kelly, 2013). This framework illuminates the mechanism through which diverse categories of young offenders become subjects of disciplinary intervention, reflecting contradictory and hybrid forms of youth governance. Responsibilisation in this context is seen as an *ethical reconstruction* of the neoliberal subject. The strategic imperative is to implement technologies of governance upon individual social actors, facilitating their transformation into *ideal* non-deviant neoliberal exemplary citizens (Hannah-Moffat, 1999, 2001; Kelly, 2001; Kemshall, 2008; O'Malley, 1992; Rose, 2000). Within the context of YJC, this is exemplified by a focus on victims' needs and encouraging young offenders to assume responsibility for their actions.

The emphasis is on individuals as rational agents, makers of their own worlds, 'making decisions according to calculations of risk and opportunity' (Petersen, 1996, p. 47). This discourse individualises risk through a process of responsibilisation, transferring governance obligations to young people and their families, expecting them to self-rule (Briggs, 2013; Kelly, 2001; Kemshall, 2008). Those who fail or 'refuse to do so, are demonized and excluded' (Briggs, 2013, p. 19). This premise clearly underpins the legislation regulating diversion, wherein individual responsibilisation is operationalised through the procedural requirement of an 'admission of guilt'—a stipulation that raises significant concerns regarding children's rights. For example, a central technique of risk management embedded within the YOA is that of responsibilisation through restorative justice interventions, such as YJCs, which function to challenge perceived deficits in young people's moral reasoning (Gray, 2005)—an issue that will be further explored in subsequent sections of this chapter.

It is also imperative to recognise how the regulation of youth, and more recently the category of youth *at risk* oscillates between competing paradigms of blame/responsibility and exculpation/diminished-responsibility—a fundamental tension that persistently characterises criminological discourses about juvenile offenders. Since the 1980s, international human rights instruments have progressively shaped youth justice frameworks, exerting significant influence on policy development—a normative evolution that has unfolded concurrently with the ascendence of neoliberal risk discourses. The development of global treaties and conventions was discussed previously (see Chapter 2), yet the significant point to emphasise here is that the movement towards a 'child-friendly justice' system, driven by globalised human rights concerns, contrasts with neoliberal justice practices (Muncie, 2013). When it comes to children's rights, the emphasis shifts toward state protection rather than individual responsibility. In contrast with the typical expansion of the penal sphere seen in neoliberal practices, systems focused on children's rights advocate for the reduction of punitive measures by promoting child dignity and viewing prison or punishment as a last resort.

Simultaneously, the global narratives, neoliberal penality and children's rights contribute to the incoherence observed in youth justice policies. Consequently, these policies and practices are applied in fragmented ways. Political, economic and cultural contexts shape the decisions of police, magistrates and juvenile justice staff regarding diversion. Furthermore, shifting perspectives on determinism/risk versus blame (responsibility) sometimes operate together rather than as extreme opposites. For example, First Nations youth are simultaneously positioned as disadvantaged victims of circumstances who are *at-risk* and in *need of* care, while also being viewed as aware of their offences and the harm caused to their victims. The criminal justice system struggles to adequately capture the nuanced intersections of these issues due to its reliance on dichotomous understandings.

Returning to the discussion of risk, at the intersections of 'risk society' concepts and neoliberal techniques of preventive and individualised risk management, 'crime control' becomes a project focused on predicting crime and identifying which groups within society should be classified as most *risky* (Cunneen & White, 2002; O'Malley, 2012). A broader preoccupation with risk in social theory is reflected in criminal justice practices, whereby risk management technologies have replaced earlier emphases on rehabilitation and disciplinary styles of social control (Cohen, 1985; Feeley & Simon, 1992; Kemshall et al., 1997; O'Malley, 1992; Robinson, 1999, 2002; Shearing & Stenning, 1985; Sparks, 2001; Walklate & Mythen, 2011). The notion of crime as a 'normal social fact' of risk societies (Cohen, 1985; Feeley & Simon, 1992; Garland, 1996; Reichman, 1986) has generated narratives centred on crime prevention through the identification of 'risk factors.' As defined by Farrington (2002, p. 664), risk factors are 'prior factors that increase the risk of occurrence of the onset, frequency, persistence, or duration of offending.' This focus is supported by risk assessment and management techniques (Bessant et al., 2005; Sparks, 2001). However, as noted by Garland, '[o]ver time the accumulation of large databases, and a predictive knowledge of risk probabilities has produced a new way of reasoning that has significant social implications' (1997, p. 181). For instance, police reports are increasingly structured around issues of risk, shaping the information recorded and leading to the non-recording of other types of data, thereby silencing alternative knowledge (Ericson & Haggerty, 1997; O'Malley, 2012).

As Ericson and Haggerty (1997) note, in crime control, police adopt a strategic position as governors of security, emphasising the gathering, sorting and forwarding of information. Consequently, much of police work concentrates on 'informational transactions concerned with risks' (p. 69), rather than crime control. Risk discourses in juvenile offending are influenced by social, economic and political conditions (Cunneen & White, 2002), under which communication exchanges occur. This context can shape discretionary inclusion/exclusion decisions within frameworks like the YOA, especially when attention shifts from individual to group-related information. As explored in the next section, those labelled as 'risky subjects' tend to be the most marginalised and disadvantaged youth, who, in turn, are less likely to receive opportunities for diversion.

According to Feeley and Simon's work on the 'new penology,' better known as 'actuarial justice,' the criminal justice system had transitioned from focusing on the 'individual' to a 'unit of analysis.' The new penology is 'markedly less concerned with responsibility, fault, sensibility, diagnosis, or intervention and treatment of the individual offender. Rather, it is concerned with techniques to identify, classify and manage groupings sorted by dangerousness' (Feeley & Simon, 1992, p. 452).

Within these risk discourses, 'problems are being governed in terms of aggregates, populations and distributions rather than individuals' (O'Malley, 1998, p. xi). This systems approach to criminal justice has been increasingly challenged, particularly by the emergence of a 'what works' narrative (Priday, 2006). In contrast to welfare ideologies, which emphasise collective responsibility, as previously discussed, neoliberalism reorients the focus towards individual responsibility for risk management, applying tailored actuarial risk management strategies to aggregate populations rather than individuals. This largely driven cost-effective approach drives current policy on detention, retribution, incapacitation and the privatisation of corrections. Simultaneously, it supports the increased use of alternative strategies such as community-based options and diversion techniques for lower-risk offenders.

However, with risk management and growing punitive sentiments in law and order, the definition of criminal behaviour has become looser to include 'nuisance behaviour and incivilities' (Bell, 2011, p. 5), the most likely type of behaviour defining 'lower-risk' offenders. Thus, not surprisingly, diversionary practices have been criticised on the grounds of net-widening—the claim being made that the boundaries of social control are expanded to individuals that would not have been otherwise drawn into the system (Chapin & Griffin, 2005). The issue of net-widening within the context of the YOA is explored in forthcoming sections of this chapter. The significant point to conclude here is that, overall, these techniques are grounded on risk assessment, regulation and management aligning within a neoliberal ideology emphasising minimal state intervention, individualisation and privatisation.

Neoliberal ethos in NSW youth governance and the YOA

Australia, like many Western nations, has embraced the political ethos of neoliberalism. Under this political ideology, and through the adoption of evidence-based policies, the government seeks to responsibilise individuals, communities and other agencies within a mixed model of crime control (Sparks, 2001). Despite limited empirical support for the efficacy of such interventions (Allard et al., 2007), community-based approaches are promoted to prevent the emergence of so-called 'risk behaviours' through early intervention and diversion programs (Bessant et al., 2005; Sparks, 2001). The neoliberal strategies of responsibilisation and managerialism via risk governance manifest themselves in the diversion practices characterising juvenile justice in Australia.

In a risk-oriented neoliberal context, YJC has emerged as the preferred model of restorative justice (Cunneen, 2008a, 2012; Gray, 2005, 2009; Hudson, 2006), promising to foster responsible and autonomous citizens, rather than welfare-dependent ones (O'Malley, 2001). However, in NSW, this transition towards *risk-based* policy frameworks occurred simultaneously with the political deployment of law-and-order rhetoric and tough-on-crime approaches as strategies for crime control. This trend is evidenced by the surge of legislation introduced since the 1990s, which predominantly expanded police powers and tightened control over public spaces.

Three broad explanations have been proposed for the expansion of police powers enacted through the legislation. First, persistent penal populism fuels this expansion by drawing on public insecurities from 'moral panics,' characterised by repeated media and political claims about crime waves and an increasingly violent society (Hogg & Brown, 1998). This phenomenon persists irrespective of youth crime trends, as the public's fascination with crime news frequently results in media representations of offending that contradict official crime statistics (Potter & Kappeler, 2006; Reiner, 1997; Urwin, 2025). A second explanation put forward for the expansion of police powers has been the need to restore public confidence in the police following the Wood Royal Commission's (Wood, 1997) exposure of corruption within NSW's police (Anderson, 2001). Lastly, the growing privatisation of public spaces has led property owners to demand greater regulation, control and surveillance in the public sphere (Anderson, 2001). Indeed, security concerns have often been used to justify the complementary regulations and legislative actions that may encroach on civil rights (Anderson, 2001).

As observed by Cunneen and White (2011), certain legislation, while technically non-age-specific, disproportionately impacts young people upon implementation. For instance, under the *Crimes Legislation Amendment (Police and Public Safety) Act 1998* (NSW), carrying a knife or other implements such as scissors in public spaces constitutes an offence. Additionally, the *Law Enforcement (Powers and Responsibilities) Act 2002* (NSW) [LEPRA] grants the police discretionary powers to stop and search young people for prohibited implements, while parents can be held liable if their children carry these items (Fitzgerald, 2000). This allowance for charging parents illustrates the shift of responsibility from state to individuals. A significant concern is the wide discretionary powers given to police officers, authorising them to carry out random searches and perform other duties that raise questions within a civil-rights framework, but are authorised by the law. Given the tendency of youth to frequent public spaces and their visibility therein, these discretionary powers are most extensively applied to young people, significantly increasing their likelihood of involvement in the criminal justice system (NSWLRC, 2005; Parker & Sarre, 2008). This issue is further 'exacerbated when fears of young people are also racialised' (Cunneen, 2008b, p. 44). For example, the historical pattern of interactions between First Nations people and police, and the enduring consequences of these encounters, demonstrate systemic differential treatment based on racial identity. Such practices undermine 'the spirit of the YOA' (NSWLRC, 2005, p. 53).

At the core of this new paradigm for crime control, 'needs' have been redefined as 'criminogenic needs.' These criminogenic needs encompass dynamic risk factors, such as antisocial attitudes or ineffective parenting, that are associated with criminal behaviour and are believed to be modifiable to reduce the recidivism risk (Hannah-Moffat, 1999). Within this framework, the central aim is to place responsibility on offenders through tailored psychological interventions designed to develop in them the characteristics of 'rational agents' (Cunneen & Luke, 2007; Kemshall, 2002). Critically, while offenders' choices and decisions are constrained by socio-economic factors, these social justice considerations are largely ignored within risk management that emphasises individual responsibility.

The emphasis on responsibility that pervades YJC has been noted in the previous chapter. Under the YOA, the central objective of conferencing is to emphasise the acceptance of responsibility by the offender and provide a community-based negotiated response that emphasises participation and restitution for victims and offenders (YOA, s. 3, pt. 1). As previously discussed, this aspect of responsibilisation is problematic as it conflicts with the doctrine of *doli incapax* in NSW (NSW Commission for Children and Young People (CCYP), 2011; Urbas, 2000). Moreover, the responsibilisation model has been criticised for exerting pressure on young people to admit an offence to obtain the presumed benefit of diversion and, in turn, the avoidance of a criminal record. This compromises the mental element of the offence (*mens rea)* and due process rights more broadly (Cunneen, 2008a). This issue is particularly problematic in Australia, where the MACR remains at ten years in all states and territories except the ACT (Cunneen & Goldson, 2015). Furthermore, this low age of criminal responsibility creates an incoherent framework when compared with how other legal responsibilities and social rights are allocated in Australian legislation (Cunneen & Goldson, 2015). Consequently, there exists a significant risk that young people's rights may be violated and the principle of the child's best interests disregarded.

A further concern regarding the responsibilisation of young offenders through restorative justice processes like YJC is the crucial need for effective communication. Without adequate communication skills, young people cannot articulate the reflective narratives that might demonstrate genuine remorse (Cunneen & Goldson, 2015). Evidence suggests that for young people in general, low levels of confidence/self-esteem, educational deficits, mental disabilities and/or substance misuse are likely to negatively impact a child's ability to communicate (Cunneen, 2010; Cunneen & Goldson, 2015). Such difficulties can be intensified for children whose first language differs from the program's language. For example, as observed among First Nations children, linguistic problems can lead to silence, which may then be interpreted as disregard or unwillingness to assume responsibility (Cunneen & Goldson, 2015). This can result in unsatisfied or unforgiving victims and unremorseful offenders.

Finally, significant implications emerge when considering gender differences in responsibilisation practices, particularly when the offender is a girl or young woman rather than a young boy. It is well established that behaviours are 'judged, controlled, and disciplined through gendered scripts in the justice arena' (Cunneen & Goldson, 2015). Additionally, according to Cook et al. (2006, p. 21), 'the socially constructed categories of difference,' created through class, gender and ethnicity, 'are not eliminated but instead used as subtle devices of domination' in restorative YJCs.

Despite these difficulties, several criminologists argue that restorative justice and diversion programs, such as conferencing within contemporary juvenile justice, should be viewed positively. They regard these approaches as the most inclusionary criminal justice options available, committed to the aims of social justice (O'Malley, 2001; Stenson, 2001). According to Braithwaite, restorative justice holds the potential to restore the 'deliberative control of justice by citizens' and to restore 'harmony based on a feeling that justice has been done' (2003, p. 57).

Further, Gray (2005) has argued that current juvenile justice initiatives are about the responsibilisation of individuals through the management of their own risks, which can be regulated through inclusionary programs. These youth restorative justice responses are premised on collaborative solutions involving all parties, including victims, offenders and the wider community. Indeed, YJC has been recognised as providing a platform for developing alternative discourses that focus on 'social harm,' 'social conflict' and 'redress,' hence providing a counterpart to the traditional punitive and retributive justice frameworks (Consedine, 1995; De Haan, 1990; Van Ness et al., 2022; Walgrave, 1995). At the same time, the YOA has led to the growth of confusing and sometimes unfair diversionary options. The legislation may also have 'widened the net' to capture children who have committed relatively minor offences (and who are likely to grow out of offending) while detracting attention and resources from the most serious and persistent offenders who inevitably end up in the formal court process (CCYP, 2011, p. 4).

It is well-documented within the current policy framework that youth justice is fraught with contradictions and confusing strategies (Ball, 1999; Fionda, 1999). Underpinning the YOA is the fundamental tactic of dividing young offenders into two groups: those deemed to benefit from diversionary restorative justice and those directed to court proceedings resulting in punitive and stigmatising processes, including bail refusal, mandatory supervision or incarceration (Cunneen, 2008a). An analogy can be noted here to Nil Christie's (1986) work on the notion of the 'ideal victim' and the 'ideal offender.' As established by Christie (1986) and others (see Rock, 2004), these ideals legitimate the experiences of some individuals while dismissing those of others. Omnipresent within social discourse, notions of ideal offender identities serve as a form of social control (Balfour, 2008; Chesney-Lind, 2002). Thus, risk mechanisms—ranging from simple recognition of a prior criminal record to the application of specifically designed risk assessment tools—have intensified such processes of bifurcation in the juvenile system. Consequently, the YOA has emerged amid a potentially radical shift from exclusionary and punitive approaches to becoming inclusionary and restorative—at least in principle and rhetoric. Yet, in practice, these ideals are neither consistently applied nor available to all young offenders. Thus, there is substantial debate about whether the YOA's framework permits authentic restorative justice. Indeed, as noted earlier, while there are strong restorative elements within the YOA framework, punitive measures also exist, even where the use of imprisonment is outlined as a *last resort*.

Evaluations and empirical evidence have demonstrated that the YOA provides a system that is, at times, unfair, disproportionate and unnecessarily stigmatising by drawing certain offenders into the juvenile system more than others (Cunneen, 2006; Cunneen et al., 2006; McAlinden, 2010). As noted elsewhere, diversionary measures bypass some groups of young people in trouble with the law altogether, specifically those considered the *risky subjects* (Richards & Lee, 2013). For example, young people who breach bail conditions are precluded from the YOA and must be dealt with by way of arrest (Richards & Renshaw, 2013). This is significant because trends, despite fluctuations, consistently show that more than half of the young people in detention in Australia are on remand (AIHW, 2012a, 2023). The latest figures show that, for an average day in 2023–2024, four out of five young people aged 10 and over in detention (80%) were held on remand (AIHW, 2024b). The primary factor driving the increase in remand is a rise in bail refusals (BOCSAR, 2024). This issue of disproportionality affects young First Nations people, who represent one of the most disadvantaged groups within the criminal justice system. For instance, from December 2023 to December 2024, there was a 21.7% increase in the number of young First Nations young people in detention, driven by a 22.6% rise in the number of First Nations youth on remand during that period (BOCSAR, 2024). Notably, exclusion from diversionary alternatives due to bail conditions has been recognised as contributing to increased youth remand numbers (Richards & Renshaw, 2013).

Under the YOA, first-time offenders benefit from conferencing models and other diversionary schemes, while those classified as *serious and repeat* offenders are ineligible for these programs (Allard et al., 2010; Cunneen, 2008a; Snowball, 2008a,

2008b; Snowball & Weatherburn, 2007). The concept of a serious and repeat offender is skewed and reflects a reality that is far more banal; such categorisations can include minor offences like being caught stealing biscuits or a packet of chewing gum as a second offence. This logic of grouping offenders with a second offence into the *serious* category, is also characteristic of punitive sentencing regimes such as mandatory sentencing and three-strike laws (see Garland, 2001).

Furthermore, the impact of the *Bail Act 1978* (NSW) has intensified bifurcation between those classified as 'low' and 'high' risk over the last decade. Changes to the legislation have contributed to an increasing number of children in remand and greater restrictions on eligibility for YJC and other diversionary programs (CCYP, 2011; Cunneen, 2008a). For example, First Nations youth 'are often held in detention on remand simply due to lack of suitable accommodation and support to comply with bail conditions' (Amnesty International, 2015, p. 5).

Data from 2022 to 2023 shows that at a national level, First Nations youth were 29 times more likely to be in detention than non-Indigenous young people and 42 times more likely to be in unsentenced detention (AIHW, 2024). Despite representing just over 5% of the Australian population aged 10–17 years, First Nations youth accounted for 58% of those in detention (AIHW, 2024). The situation is even more severe for the youngest First Nations children, with those aged 10–13 years comprising more than 73% of all detained children in that age group in Australia in 2023, making them 46 times more likely to be in detention than non-Indigenous young people in the same age range (AIHW, 2023).

Although, the detention rate of First Nations young people aged 10–17 in NSW is slightly lower than the national average—20.7 per 10,000 compared to 27.3 per 10,000 nationally in the June quarter 2024—First Nations young people remain severely over-represented, being 23 times more likely to be in detention than their non-Indigenous counterparts (AIHW, 2024). First Nations youth constitute approximately 65.3% of the total youth detention population in NSW, despite comprising only 7.5% of the population aged 10–17 years in NSW (AIHW, 2024).

Several plausible factors contribute to this over-representation, including insufficient diversionary alternatives in regional and remote areas (Snowball, 2008a, 2008b) and policy constraints within the jurisdictional context relating to First Nations over-representation. Nonetheless,

> the relationship between risk and bail is a good example of how Indigenous youth lose out in generic measures of risk based on previous offending. Falling into a high-risk category for re-offending allows for the suspension of the right to bail and the presumption of innocence. Predicting the likelihood of re-offending determines access to what were once seen as fundamental rights and protections of the system. The offending histories of Indigenous young people young people place them outside these protections and redefine them as a group that society needs protection from and therefore justifies their pretrial detention.
>
> (Cunneen, 2008a, p. 52)

As Cunneen (2001, 2008a) argues, one of the critical issues with risk discourses is their neglect of historical, socio-political and economic structures that contextualise juvenile criminalisation, while narrowly focusing on neoliberal prescriptions for individual deviance and family failure. In the case of First Nations youth, this assumption appears absurd given the long history of state intervention in First Nations family and community life (Cunneen, 2008a). Cunneen further observes, an Australian longitudinal study examining criminal recidivism and associated risk factors found that: '[o]ver time, the probability of those juveniles on supervised orders in 1994–95 who are subject to multiple risk factors (e.g. Male, Indigenous care and protection orders) progressing to the adult corrections system will closely approach 100 per cent' (Lynch et al., 2003, p. 5).

Reduction of structural circumstances and a person's gender and cultural identity to 'risk factors' reduces 'identity' to an equation of probability requiring management (Cunneen, 2008a). This reductive approach further perpetuates marginalisation based on gender and racial/ethnic identity. Hudson (2006) argues that the marginalisation of ethnic minorities and women stems from conceptualising white male middle class identity as the universal norm. Within contemporary actuarial techniques of risk management, women, First Nations people and people of colour—categorised as 'Other'—experience significant disadvantages and inequitable outcomes (Cunneen, 2008b, 2012; Hudson, 2006).

According to the YOA, measures for dealing with children are to be culturally appropriate 'wherever possible' (s. 34, pt.1(a)) and the sanctions imposed are to 'take into account gender, race and sexuality' (s. 34, pt. 1(c)). However, the legislation provides no definition of what constitutes 'culturally appropriate' measures, nor does it specify who determines when or how such measures should be implemented (Cunneen, 2008a). Consequently, there is limited scope for these decisions to be framed from a perspective that authentically reflects the cultural experiences of the young people involved. For example, while circle sentencing and healing programs in NSW represent First Nations' initiatives that strive for justice aligned with First Nations' aspirations (Stubbs, 2000), these customary laws are inevitably interpreted through and constrained by dominant white criminal justice narratives (Daly & Stubbs, 2007). While individual responsibilisation dominates the focus of restorative justice alternatives (Gray, 2005; McAlister & Carr, 2014), First Nations communities frequently advocate for broader visions of justice that encompass collective self-determination (Cunneen, 2003; Stubbs, 2010). Additionally, the actuarial techniques underpinning evidence-based policy frameworks such as the YOA obscure the power/knowledge dynamics related to gender, ethnicity and race (Chan & Rigakos, 2002; Cunneen, 2008a; Hudson, 2006). When combined with the well-documented tendency toward punitive solutions in policy and legislation (see Cunneen, 1997, 2008a; Hogg, 2001; Hunyor, 2015), this results in a diversionary system that, as previously noted, systematically excludes disadvantaged minorities.

Gendered inequities and diversion

Gender compounds the structural marginalisation already experienced by juvenile offenders due to constraints of class, age and race/ethnicity. Young women, particularly young First Nations women, represent some of the most disadvantaged groups within the criminal justice system. While research generally indicates that risk factors contributing to crime involvement are similar for young men and women, some have been specifically identified as having greater significance for young women (AIHW, 2012b). Young girls involved in crime are likely to have experienced childhood abuse or neglect, psychological or mental health challenges such as anxiety, self-harm, and attempted suicide, experience out-of-home care, chronic illness or disability, socioeconomic disadvantages and difficulties with school (AIHW, 2012b).

For example, girls involved in the Australian juvenile justice system are approximately one and a half times more likely than boys to have been part of the protection system (McFarlane, 2011). In 2024, the AIHW published a report analysing data on youth under supervision during 2022–2023 who had prior contact with child protection services within the decade before 2023. The findings revealed that approximately two-thirds (65%) of young people in the youth justice system had interacted with child protection services over this ten-year period. For young females, the percentage was even higher, at about three-quarters (76%), and a similar proportion (76%) of First Nations youth had experienced such interactions (AIHW, 2024a, p. 7). Additionally, a study involving a random sample from the NSW Children's Court on criminal matters concerning young women in out-of-home care found that 80% of young women in detention reported having a psychological disorder (Justice Health & Forensic Mental Health Network and Juvenile Justice NSW (JHFMHN), 2017).

The combination of high rates of prior abuse and overly punitive responses to low-level offending often leads to the incarceration of many young women. For instance, the aforementioned study revealed that 50% of these young women were appearing in court for property damage offences (JHFMHN, 2017). In both, Australian jurisdictions and other Western countries, young women's involvement in crime tends to be less serious and of shorter duration than that of young men. Young women are most commonly charged with minor assaults, property offences such as shoplifting, and public order violations (Batchelor & Burman, 2004; Wundersitz, 2000b).

Except for the recent increase in youth detention numbers in 2024, the number of young people under supervision among both males and females has steadily decreased over the last decade across most Australian jurisdictions, including NSW (AIHW, 2021). Despite these declining rates, the proportion of young women involved in crime compared to young boys has grown significantly. For instance, in NSW, research shows a 40% increase in the number of females who were criminally proceeded against by NSW Police during the decade leading up to 2023 (Donnelly, 2024, p. 1). In the juvenile justice system, legal actions against young females aged 10–17 also grew by 20% over the same period, compared to relatively stable trends for their male counterparts (Donnelly, 2024, p. 1). There was a notable decline in the number of offences during the COVID-19 period and associated government responses in 2020–2021; however, from 2022 onwards, the number of offences committed by young females increased again (Donnelly, 2024). Furthermore, young women are over-represented in remand. For example, during the four-year period from June 2019 to March 2023, a higher proportion of females ranging from 71% to 83%, compared to 61% to 73% for males, were held in unsentenced detention (AIHW, 2023).

Additionally, there is evidence indicating that young women's involvement in violent crime has increased over the years, both in Australia and internationally (Kong & AuCoin, 1982; Youth Justice Board, 2009). For example, research shows that from 1999 to 2010, the increase in charges for violent offences against young women in NSW surpassed that of their young men counterparts (Carrington & Pereira, 2009; Holmes, 2010).

Explanations proposed for these changes have focused on the sexualisation of young women's behaviour, their participation in youth subcultures (Carrington & Pereira, 2009; Chesney-Lind, 1998), and the rise of cyberbullying coupled with the media's role in amplifying girls' violence (Carrington & Pereira, 2009). However, it has also been argued that the changes reflect legislation and policy changes rather than an actual change in girls' criminal behaviour (AIHW, 2012b; Steffensmeier et al., 2023). For instance, in NSW, high-volume offences such as domestic violence (DV) assault, breaches of Apprehended Violence Orders (AVO), intimidation, stalking and harassment, and breach of bail have driven the increase in female offending over the last decade. However, these increases likely reflect significant changes that have occurred in policing and legislation targeting DV during this period (Holmes & Fitzgerald, 2017). Nonetheless, social concerns regarding girls' sexuality and independence, along with shifts in policy, have resulted in cases where young women who might previously have appeared in court for welfare related matters are now entering the criminal justice system on criminal charges (Carrington & Pereira, 2009; Creaney, 2012; Gelsthorpe & Worrall, 2009).

Bias against young women in the criminal justice system is well documented (see for example, Chesney-Lind, 1998; Eaton, 1986; Federle & Chesney-Lynd, 1992). This tendency persists as an ongoing practice, 'young women continue to be arrested and incarcerated for behaviours that would not trigger a similar response for young males' (Krisberg & Austin, 1993, p. 140). As discussed in Chapter 2, the gendered approach to juvenile justice extends from the paternalistic nature of the law (Federle & Chesney-Lynd, 1992; Graycar, 1995), and the 'male-centricity of its form, language, and substance' (Snider, 1998, p. 247). Within this continuum, restorative justice has the potentially problematic consequence of net widening for young female offenders. Although female offenders constitute a minority group in the criminal justice system, as noted earlier in this chapter, Richards' study in 2010 found that similar proportions of male and female juveniles who come into contact with the police were referred to restorative measures under the YOA in NSW. This suggests 'that the restorative measures may be having a net-widening impact on female offenders' (Richards, 2010, p. 6).

The appropriateness of restorative conferences for women as offenders or victims has been highly debated in the literature and briefly discussed in this chapter (Cook et al., 2006; Daly, 2011; Ptacek, 2010). The focus here, however, is on the narrowly gendered framework criminology has assigned to the concept of risk. Feminist writers, highlighting the limitations of the concept of risk, note that risk analyses tend to reduce the relationship between women and risk to the context of risk avoidance while neglecting risk-taking-activities (Miller, 1991). This prejudice reinforces stereotypical images of women as crime victims, while failing to acknowledge them as risk takers (Chan & Rigakos, 2002; Miller, 1991) and individual agents. Adding to this, the 'unacknowledged gendered nature of risk assessments' has metamorphosed into the 'unacknowledged needs assessments for females at risk of offending' (Hannah-Moffat, 2006, p. 106). As Douglas (1992) notes, constructions of risk are socially and culturally engineered. Consequently, risk perceptions are subjective and shaped by politically negotiated outcomes.

Furthermore, as noted earlier in this chapter, young women who engage in risk-taking activities are often harshly judged since such behaviours deviate from traditional feminine gender norms (Jewkes, 2004). Traditional stereotypes of femininity influence how the police treat female offenders (Horn & Wincup, 1995). In particular, women who come in contact with the police for violent behaviour are viewed as *bad*, and research has found that normative gendered expectations guide how some police officers exercise their discretion in responding to women who offend. For instance, police are more likely to arrest and charge women who engage in violence because violence is traditionally seen as a behaviour associated with men (Collier & Hall, 2000; Horn & Wincup, 1995; Miller & White, 2004). Similar processes operate in relation to groups that are racialised, whether men or women (Cunneen, 1995; Hagan et al., 2005; White, 1994, 1997, 2009).

Police discretion and the issue of police culture(s)

Social and political forces guide decision-making processes based on police discretion. For instance, policing outcomes can vary significantly based on shifts in political and organisational priorities, structural changes, and the allocation of resources to different issues over time. Such taskforces may subsequently contribute to the criminalisation of young people in public spaces. Examples include the criminalisation of antisocial behaviour (Crawford, 2009) and graffiti (White, 2001).

Additionally, Cunneen and White (2007) note the salience of this in the treatment of those classified as ethnically and culturally 'Other', including First Nations, Arabic, and more recently, as noted by Coventry et al. (2014), Sudanese Australians. As primary gatekeepers to diversionary alternatives, police discretionary powers are not carte blanche (Cunneen & White, 2007; Parker & Sarre, 2008). As noted earlier in this chapter (and in Chapter 2), according to legislation, police are required to consider factors such as the seriousness of the offence, the offender's criminal record, and whether the offender admits to the offence (YOA, s. 37).

Additionally, police are also given license to treat offenders in accordance with 'any other matter the official thinks appropriate in the circumstances' (YOA, s. 37(e)). Hence, the legislation provides an open window for unchecked police discretion regarding whether to divert or not to divert offenders, despite the legislative boundaries of the YOA. Within this context, Shearing (1993) argues, that police attitudes have the potential to subvert legislative objectives. The dominance of police in risk management contexts has been accompanied by a lack of accountability or oversight over their roles (Cunneen, 2008a), resulting in more individuals being labelled as 'risky,' particularly along gender and racial lines.

The shift to a risk management paradigm instead of crime control exposes police officers to the double-edged discourses embedded within risk society narratives and actuarial techniques, such as risk assessment tools, that have shaped current policy (Campbell, 2004; Stahlkopf, 2008). Existing risk discourses not only arrange offenders' identities in sequences from less to more 'risky'—filtered through structures of class, race/ethnicity and gender—but they also determine the consequences (Atkinson, 1990). For police officers, in general, decision-making processes are routine activities that produce and disseminate the methodological message embedded in current discourses around youth justice (Cunneen & White, 2007).

An officer engaged in police decision-making continuously struggles with 'the *discursive* boundaries of desirable and acceptable policing and thereby sustaining and generating the integrity of its corporate reputation and identity' (Campbell, 2003, p. 318). Thus, decisional choices are not reducible to legislative criteria and cannot be entirely explained in terms of their presence or absence (Campbell, 2003). Rather, criteria listed in the YOA, such as offender history, seriousness of the offence, degree of violence involved and harm to the victim, are likely to be considered or made meaningful within a mythology of police accomplishment within the prevailing culture of the Police Force.

As noted by Black and Wilkie (1997), the notion of policing success is often constructed in terms of arrest rates, 'adding to the belief that 'real policing' necessarily requires the arrest and prosecution of individual offenders, rather than crime prevention or reduction' (p. 20). While police discretion is essential to foster fairness by considering individual circumstances of each case, this approach poses challenges because decisions on whether to divert or not depend heavily on an officer's motivations. Thus, diversion has the potential to be omitted as an option (Jordan & Farrell, 2013). Moreover, as it is well documented, youth crime is highly politicised and subject to moral panics spurred by reports of crime waves (Cohen, 1972; Collins et al., 2000; Simpson, 1997). Consequently, policing practices become susceptible to political 'law and order' agendas.

As previously noted, the legislation grants police broad discretion to make decisions about whether to divert youth from court proceedings. However, as noted in the 2002 review of the YOA by the NSW Attorney General's Office, police are not required to record the reasons for their decisions, thus making it difficult to identify the factors motivating such decisions. Consequently, the review recommended that the Police Service—since renamed as the Police Force—should establish guidelines governing the exercise of discretion under the YOA.

A shift in police culture(s) is necessary to become more accommodating to diversionary practices. As previously noted, statistical data indicate that courts continue to make more referrals to YJC than the police do, suggesting missed opportunities for diversion within the policing practices. The Noetic Solutions Review of 2010 highlighted a lower referral rate to YJC by the NSW Police Force compared to court-made referrals and suggested that diversionary options were not being utilised uniformly and equitably across NSW. Additionally, research conducted by Ringland and Smith (2013) aimed at assessing variation across LACs revealed general adherence to the general principles of the YOA but identified 'some LACs had unexpectedly low rates of diversion' (p. 10).

In response to criticisms regarding the low level of police referrals highlighted by the Noetic Solutions Review, the NSW Police Force noted that a key factor contributing to this issue is the legislative requirement for an admission of guilt under the YOA (YOA s. 36, pt. b). This requirement was highlighted as 'the predominant causal factor in the lower referral rate of police-initiated conferences as opposed to Court-ordered conferences' (Police Association of New South Wales, 2011, p. 11). To address this issue, the Protected Admissions Scheme (PAS) was introduced as a mechanism designed to enable young offenders to make admissions to an offence whilst preserving their rights not to provide self-incriminating evidence. Designed to remove the apparent blockage to cautioning and YJC referral options by the police, the PAS was approved by the NSW Police Force to be used for cautions in April 2014, extending this approval to YJCs in July 2015 (NSW Police Force, 2015). However, the effectiveness of the PAS remains under-researched. At the time of data collection for the study on which this book is based, no evaluations of the PAS had been conducted. Subsequently, drawing on a small subset of data from interviews conducted with members of the NSW Police Force—which form part of the analysis in this book, and will be presented in upcoming chapters—a study by Pearce (2021) highlights that 'the introduction of PAS has not removed the constraints created by the legislative requirement of an admission of guilt for the purposes of diversion under the YOA' (p. 295).

Nonetheless, a protected admission can be offered to an offender if the police officer believes a caution or YJC is appropriate, and the young offender refuses to admit to the offence. Upon signing a Protected Admissions Form—which is provided with a Protection Admission Information Sheet—the young offender can be questioned about the offences listed in the form, and the information gathered may not be used in any criminal proceedings (NSW Police Force, 2015).

However, if during the interview the young offender admits to additional or more serious crimes, 'police may elect to suspend the interview and commence a separate interview to ask about those offences. If this occurs, police will make it clear to the young person that what they say in the new interview is not 'protected' and can be admissible in criminal proceedings' (NSW Police Force, 2015, p. 9). This practice raises significant concerns related to due process and the individual responsibilisation of young offenders.

As previously noted, in other areas of the law—such as medical consent, voting rights, and sexual consent—young people are not deemed capable of making moral and civil decisions. However, the ideology underlying the PAS assumes that young individuals can comprehend and evaluate its complexities and the inherent consequences of participating in such a process. As already established, the use and/or misuse of the PAS, as well as its impact on police referrals to YJC, remain largely unexplored. Nevertheless, with or without the PAS, the discretion as to whether to divert remains with the police officer, and as previously noted, decisions made by police at their first point of contact with a young person are highly likely to influence subsequent judicial decisions and ultimately affect sentencing outcomes.

Magistrates' decision-making under the YOA: the little we know

Magisterial decision-making concerning diversion under the YOA remains an unexplored area. According to the legislation, magistrates, acting as 'gatekeepers' for diversionary alternatives, are required to consider the same factors as those considered by the police: the seriousness of the offence, the offender's criminal history, whether the offender admits to the offence (YOA, s. 40), and 'any other matter the Director or court thinks appropriate in the circumstances' (YOA, s. 40 (e)). Thus, from a legislative standpoint, magistrates operate within the same risk paradigm previously discussed. As with the police, magistrates are also given ample latitude for decision-making, thus raising questions about magisterial differences in decision-making and factors that might affect decisions within this context.

Children's courts in Australia are vital institutions 'for holding young offenders accountable for their behaviour, helping rehabilitate them and protecting the community and for advancing the "best interest of the child" and protecting them from harm' (Borowski, 2013, p. 184). The Children's Court faces a significant challenge in balancing welfare and justice to achieve its desired objectives (see Chapter 2). Amidst the rise of the justice model—characterised by its focus on 'just deserts' and 'moral panics' over youth crime fuelled by politicians and the media—restorative justice has often been misrepresented as a *soft option* (O'Connor, 1997). Despite extensive research demonstrating that restorative justice, in its various forms and uses, including YJC, is far from a soft option (see Bottoms & Dignan, 2004; Walgrave, 2004), this misconception can at times unsettle a community that focuses on retributive justice. Consequently, this places magistrates in the difficult position of balancing community expectations and the *best interests* of the child.

The most recent comprehensive study of the Children's Courts in NSW revealed that outcomes for young people appearing in court were contingent on 'how the legislation is applied by individual judicial officers and practitioners, resources available, geographical considerations and orientations of the magistrates and other stakeholders' (Fernandez et al., 2013, p. 31). For example, magistrates expressed concern and frustration over potential differences in court processes and outcomes based on geographical location, primarily due to 'inequities in access to resources and services across the rural/city divide in NSW' (Fernandez et al., 2013, p. 41). Additionally,

> [g]eneralist judicial officers (most often those that preside over Magistrate's or Local Courts in regional and remote locations) lack of knowledge and skill was seen as producing geographic variability in case processing and decision-making, for example, in criminal sentencing (typically harsher in regional and remote locations) and reviews of child protection cases.
>
> (Borowski, 2013, p. 172)

The aforementioned study included insights into diversionary measures within the Children's Court, revealing that magistrates support extending YJC to more serious offences (Fernandez et al., 2014). However, they emphasised that 'this must be coupled with an increase in services for young people to be referred to, addressing causes of juvenile crime' (Fernandez et al., 2013, p. 37). Furthermore, there was a consensus amongst magistrates that the punitive nature of the *Bail Act 1978* (NSW) undermines the Court's role in acting in the *best interest of the child* (Fernandez et al., 2014). Thus, as argued in this chapter, legislation subscribing to risk governance paradigms hinders the effective application of the YOA.

Conclusion

Traditional crime control ideologies have given way to the 'crime as risk' ethos, which underpins what scholars such as Feeley and Simon (1992) refer to as the 'managerialist turn' within criminal justice practice. Juvenile justice has not escaped this shift; diversion interventions under the YOA may partly reflect techniques that have come to dominate the risk management ethos. These risk governance strategies focus on classifying and managing individuals based on perceived levels of dangerousness (Castel, 1991), rather than aiding young offenders in 'making good' (Maruna, 2001).

Neoliberal ideologies have significantly influenced the management of crime as risk. Neoliberalism's apolitical stance towards social divisions such as class, race/ethnicity, and gender reduces structural constraints and identity to actuarial calculations of probability and risk. This leads to increased management of certain groups perceived as more *risky* due to factors of structural disadvantage. Meanwhile, the neutral, unquestioned identity that determines who is more risky than others is portrayed as universal; this leads to the marginalisation of 'Others' who fall outside the narrow ambit of the white male justice narrative (Hudson, 2006).

The question of how these risk-oriented approaches to crime affect diversion is one that is crucial. The ambiguous nature of the YOA prescriptions regarding diversion grants *gatekeepers* wide discretionary powers. As a result, decisions about diversion are influenced by police officers' and magistrates' decision-making processes, which must balance broad objectives related to risk management with the cultural and institutional constraints within which they operate. These cultural and institutional constraints will be analysed in the subsequent chapters of this book.

The empirical data indicates that police diversion decision-making remains faithful to the exclusionary system that marginalises individuals categorised as 'high risk'. Here, the potential of risk management techniques to subvert the inclusionary objectives of restorative justice schemes becomes apparent. The preoccupation of risk management with bureaucratic efficiency results in pre-emptive action and the diversion of certain groups *into* the traditional criminal justice system rather than away from it. These groups often include individuals who have already been processed through the system and are least likely to benefit from conventional criminal justice measures. It is at this point that diversion fails; risk management disables the potential of restorative justice. The immobilisation of restorative justice through the conflicting imperatives of dominant risk management paradigms occurs in context-specific ways within different institutional cultures. It is to the specific institutional imperatives of the NSW Police Force and the NSW Children's Court that the remainder of this book is devoted.

References

Allard, T., Ogilvie, J., & Stewart, A. (2007). *The efficacy of strategies to reduce juvenile offending*. Griffith University.

Allard, T., Stewart, A., Chrzanowski, A., Ogilvie, J., Birks, D. J., & Little, S. (2010). *Police diversion of young offenders and Indigenous over-representations* (Trends and Issues in Crime and Criminal Justice, No. 390). Australian Institute of Criminology.

Amnesty International. (2015). *A brighter tomorrow: Keeping Indigenous kids in the community and out of detention in Australia.*

Anderson, T. (2001). Policing and civil rights since the NSW police Royal Commission. *University of Western Sydney Law Review, 5*, 75–82.

Aradau, C., Lobo-Guerrero, L., & Van Munster, R. (2008). Security, technologies of risk, and the political: Guest editors' introduction. *Security Dialogue, 39*(2–3), 147–154.

Armstrong, D. (2005). A risky business? Research, policy, governmentality and youth offending. *Youth Justice, 4*(2), 100–116.

Atkinson, P. (1990). *The ethnographic imagination: Textual constructions of reality*. Routledge.

Australia Institute of Health and Welfare. (2012a). *Juvenile detention population in Australia 2012* (Juvenile Series, 11). Australian Government. https://www.aihw.gov.au/reports/youth-justice/juvenile-detention-population-in-australia-2012

Australia Institute of Health and Welfare. (2012b). *Girls and young women in the criminal justice system* (Bulletin 107). Australian Government. https://www.aihw.gov.au/getmedia/d6cacfce-86ab-41de-af14-876ad7af78a5/14594.pdf.aspx?inline=true

Australian Institute of Health and Welfare. (2021). *Youth detention population in Australia, 2021.* https://www.aihw.gov.au/reports/youth-justice/youth-detention-population-in-australia-2021/contents/summary

Australian Institute of Health and Welfare. (2023). *Youth detention population in Australia 2023.* https://www.aihw.gov.au/reports/youth-justice/youth-detention-population-in-australia-2023

Australian Institute of Health and Welfare. (2024a). *Young people under youth justice supervision and their interaction with the child protection system, 2022–2023.* https://www.aihw.gov.au/reports/youth-justice/young-people-youth-justice-supervision-2022-23/summary

Australian Institute of Health and Welfare. (2024b). *Youth justice in Australia 2022–23.* https://www.aihw.gov.au/reports/youth-justice/youth-justice-in-australia-annual-report-2022-23

Bail Act 1978 (NSW). https://www.austlii.edu.au/cgi-bin/viewdb/au/legis/nsw/repealed_act/ba197841/

Balfour, G. (2008). Falling between the cracks of retributive and restorative justice: The victimization and punishment of Aboriginal women. *Feminist Criminology, 3*(2), 102–120.

Ball, C. (1999). The *Youth Justice and Criminal Evidence Act 1999*: Part I: A significant move towards restorative justice, or a recipe for unintended consequences? *Criminal Law Review*, 211–222.

Bargen, J. (2001, October 8–9). Diverting ATSI young offenders from court and custody in New South Wales: Practices, perspectives and possibilities under the Young Offenders Act 1997. In *The best practice interventions in corrections for Indigenous people conference.* https://rb.gy/469bmz

Barry, A., Thomas, O., & Rose, N. (1996). *Foucault and political reason: Liberalism, neoliberalism and rationalities of government*. UCL Press.

Batchelor, S., & Burman, M. (2004). Working with girls and young women. In G. McIvor (Ed.), *Women who offend* (pp. 266–288). Jessica Kingsley Publishers.
Bauman, Z. (1998). *Globalisation: The human consequences*. Polity Press.
Beck, U. (1992). *Risk society: Towards a new modernity*. Sage.
Beck, U. (2006). *Power in the global age*. Polity Press.
Bell, E. (2011). *Criminal justice and neoliberalism*. Palgrave Macmillan.
Bessant, J., Hill, R., & Watts, R. (2005). *Discovering 'risk': Social research and policy making*. Peter Lang.
Black, H., & Wilkie, M. (1997). Young people and policing in Australia: The relevance of the United Nations Convention on the Rights of the Child. *Australian Journal of Human Rights*, *8*(2), 134–158.
Borowski, A. (2013). A portrait of Australia's Children's Courts: Findings of a national assessment. In R. Sheehan & A. Borowski (Eds.), *Australia's Children's Courts today and tomorrow*. Springer.
Bottoms, A., & Dignan, J. (2004). Youth justice in Great Britain. In M. Tonry & A. Doob (Eds.), *Crime and justice, a review of research, volume 31: Youth crime and youth justice: Comparative and cross-national perspectives* (pp. 21–183). University of Chicago Press.
Braithwaite, J. (2003). Restorative justice and a better future. In E. McLaughlin, R. Fergusson, G. Hughes, & L. Westmarland (Eds.), *Restorative justice: Critical issues* (pp. 82–97). Sage.
Briggs, D. B. (2013). Conceptualising risk and need: The rise of actuarialism and the death of welfare? Practitioner assessment and intervention in the youth offending service. *Youth Justice*, *13*(1), 17–30.
Burchell, G. (1996). Liberal government and techniques of the self. In A. Barry, T. Osborne, & N. Rose (Eds.), *Foucault and political reason* (pp. 19–36). UCL Press.
Burchell, G., Colin, G., & Miller, P. (Eds.). (1991). *The Foucault effect: Studies in governmentality*. University of Chicago Press.
Campbell, E. (2003). Police narrativity and discretionary power. *International Journal of the Sociology of Law*, *31*(4), 295–322.
Campbell, J. (2004). Helping women understand their risk in situations of intimate partner violence. *Journal of Interpersonal Violence*, *19*(2), 1464–1477.
Carrington, K., & Pereira, M. (2009). *Offending youth: Sex, crime and justice*. Federation Press.
Case, S., & Haines, K. (2015). Children first, offenders second: The centrality of engagement in positive youth justice. *The Howard Journal of Criminal Justice*, *54*(2), 157–175.
Castel, R. (1991). From dangerousness to risk. In G. Burchell, C. Gordon, & P. Miller (Eds.), *The Foucault effect: Studies in governmentality* (pp. 281–298). University of Chicago Press.
Chan, W., & Rigakos, G. S. (2002). Risk, crime and gender. *British Journal of Criminology*, *42*, 743–761.
Chapin, D. A., & Griffin, P. A. (2005). Juvenile diversion. In K. Heilbrun, N. E. S. Goldstein, & R. E. Redding (Eds.), *Juvenile delinquency: Prevention, assessment, and intervention* (pp. 161–178). Oxford University Press.
Chesney-Lind, M. (1998). The forgotten offender. *Corrections Today*, *60*(7), 66–73.
Chesney-Lind, M. (2002). Criminalizing victimization: The unintended consequences of pro-arrest policies for girls and women. *Criminology & Public Policy*, *2*(1), 81–90.
Christie, N. (1986). The ideal victim. In E. Fattah (Ed.), *From crime policy to victim policy* (pp. 17–30). Macmillan.
Cohen, S. (1972). *Folk devils and moral panics: The creation of the mods and rockers*. Martin Robertson.
Cohen, S. (1985). *Visions of social control: Crime, punishment and classification*. Polity Press.

Collier, R., & Hall, S. (2000). Masculinities and violence. *Criminal Justice Matters, 42*(1), 8–11.
Collins, J., Noble, G., Poynting, S., & Taber, P. (2000). *Kebaks, kids, cops and crime: Youth, ethnicity and crime*. Pluto Press.
Consedine, J. (1995). *Restorative justice: Healing the effects of the crime*. Ploughshares.
Cook, K., Daly, K., & Stubbs, J. (2006). Gender, race and restorative justicc [Special issue]. *Theoretical Criminology, 10*(1), 9–28.
Coventry, G., Dawes, G., Moston, S., & Palmer, D. (2014). *Sudanese Australians and crime: Police and community perspectives* (Trends and Issues in Crime and Criminal Justice, No. 477). Australian Institute of Criminology.
Crawford, A. (2009). Criminalizing sociability through anti-social behaviour legislation: Dispersal powers, young people and the police. *Youth Justice, 9*(1), 5–26.
Creaney, S. (2012). Risk, prevention and early intervention: Youth justice responses to girls. *Safer Communities, 11*, 111–120.
Crime and Disorder Act 1998 (UK). https://www.legislation.gov.uk/ukpga/1998/37/contents
Crimes Legislation Amendment (Police and Public Safety) Act 1998 (NSW). https://classic.austlii.edu.au/au/legis/nsw/num_act/claapsa1998n38498/
Cunneen, C. (1995). Ethnic minority youth and juvenile justice: Beyond the stereotype of ethnic gangs. *Current Issues in Criminal Justice, 6*(3), 387–394.
Cunneen, C. (1997). Community conferencing and the fiction of indigenous control. *The Australian and New Zealand Journal of Criminology, 30*, 292–311.
Cunneen, C. (2001). *Conflict, politics and crime: Aboriginal communities and the police*. Allen & Urwin.
Cunneen, C. (2003). Thinking critically about restorative justice. In E. McLaughlin, R. Ferguson, G. Hughes, & L. Westmarland (Eds.), *Restorative justice: Critical issues* (pp. 182–194). SAGE in association with the Open University.
Cunneen, C. (2006). Racism, discrimination and the over-representation of Indigenous people in the criminal justice system: Some conceptual and explanatory issues. *Current Issues in Criminal Justice, 17*(3), 329–346.
Cunneen, C. (2008a). Understanding restorative justice through the lens of critical criminology. In T. Anthony & C. Cunneen (Eds.), *The critical criminology companion* (pp. 290–302). Hawkins Press.
Cunneen, C. (2008b). Changing neo-colonial impacts of juvenile justice. *Current Issues in Criminal Justice, 20*(1), 43–58.
Cunneen, C. (2010). The limitations of restorative justice. In C. Cunneen & C. Hoyle (Eds.), *Debating restorative justice* (pp. 101–188). Hart Publishing.
Cunneen, C. (2012). Restorative justice, globalization and the logic of empire. In J. McCulloch & S. Pickering (Eds.), *Borders and crime pre-crime, mobility and serious harm in an age of globalization* (pp. 147–162). Palgrave Macmillan.
Cunneen, C., & Goldson, B. (2015). Restorative justice? A critical analysis. In B. Goldson & J. Muncie (Eds.), *Youth crime and justice* (2nd ed., pp. 137–156). Sage.
Cunneen, C., & Luke, G. (2007). Recidivism and the effectiveness of criminal justice interventions: Juvenile offenders and post release support. *Current Issues in Criminal Justice, 19*(2), 197–210.
Cunneen, C., Luke, G., & Ralph, N. (2006). *Evaluation of the Aboriginal over-representation strategy report to the NSW Department of Juvenile Justice Sydney*. Institute of Criminology University of Sydney Law School.
Cunneen, C., & White, R. (2002). *Juvenile justice: Youth and crime in Australia*. Oxford University Press.
Cunneen, C., & White, R. (2007). *Juvenile justice: Youth and crime in Australia* (3rd ed.). Oxford University Press.
Cunneen, C., & White, R. (2011). *Juvenile justice: Youth and crime in Australia* (4th ed.). Oxford University Press.

Daly, K. (2011). Gendered violence and restorative justice: The views of New Zealand opinion leaders. *Contemporary Justice Review*, *14*(3), 269–290.

Daly, K., & Stubbs, J. (2007). Feminist theory, feminist and anti-racist politics, and restorative justice. In J. Johnstone & D. V. Van Ness (Eds.), *Handbook of restorative justice* (pp. 149–170). Willan.

De Haan, W. (1990). *The politics of redress*. Unwin Hyman.

Donnelly, N. (2024). *Trends in female offending in New South Wales: 2014 to 2023* (Bureau Brief No. 173). NSW Bureau of Crime Statistics and Research.

Douglas, M. (1992). *Risk and blame: Essays in cultural theory*. Routledge.

Eaton, M. (1986). *Justice for women*. Open University Press.

Ericson, R. V., & Haggerty, K. D. (1997). *Policing the risk society*. Clarendon Press.

Farrington, D. P. (2002). Developmental criminology and risk-focused prevention. In M. Maguire, R. Morgan, & R. Reiner (Eds.), *The Oxford Handbook of Criminology* (pp. 655–701). Oxford University Press.

Federle, K. H., & Chesney-Lynd, M. (1992). *Special issues in juvenile justice: Gender, race, and ethnicity from juvenile justice and public policy: Toward a national agenda*. Macmillan.

Feeley, M., & Simon, J. (1992). The new penology: Notes on the emerging strategy of corrections and its implications. *Criminology*, *30*(4), 449–474.

Feeley, M., & Simon, J. (1994). Actuarial justice: The emerging new criminal law. In D. Nelken (Ed.), *The futures of criminology* (pp. 173–201). Sage.

Fernandez, E., Bolitho, J., Hansen, P., & Hudson, M. (2013). The Children's Court in New South Wales. In R. Sheehan & A. Borowski (Eds.), *Australia's Children's Court today and tomorrow* (pp. 27–44). Springer.

Fernandez, E., Bolitho, J., Hansen, P., Hudson, M., & Kendall, S. (2014). *A study of the Children's Court of New South Wales. Part of a national assessment of Australia's Children's Courts*. University of New South Wales Australia. https://childrenscourt.nsw.gov.au/documents/other/chcourt%20assessment.pdf

Fionda, J. (1999). Crime and Disorder Act 1998: New Labour, old hat: Youth justice and the Crime and Disorder Act 1998. *Criminal Law Review*, *Jan*, 36–47.

Fitzgerald, J. (2000). *Graffiti in New South Wales* (Bureau Brief Issue no. 5). NSW Bureau of Crime Statistics and Research.

Foucault, M. (1991). Governmentality. In G. Burchell, C. Gordon, & P. Miller (Eds.), *The Foucault effect: Studies in governmentality* (pp. 87–104). University of Chicago Press.

Gandy, O. H. (1993). *The panoptic sort: A political economy of personal information*. Westview Press.

Gandy, O. H. (2021). *The panoptic sort: A political economy of personal information* (2nd ed.). Oxford University Press.

Garland, D. (1996). The limits of the sovereign state. *British Journal of Criminology*, *36*(4), 445–471.

Garland, D. (1997). 'Governmentality' and the problem of crime. *Theoretical Criminology*, *1*, 173–214.

Garland, D. (2001). *The culture of control: Crime and social order in contemporary society*. University of Chicago Press.

Gelb, K. (2008). *More myths and misconceptions*. Sentencing Advisory Council. https://www.sentencingcouncil.vic.gov.au/sites/default/files/2019-08/More_Myths_and_Misconceptions.pdf

Gelsthorpe, L., & Worrall, A. (2009). Looking for trouble: A recent history of girls, young women and youth justice. *Youth Justice*, *9*, 209–223.

Giddens, A. (1990). *The consequences of modernity*. Polity Press.

Giddens, A. (1991). *Modernity and self-identity: Self and society in the late modern age*. Polity Press.

Goldson, B. (2000). 'Children in need' or 'young offenders'? Hardening ideology, organizational change and new challenges for social work with children in trouble. *Child and Family Social Work*, *5*(3), 225–265.

Goldson, B. (2002). New Labour, social justice and children: Political calculation and the deserving-undeserving schism. *British Journal of Social Work, 32*, 683–695.

Goldson, B. (2005). Taking liberties: Policy and the punitive turn. In H. Hendrick (Ed.), *Child welfare and social policy: An essential reader* (pp. 255–267). Polity Press.

Goldson, B., & Muncie, J. (2006). Critical anatomy: Towards a principled youth justice. In B. Goldson & J. Muncie (Eds.), *Youth, crime and justice* (pp. 203–231). Sage.

Gray, P. (2005). The politics of risk and young offenders' experiences of social exclusion and restorative justice. *British Journal of Criminology, 5*, 938–957.

Gray, P. (2009). The political economy of risk and the new governance of youth crime. *Punishment and Society, 11*(4), 443–458.

Graycar, R. (1995). The gender of judgments: An introduction. In M. Thornton (Ed.), *Public and private: Feminist legal debates* (pp. 262–268). Oxford University Press.

Hagan, J., Shedd, C., & Payne, M. R. (2005). Race, ethnicity, and youth perceptions of criminal injustice. *American Sociological Review, 70*(3), 381–407.

Hannah-Moffat, K. (1999). Moral agent or actuarial subject: Risk in Canadian women's imprisonment. *Theoretical Criminology, 3*(1), 71–94.

Hannah-Moffat, K. (2001). *Punishment in disguise: Penal governance and federal imprisonment of women in Canada*. University of Toronto Press.

Hannah-Moffat, K. (2006). Pandora's box: Risk/need and gender responsive corrections. *Criminology and Public Policy, 5*(1), 183–191.

Harcourt, B. (2010). Neoliberal penality: A brief genealogy. *Theoretical Criminology, 14*, 74–92.

Hogg, R. (2001). Penality and modes of regulating Indigenous peoples in Australia. *Punishment and Society, 3*(3), 355–379.

Hogg, R., & Brown, D. B. (1998). *Rethinking law and order*. Pluto Press.

Holmes, J. (2010). *Female offending: Has there been an increase?* (Crime and Justice Statistics no. 46). NSW Bureau of Crime Statistics and Research.

Holmes, J., & Fitzgerald, J. (2017). *Trends in NSW Police clear up rates* (Bureau Brief No. 129). NSW Bureau of Crime Statistics and Research.

Horn, R., & Wincup, E. (1995). Not real criminals: Police perceptions of women offenders. *Criminal Justice Matters, 19*, 17–19.

Hudson, B. (2006). Beyond white man's justice: Race, gender and justice in late modernity. *Theoretical Criminology, 10*, 29–48.

Hunyor, J. (2015). Imprison me NT: Paperless arrests and the rise of executive power in the Northern Territory. *Indigenous Law Bulletin, 8*(21), 3–9.

Jewkes, Y. (2004). *Media and crime*. Sage.

Jones, C., Weatherburn, D., & McFarlene, K. (2008). *Public confidence in the New South Wales criminal justice system* (Crime and Justice Bulletin No. 118). NSW Bureau of Crime Statistics and Research.

Jordan, L., & Farrell, J. (2013). Juvenile justice diversion in Victoria: A blank canvas? *Current Issues in Criminal Justice, 24*(3), 419–437.

Justice Health & Forensic Mental Health Network and Juvenile Justice NSW. (2017). *2015 Young people in custody health survey* (Full Report). Justice Health & Forensic Mental Health Network and Juvenile Justice.

Karstedt, S. (2002). Social ontology and research strategy. *Theoretical Criminology, 6*(3), 255–278.

Kelly, P. (2001). Youth at risk: Processes of individualisation and responsibilisation in the risk society. *Discourse: Studies in the Cultural Politics of Education, 22*(1), 100–116.

Kempf-Leonard, K., & Peterson Sparks, E. (2000). Expanding the realms of the new penology: The advent of actuarial justice for juveniles. *Punishment and Society, 2*(1), 66–97.

Kemshall, H. (2002). *Risk, social policy and welfare*. Open University Press.

Kemshall, H. (2003). *Understanding risk in criminal justice*. Open University Press.

Kemshall, H. (2008). Risks, rights and justice: Understanding and responding to youth risk. *Youth Justice*, *8*(1), 21–37.

Kemshall, H., Parton, N., Walsh, M., & Waterson, J. (1997). Concepts of risk in relation to organizational structure and functioning within the personal social services and probation. *Social Policy and Administration*, *31*(3), 213–232.

Keyzer, P., & McSherry, B. (2015). The preventive detention of sex offenders: Law and practice. *The University of New South Wales Law Journal*, *38*(2), 792–882.

Kong, R., & AuCoin, K. (1982). *Female offenders in Canada* (Juristat, 28(1)). Statistics Canada.

Krisberg, B., & Austin, J. F. (1993). *Reinventing juvenile justice*. Sage.

Laster, K., & O'Malley, P. (1996). Sensitive new-age laws: The reassertion of emotionality in law. *International Journal of the Sociology of Law*, *24*(1), 21–40.

Law Enforcement (Powers and Responsibilities) Act 2002 (NSW). https://classic.austlii.edu.au/au/legis/nsw/consol_act/leara2002451/

Lynch, M., Buckman, J., & Krenske, L. (2003). *Youth justice: Criminal trajectories* (Research and Issues Paper No 4 July 2003). Crime and Misconduct Commission.

Maruna, S. (2001). *Making good: How ex-convicts reform and rebuild their lives*. American Psychological Association.

McAlinden, A. (2010). Transforming justice: Challenges for restorative justice in an era of punishment-based corrections. *Contemporary Justice Review: Issues in Criminal, Social, and Restorative Justice*, *14*(4), 383–406.

McAlister, S., & Carr, N. (2014). Experiences of youth justice: Youth justice discourses and their multiple effects. *Youth Justice*, *14*(3), 241–254.

McFarlane, K. (2011). From care to custody: Young women in out-of-home care in the criminal justice system. *Current Issues in Criminal Justice*, *22*(3), 345–353.

Miller, B. (1991, June 4–6). Working together for crime prevention. In *Australian Institute of Criminology Conference*. Alice Springs. https://www.aic.gov.au/publications/proceedings/proceedings5

Miller, J., & White, N. A. (2004). Situational effects of gender inequality. In C. Alder & A. Worrall (Eds.), *Girls' violence: Myths and realities* (pp. 167–190). State University of New York Press.

Moore, E. (2012). *Restorative justice initiatives: Public opinion and support in NSW* (Criminal Justice and Statistics Bureau Brief 77). NSW Bureau of Crime Statistics and Research.

Muncie, J. (2005). The globalisation of crime control: The case of youth and juvenile justice: Neo-liberalism, policy convergence and international conventions. *Theoretical Criminology*, *9*(1), 35–64.

Muncie, J. (2006). Governing young people: Coherence and contradiction in contemporary youth justice. *Critical Social Policy*, *26*(4), 770–793.

Muncie, J. (2013). International juvenile (in)justice: Penal severity and rights compliance. *International Journal for Crime, Justice and Social Democracy*, *2*(2), 43–62.

Muncie, J., Coventry, G., & Walters, R. (1995). The politics of youth crime prevention: Developments in Australia and England and Wales. In L. Noaks, M. Maguire, & M. Levi (Eds.), *Contemporary issues in criminology* (pp. 338–361). University Press.

New South Wales Attorney General and Justice. (2002). *Report on the review of the Young Offenders Act 1997*. NSW Government. https://dcj.nsw.gov.au/documents/about-us/engage-with-us/public-consultations/unsorted/young_offenders_act_review.pdf

New South Wales Bureau of Crime Statistics and Research. (2024). *NSW Custody Statistics: Quarterly update December 2024*. https://bocsar.nsw.gov.au/documents/publications/custody/2024_12_NSW_Custody_Statistics_Dec_2024.pdf

New South Wales Commission for Children and Young People. (2011). *Submission to the review of the Young Offenders Act 1997 and the Children (Criminal Proceedings) Act 1987*. NSW Government. https://dcj.nsw.gov.au/content/dam/dcj/dcj-website/documents/about-us/engage-with-us/public-consultations/unsorted/nswccyp.pdf

New South Wales Law Reform Commission. (2005). *Young Offenders* (Report No 104). NSW Law Reform Commission. https://lawreform.nsw.gov.au/documents/Publications/Reports/Report-104.pdf

New South Wales Police Force. (2015). *Protected Admissions Young Offenders Act 1997* (Corporate Sponsor: Youth D/2013/218882 [Unpublished]). NSW Police Force.

Noetic Solutions. (2010). *A strategic review of the New South Wales juvenile justice system: Report for the Minister for Juvenile Justice*. New South Wales Department of Human Services.

O'Connor, I. (1997). Models of juvenile justice. In A. Borowski & O. O'Connor (Eds.), *Juvenile crime, justice and corrections* (pp. 229–253). Longman.

O'Malley, P. (1991). Legal networks and domestic security. *Studies in Law, Politics and Society, 11*, 171–190.

O'Malley, P. (1992). Risk, power and crime prevention. *Economy and Society, 21*, 252–275.

O'Malley, P. (1998). Introduction: Crime and the risk society. In P. O'Malley (Ed.), *Crime and the risk society* (pp. 3–98). Aldershot.

O'Malley, P. (2001). Crime, risk and prudentialism revisited. In K. Stenson & R. R. Sullivan (Eds.), *Crime, risk and justice: The politics of crime control in Liberal democracies* (pp. 89–103). Willan.

O'Malley, P. (2006). *Riesgo, justicia penal y neoliberalism*. Ad Hoc Press.

O'Malley, P. (2010). *Crime and risk*. Sage.

O'Malley, P. (2012). Neo-liberalism and risk in criminology. In T. Anthony & C. Cunneen (Eds.), *The critical criminology companion* (pp. 55–67). Hawkins Press.

Pali, B., & Pelikan, C. (2010). *Building social support for restorative justice*. European Forum for Restorative Justice. https://www.euforumrj.org/sites/default/files/2019-11/final_report_building_social_support_for_rj.pdf

Parker, A. L., & Sarre, R. (2008). Policing young offenders: What role discretion? *International Journal of Police Science and Management, 10*(4), 478–485.

Pearce, E. (2021). Why 'admission of guilt' is not working in youth diversionary schemes in NSW – exploratory findings from interviews with police officers. *Current Issues in Criminal Justice, 33*(3), 285–299.

Petersen, A. (1996). Risk and the regulated self: The discourse of health promotion as politics of uncertainty. *Australian and New Zealand Journal of Sociology, 32*(1), 44–57.

Phoenix, J., & Kelly, L. (2013). 'You have to do it for yourself': Responsibilisation in young people's situated knowledge of youth justice practice. *British Journal of Criminology, 53*, 419–437.

Police Association of New South Wales. (2011). *Review of the Young Offenders Act 1997 and the Children (Criminal Proceedings) Act 1987: Police Association of NSW response to the NSW Department of Attorney General and Justice review on laws for child offenders*. NSW Government. https://dcj.nsw.gov.au/documents/about-us/engage-with-us/public-consultations/unsorted/policeassociation.pdf

Potter, G. W., & Kappeler, V. E. (2006). *Constructing crime: Perspectives on making news and social problems*. Waveland Press.

Priday, E. (2006). Thinking about new directions in juvenile justice: Risk and cognitive behaviourism. *Current Issues in Criminal Justice, 17*(3), 413–430.

Prison Reform Trust. (2011). *Public want offenders to make amends*. https://prisonreformtrust.org.uk/wp-content/uploads/old_files/Documents/public%20want%20offenders%20to%20make%20amends.pdf

Ptacek, J. (2010). Resisting co-optation: Three feminist challenges to antiviolence work. In J. Ptacek (Ed.), *Restorative justice and violence against women* (pp. 5–36). Oxford University Press.

Reichman, N. (1986). Managing crime risks: Towards an insurance-based model of social control. *Research in Law, Deviance and Social Control, 8*, 151–172.

Reiner, R. (1997). Media made criminality. In M. Maguire, R. Morgan, & R. Reiner (Eds.), *The Oxford Handbook of Criminology* (pp. 189–231). Oxford University Press.

Reiner, R. (2007). *Law and order: An honest citizen's guide to crime and control*. Polity Press.

Richards, K. (2010). Police-referred restorative justice for juveniles in Australia. *Current Issues in Criminal Justice, 398*, 1–8.
Richards, K., & Lee, M. (2013). Beyond the 'three dogmas of juvenile justice': A response to Weatherburn, McGrath and Bartels. *University of New South Wales Law Journal, 36*(3), 839–862.
Richards, K., & Renshaw, L. (2013). *Bail and remand for young people in Australia: A national research project* (AIC Reports: Research and Public Series 125). Australian Institute of Criminology.
Ringland, C., & Smith, N. (2013). *Police use of court alternatives for young persons in NSW* (Contemporary Issues in Crime and Criminal Justice, No. 167). NSW Bureau of Crime Statistics and Research.
Roberts, J. V., Stalans, L. J., Indermaur, D., & Hough, M. (2003). *Penal populism and public opinion: Lessons from five countries*. Oxford University Press.
Robinson, G. (1999). Risk management and rehabilitation in the probation service: Collision and collusion. *The Howard Journal, 38*(4), 421–433.
Robinson, G. (2002). Exploring risk management in probation practice: Contemporary developments in England and Wales. *Punishment and Society, 4*(1), 5–25.
Rock, P. (2004). On becoming a victim. In C. Hoyle & R. Young (Eds.), *New visions of crime* (pp. 1–22). Hart Publishing.
Rose, N. (1999). *Powers of freedom: Reframing political thought*. Cambridge University Press.
Rose, N. (2000). Government and control. *British Journal of Criminology, 40*, 321–339.
Rose, N. (2001). The politics of life itself. *Theory, Culture and Society, 18*(6), 1–30.
Rose, N., & Miller, P. (1992). Political power beyond the state: Problematics of government. *British Journal of Sociology, 43*, 173–205.
Rose, N., & Miller, P. (2008). *Governing the present: Administering economic, social and personal life*. Polity Press.
Roth, L. (2014). *Public opinion on sentencing: Recent research in Australia* (NSW Parliamentary Research Service e-brief 08/2014). New South Wales Parliament. https://www.parliament.nsw.gov.au/researchpapers/Documents/public-opinion-on-sentencing-recent-research-in-/public%20opinion%20on%20sentencing.pdf
Schehr, R. C. (2005). Conventional risk discourse and the proliferation of fear. *Criminal Justice Policy Review, 16*(1), 38–58.
Shearing, C. (1993). Policing: Relationships between public and private. In M. Findlay & Z. Uglje (Eds.), *Alternative policing styles: Cross-cultural perspectives* (pp. 203–227). Kluwer Law and Taxation Publishers, United Nations Interregional Crime and Justice Research Institute.
Shearing, C. D., & Stenning, P. C. (1985). From the panopticon to Disney World: The development of discipline. In A. N. Doob & E. L. Greenspan (Eds.), *Perspectives in criminal law* (pp. 335–346). Canada Law Book.
Sherman, L. M. (2003). Reason for emotion: Reinventing justice with theories, innovations, and research – The American Society of Criminology 2002 Presidential Address. *Criminology, 41*(1), 1–38.
Simon, J. (1987). The emergence of a risk society: Insurance, law, and the state. *Socialist Review, 95*, 61–89.
Simpson, B. (1997). Youth crime, the media and moral panic. In J. Bessant & R. Hill (Eds.), *Youth, crime and the media* (pp. 9–15). Australia Clearing House for Youth Studies.
Sir Mason, A. (2019, March 20). *The courts and public opinion*. National Institute of Government and Law Public Lecture, Parliament House.
Snider, L. (1998). Feminism, punishment and the potential for empowerment. In K. Daly & L. Maher (Eds.), *Criminology at the crossroads: Feminism readings in crime and justice* (pp. 246–261). Oxford University Press.

Snowball, L. (2008a). *Diversion of Indigenous juvenile offenders* (Trends and Issues in Crime and Criminal Justice, No 355). Australian Institute of Criminology.

Snowball, L. (2008b). *Juvenile diversion of Indigenous offenders: A study examining juvenile offenders in Western Australia, South Australia and New South Wales* (Trends and Issues in Crime and Criminal Justice, No. 355). Australian Institute of Criminology.

Snowball, L., & Weatherburn, D. (2007). Does racial bias in sentencing contribute to Indigenous overrepresentation in prison? *The Australian and New Zealand Journal of Criminology*, *40*(3), 272–290.

Sparks, R. (2001). Degrees of estrangement: Cultural theory of risk and comparative penology. *Theoretical Criminology*, *5*(2), 159–176.

Stahlkopf, C. (2008). Political, structural and cultural differences on England Youth Offending Team Practices. *International Criminal Justice Review*, *18*, 455–471.

Steffensmeier, D., Schwartz, J., Slepickla, J., & Zhong, H. (2023). Twenty-first century trends in girls' violence and the gender gap: Triangulated findings from official and unofficial longitudinal sources. *Journal of Interpersonal Violence*, *38*(17–18), 9818–9844.

Stenson, K. (2001). The new politics of crime control. In K. Stenson & R. K. Sullivan (Eds.), *Crime, risk and justice, the politics of crime control in liberal democracies* (pp. 15–28). Willan Publishing.

Stubbs, J. (2000). Restorative justice, gendered violence and Indigenous women. In J. Ptacek (Ed.), *Feminism, restorative justice and violence against women* (pp. 103–122). Oxford University Press.

Stubbs, J. (2010). Restorative justice, gendered violence and Indigenous women. In J. Ptacek (Ed.), *Restorative justice and violence against women*. Oxford University Press.

Tilley, N. (2008). Modern approaches to policing: Community, problem oriented and intelligence-led. In T. Newburn (Ed.), *Handbook of policing* (pp. 372–403). Willan Publishing.

Turnbull, G., & Spence, J. (2011). What's at risk? The proliferation of risk across child and youth policy in England. *Journal of Youth Studies*, *14*(8), 939–959.

Urbas, G. (2000). *The age of criminal responsibility*. Australian Institute of Criminology.

Urwin, J. (2025). *A popular criminology of youth justice: Youth on film*. Routledge.

Van Ness, D. V., Strong, K. H., Derby, J., & Lynetter Parker, L. (2022). *Restoring justice: An introduction to restorative justice* (6th ed.). Routledge, Taylor & Francis Group.

Wacquant, L. (2008). Ordering insecurity: Social polarisation and the punitive upsurge. *Radical Philosophy Review*, *11*(1), 9–27.

Walgrave, L. (1995). Restorative justice for juveniles: Just a technique or a fully fledged alternative? *Howard Journal*, *34*(3), 228–249.

Walgrave, L. (2004). Restoration in youth justice: Youth crime and youth justice: Comparative and cross-national perspectives. *Crime and Justice*, *31*, 543–597.

Walklate, S., & Mythen, G. (2011). Beyond risk theory: Experiential knowledge and 'knowing otherwise'. *Criminology and Criminal Justice*, *11*(2), 99–113.

Warner, K., Davies, J., Walter, M., Bradfield, R., & Vermey, R. (2011). *Public judgement on sentencing: Final results from the Tasmania Jury Sentencing Study* (Trends and Issues in Crime and Criminal Justice, No. 407). Australian Institute of Criminology.

White, R. (1994). Shaming and reintegrative strategies: Individuals, state power and social interests. In C. Alder & J. Wundersitz (Eds.), *Family conferencing and Juvenile Justice: The way forward or misplaced optimism?* Australian Institute of Criminology.

White, R. (1997). Police practices, punishment and juvenile crime prevention. In A. Borovski & I. O'Connor (Eds.), *Juvenile crime, justice and corrections* (pp. 254–269). Addison Wesley Longman.

White, R. (2001). Graffiti, crime prevention and cultural space. *Current Issues in Criminal Justice*, *12*(3), 253–266.

White, R. (2009). Ethnic diversity and differential policing in Australia: The good, the bad and the ugly. *Journal of International Migration and Integration*, *10*(4), 359–375.

Wilkinson, I. (2009). *Risk, vulnerability and everyday life*. Routledge.

Wood, J. R. T. (1997). *Royal Commission into the New South Wales Police Service*. Final Report (Vol. 1, pp. 183). https://catalogue.nla.gov.au/catalog/3011481
Wundersitz, J. (2000b). Juvenile delinquency, Australia. In R. H. Rafter (Ed.), *Encyclopedia of women and crime* (pp. 131–132). Oryx Press.
Young Offenders Act 1997 (NSW). https://www.austlii.edu.au/cgi-bin/viewdb/au/legis/nsw/consol_act/yoa1997181/
Youth Justice Board. (2009). *Girls and offending—Patterns, perceptions and interventions*.
Zehr, H. (2015). *Changing lenses, restorative justice for our times* (25th Anniversary ed.). Herald Press. http://www.abs.gov.au/AUSSTATS/abs@.nsf/7d12b0f6763c78caca257061001cc588/dfd6faea24f68ad6ca257235001cd238

4 Police Perspectives on Youth Diversion

Introduction

The previous chapters have established how the YOA legislatively positions YLOs as critical *gatekeepers* in the youth justice system. The Act establishes a hierarchy of responses to youth offending—beginning with warnings[1] and cautions to YJCs and court proceedings. Within this framework, YLOs are vested with the authority to determine whether a young person is eligible for diversion and which pathway is most appropriate. This discretion places them at the pivotal junction between informal and formal justice responses. Their decisions effectively control access to diversionary options, making them the primary arbiters of whether a young person avoids the stigma and consequences of court involvement. As such, the legislation entrusts NSW Police with significant responsibility, reinforcing their role not only as law enforcers but also as frontline decision-makers in promoting rehabilitative and restorative justice outcomes for young people.

This chapter focuses on the role of the NSW Police Force in the diversionary decision-making of young people under the YOA. It analyses data from six interviews—one conducted by telephone and five face-to-face—with five YLOs and one youth policy officer, carried out between February 2016 and April 2016. The interview questions were designed to explore respondents' views on various issues related to diversion. The questions fell into three main areas: (1) YLO's understanding of their general role, their interest in the position and perceived differences from 'general duties' officers; (2) the process of diversion to cautions and YJCs, including key decision-making points, influencing factors and strengths and weaknesses of the diversion process; and (3) experiences with other organisations involved in the decision-making process, along with recommendations for improving diversion practices.

The interview sample consisted of six participants from the NSW Police Force. This included one Youth Policy Officer—a civilian role within the NSW Police Force responsible for managing youth strategy—and five YLOs. To ensure anonymity, all participants are referred to as YLOs. The sample comprised five female participants and one male participant, with ages ranging from 36 to 50 years (two did not disclose their age). Participants had varying levels of

DOI: 10.4324/9781003470366-4

experience within the NSW Police Force, ranging from 9 to 17 years of service. Their time in their current roles varied considerably, from 2 to 15 years. Geographically, participants were distributed across different regions of NSW, including Southwest Metropolitan, Central Metropolitan, Northwest Metropolitan and Northern Region.

Negotiating access to YLOs within the NSW Police Force proved to be a lengthy and challenging process. As McGovern (2011) observes, this experience is not unique and has been echoed by numerous other researchers. Police organisations have traditionally been characterised as 'closed' institutions, marked by complex layers of bureaucracy, administration and hierarchical management (McGovern, 2011). Despite increasing rhetoric around openness, accountability and transparency, particularly in relation to external research, this closed nature persists—often due to the perception of researchers as critics of police practices (Silverman, 2001). This institutional resistance was evident in the extensive formal procedures required to gain research approval from the NSW Police Force. The process—from initial contact to the successful interviewing of YLOs—spanned 16 months. The study initially targeted 40 of the 80 LACs, with this sample size deemed both sufficient for the research objectives and manageable in scope. However, of the 40 YLOs invited to participate, only five agreed to be interviewed. This low response rate highlights a significant degree of resistance at the local level, reflecting the broader challenges of conducting research within a tightly controlled bureaucratic institution.

While the small sample size limits the ability to generalise findings, the research nonetheless offers valuable insights into expert perspectives on youth diversion. These perspectives either coalesce with or diverge from broader views within policing, the criminal justice system and the political domain. The interviews reveal recurring themes and a nuanced understanding of the complexities surrounding diversion, contributing meaningfully to the discourse on youth justice. The data collected from the NSW Police Force participants has been organised into key thematic areas related to diversion. These include interpretations of the YLO role, their position as gatekeepers to diversionary pathways and the critical decision-making points that influence the application of the YOA. The findings are presented in the following sections.

Attraction to and understandings of the YLO's role

This section explores participants' interest in their roles, their perceptions of differences between YLOs and general duties officers and their understanding of the YLO role within the framework of the YOA. Participants expressed mixed motivations for pursuing the YLO position. Some were driven by a desire to support children and held an idealistic belief in early intervention as a means of preventing youth from entering criminal pathways. Others noted more practical reasons, such as the appeal of regular working hours. Unlike general duties officers, who typically work rotating shifts, YLOs generally work standard hours—Monday–Friday, 9–5.

A background in working with young people, or a strong personal commitment to supporting youth, influenced some participants' decisions to take on the YLO role. For instance, YLO4, who had experience in Early Childhood Education, expressed a particular interest in diversionary programs available under the YOA. Similarly, YLO3, who holds a university degree in primary teaching and had previously worked as a youth group leader and sports coach, explained that her background and passion for helping children were instrumental in securing her position. According to YLO3, initial training at the NSW Police Force Academy included minimal coverage of YJC as a diversion scheme. However, it was her in-depth knowledge of YJC, combined with a strong desire for 'helping children' that led her to take on the YLO role. She particularly idealised the possibilities for intervention to lead children away from the pathways of criminal lives: 'I wanted to do something preventative and helpful for the community. To try and help people, stop people, from getting in trouble before they get to the point of getting in trouble' (YLO3).

This respondent's remark alludes to the preventative objectives of the YOA and highlights their desire to move beyond the traditional 'law enforcer' role. It reflects an awareness of the need to align policing practices with the Act's preventative intentions. Such a perspective marks a departure from the conventional and pervasive understanding of police work as primarily focused on apprehending 'wrongdoers' and gathering evidence for formal judicial proceedings. Instead, it signals a shift towards early intervention and community-based interventions.

While the desire to support young people was common among most of the respondents, the origins of their motivations varied. Many described this commitment as intrinsic, yet shaped and reinforced by their educational backgrounds and prior professional experiences. In one notable case, a participant linked their dedication to youth work to their religious beliefs:

> I worked in a before-and-after school childcare centre as a coordinator … also, I was a youth worker for a number of years… I worked with at-risk kids running activities like camps and surf camps and snow camps …as a manager of an indoor climbing centre. I've also been a youth pastor with my wife for a couple of years and I've been on youth teams in local churches down in Sydney, in youth groups and that sort of thing.
>
> (YLO5)

This YLO expressed a strong motivation to 'help' children improve their life choices 'or get back on track with their lives' (YLO5). This perspective aligns more closely with pastoral or social support roles than with traditional policing. As discussed in Chapter 2, police culture(s) traditionally emphasised a craving for crime-oriented work that promises excitement and focuses heavily on detecting and responding to crime (Reiner, 2010). This stands in contrast to the philosophy underpinning the YOA, which prioritises repairing harm and restoration over punitive measures of crime control. Clearly, YLO5's statement aligns with the restorative justice approach.

For other YLOs without prior careers outside the NSW Police Force, their interest in the role was similarly driven by a passion or *love* for working with children. For instance, when asked what initially drew them to the position, YLO2 shared:

> I assisted as the backup YLO some years ago, and loved it! So, I enjoy working with young people, they're challenging but it's very rewarding for me as well as for them. I still run into young people I worked with ten years ago who have children now. I don't know, while I still enjoy it, I'm still going to do it. And I don't know, just … love it!

For some YLOs, practical considerations played a role in their decision. YLO1, for example, noted that the more predictable hours associated with the YLO position—compared to rotating shifts of general duties—were particularly appealing due to their responsibilities as a single parent of a child with a child requiring regular hospital care.

The small number of participating YLOs limits the ability to generalise from these accounts. However, it is evident that those interviewed are driven by a passion for working with children and/or an idealistic preference for restorative opportunities over punitive justice.

YLOs as 'gatekeepers': between diversion and police culture(s)—a role in tension

The position of the YLO was established in 1998 in response to the YOA. This role was created to oversee the implementation of the legislation, provide training for general duties police officers, monitor diversion practices, serve as Specialist Youth Officers (SYOs) and promote the Act within LACs. A total of 80 YLO positions were created, with one assigned per LAC (NSWAGJ, 2002). In response to the legislation, NSW Police also established SYO positions. Under the YOA, SYOs were crucial as they would receive training to 'apply the criteria of the Act to matters before them and have the delegated authority of the Commissioner of Police to refer matters for youth justice conferencing or to court' (NSWAGJ, 2002, p. 13).

Interviewed YLOs often contrasted their roles with those of SYOs and general duties/arresting police officers. The interview findings indicate that, in practice, when a YLO is not on duty, SYOs typically assume their responsibilities. Most YLOs described their role as encompassing various activities that align with the official description on the NSW Police website, which notes:

> [YLOs] are the administrators of the [YOA] for NSW Police. As part of their duties, they are responsible for delivering cautions and referring children and young people to youth justice conferences. The [YLO] role also involves implementing strategies to reduce juvenile crime including: crime prevention and safety talks at schools, juvenile crime reduction programs;

and networking with other agencies. They are the primary point of contact between NSW Police and Juvenile Justice.'

(NSW Police Force, 2016)

Overall, YLOs highlighted several key responsibilities: engaging primary-school students by delivering school presentations; delivering cautions; making referrals and attending YJCs; liaising with young people in custody; training other police officers on the YOA. As noted by YLO2: 'doing anything from a primary age talk to maybe a behavioural school talk to a youth refuge presentation, to youth workers, to parents…also run programs in the community.' Throughout the interviews, it was consistently emphasised that the YLO role diverges significantly from the traditional view of police officers as primarily focused on crime control.

A misunderstanding or devaluation of the work done by YLOs by general duties/arresting police officers was highlighted by some respondents. For instance, YLO1 remarked:

> General duties wouldn't have the faintest idea of the background work that the Crime Management unit does. They'd have no idea how much interaction I would have with families, how much telephone work I do, what I go out and actually do, or what my job is all about. I deal with schools; I deal with the agencies that the young person might be working with. So, I have an idea of what's happening in the background in that child's life. General duties don't have that; they have one vision, 'this child is committing crime' and the child is judged under that banner. Whereas, because of my role, I come from the *softer* side, trying to put things in place to help this young person make better decisions.

The quote reflects YLOs' perception that general duty police do not consider the YLO role as *real* work (for discussions on community policing being viewed as 'not real police work,' see Garcia, 2005). It also illustrates a common sentiment among YLOs: general duties policing often fosters a negative view of young people as offenders.

The negative perception held by many police regarding the YLO role and, more specifically, the existence of the YOA, is further noted by YLO4:

> I can't just make a blanket statement and say, 'every general-duties police officer thinks that the YOA is a … heap of poo'. But there are still pockets of *that*… in NSW Police and it's … I think sometimes … sort of comes down from the more senior [officers], some of the more senior people that are very old-school about how they used to deal with juveniles back in the day. I hear a lot of: 'Well, back in the day when I was dealing with them, we would do this, this and this … and then the YOA came in'. Some of those attitudes still get passed down to junior ranking police …There is still a bit of resistance to change in the way we think about diversion and restorative justice… I just don't think that we're quite there with innovative thinking with regard to how we're managing juvenile offenders.

The quote illustrates a broader issue: some senior figures are resistant to change. This is displayed through negative attitudes towards restorative justice and diversion for juveniles, particularly repeat offenders. This finding aligns with research discussed in Chapter 2, which shows that rank is a significant predictor for punitive attitudes among police officers, whereby higher-ranking police officers have been observed to adopt more punitive approaches (Shafiq et al., 2016).

The final comments on persistent resistance highlight the YLOs' belief that police culture(s) has not sufficiently evolved to embrace the intentions of the YOA. This sentiment is encapsulated in YLO4's concluding remark: 'I just don't think that we're quite there with innovative thinking in regard to how we're managing juvenile offenders.' Concurrently, this quote reflects the YLOs' need to affirm their role's significance within a system resistant to change and innovation. Overall, the YLOs interviewed attribute the perception among general duties officers and/or senior leadership that YLO work does not constitute 'real police work' to a stagnant system that fails to embrace innovation and alternative justice procedures.

Although one YLO suggested that resistance approaches may be diminishing, there was broad agreement that such resistance remains embedded in police culture(s). Interviewed YLOs identified several contributing factors: an unwillingness to move beyond the traditional 'arrest and charge' approach; a narrow view of policing that equates law enforcement and use of force with 'real' police work; and a widespread lack of understanding among general duties officers about the value of the YOA. YLOs see themselves as crucial in re-enforcing the value of the YOA:

> The YLO role really helps the command and the young people in the community because we're *educating* officers in here by saying: 'Hey, there is a better way' … I guess, this is giving young people a chance, and yes, they do make mistakes, but we can obviously assist them – still deal with the incident and the issues around it – but they're not going to end with charges and that sort of stuff.
>
> (YLO5)

The emphasis on *educating* officers about diversionary practices reflects a broader belief among YLOs that systemic and institutional cultural change is needed—both within policing and at the political level—to shift away from conservative and punitive approaches and fully embrace diversion.

A shared concern among YLOs is that general duties officers often lack the time, training or communications skills to engage with young people. As YLO2 explained:

> My communication skills might be very different…my advantage is: I have time. I'm not bound because I have to go to the next job. I've got the advantage of following up and taking the time to make referrals…it's just the role itself that enables you a little bit more flexibility to engage more.

Similarly, YLO5 noted:

> In general duties, you're sort of a slave to the radio because whatever jobs come over, you *have to* go out and just do them. And sometimes you could have ten or so jobs outstanding and you don't *actually* get the time in general duties to actually make any impact [on] people's lives.

These accounts highlight both cultural and structural barriers to diversion. Restorative options like YJCs are often undervalued—not regarded as 'real police work'—therefore not warranting significant attention. Additionally, structural constraints arise from competing demands on their time.

The time-intensive nature of reviewing youth cases under the YOA, combined with the complexities of these processes and the realities of how policing works, emerged as a key challenge for YLOs in meeting the expectations set out by the legislation. According to the legislation, cautions and YJC referrals should be overseen by a YLO. As such, decisions made by general duties or arresting officers in this context may involve consultation with the YLO or SYO. However, when decisions are made to 'charge' rather than 'divert,' the process becomes rather complex. While the legislation requires that charges be approved by the YLO, in practice, their role is largely advisory. As YLO2 explained, 'it is up to the officers [general duties], but it has to fit the criteria and I [the YLO] provide guidance.'

YLO1 offered further insight on this dynamic:

> If I want to go above their head [general duties], then I need to go to a Crime Manager or the Commanders. But at the end of the day, it's the officer who makes the final decision…I can *only* make recommendations. Any police officer making a decision –whether they're charging or bringing a young person through the YOA: *it's their decision* because they are the ones who will have to go to court, and they are the ones who will have to give evidence. There's no sitting back there and saying: 'Oh my boss told me that I had to do this'. There is none of that! They have to take responsibility, so it's their decision.

This statement highlights the bureaucratic imperatives within the institution, where individual officers are held accountable for their decisions. It also highlights the limited formal occupational authority of YLOs, raising questions about their actual influence in diversion-related decision-making. A central issue is whether offering advice and guidance—without decision-making power—is sufficient, especially given that YLOs are the most trained officers in the application of the YOA. Despite their expertise, institutional constraints often limit their interactions with general duties, which can negatively impact diversion decision-making and ultimately its outcomes.

The extent to which YLOs can provide guidance also varies across LACs, depending on factors such as accessibility, engagement and communication between

YLOs and general duties officers. These dynamics are explored further in the following section that focuses on the diversion process itself.

'Gatekeeping' in practice: YLOs and the bureaucracy of diversion

This section examines interviewees' insights into the bureaucratic process of diversion. In doing so, it highlights the various individuals and organisations involved, critical decision-making points for YLOs, the factors influencing YLO decision-making and the strengths and weaknesses of the process as described by the YLOs.

In discussing their gatekeeping role, YLOs noted that young people aged 10–17, to whom the YOA applies, are not always brought to the police station where the YLO is based and can provide direct assistance. In some cases, general duties officers may choose to handle matters in the field, believing it to be in the young person's best interest. However, as YLO2 explained:

> If the officer makes the decision to deal with it [under the YOA], they should consult a SYO, who is not always a YLO, but is trained to give that advice. Every incident is sent to me to review. If I'm happy, then they're happy. If I think that they're missing something or potentially it's an offence that can't be dealt with under the YOA [but instead, they are charging], then I'll send it back to the officer, and they will need to make other arrangements. So literally I don't make the decision – it's up to the officer [general duties], but it has to fit the criteria [of the legislation] and I provide guidance [accordingly].

This quote highlights two significant points: firstly, that there exist markedly divergent perspectives among officers on diversion; secondly, that YLOs primarily serve in an advisory capacity rather than as active decision-makers. As a result, during the critical initial contact—when the decision to divert or charge is made—YLOs often have limited influence. This raises questions about the current training structure, where YLOs receive the most comprehensive instruction on the YOA. If general duties officers are ultimately responsible for the decision, broader training across the force may be warranted.

Interviewees were specifically eager to emphasise the distinction between YLOs and SYOs. As noted earlier, YLOs are tasked, by the legislation, with implementing the YOA, providing training, monitoring diversion, acting as a SYO (if required) and promoting the Act's provisions. SYOs, on the other hand, are trained and authorised to 'apply the criteria of the Act to matters before them and have the delegated authority of the Commissioner of Police to refer matters for youth justice conferencing or to court' (NSWAGJ, 2002, p. 13). As YLO3 explained:

> SYOs are not the same as YLOs, but they're able to make determinations on what happens to young people. They can verify if a young person is getting charged and give advice to other police. The aim is to have them [SYOs] around when we, the YLOs are not on duty, so other police [officers] can seek their advice.

SYOs were commonly described by the YLOs as key points of contact for general duties officers, particularly on weekends when YLOs are off duty, and hence unavailable. According to the participants, although SYOs have the official authority to override decisions that do not meet diversion criteria, in practice, they often act as advisors. Concerns were raised about the quality and consistency of SYO training. As YLO4 observed:

> I feel like it's really hit-and-miss with SYO's. I don't think that you should become an SYO to tick a box. You should have a genuine interest in the YOA, its place within NSW Police and its benefits…some kind of knowledge around restorative justice and its principles; It should not be a box ticking exercise: 'Yes, I've got that qualification now'. I've seen some really good SYOs and some really poor ones.

When asked to elaborate, YLO4 explained:

> Once you've become an SYO, that's it – no refresher training. You don't get anything else. That's it! You're just an SYO until the dawn of time. They're not in the same loop as the YLOs. They're not on the YLO network – what we call a *muddle* – so an email *muddle*, which is communication among YLOs across the state. The SYOs aren't a part of that, so they're not getting fresh information which means you're not going to, probably, do the best when it comes to outcomes for juveniles.

Further clarifying the role, YLO4 added:

> They SYO are sort of like *a back-up* YLO for when the YLO can't be here. When I'm here, I'll get a majority of them [requests for advice] unless an SYO feels confident enough and takes some. But many SYOs are not [confident], because of the lack of updated knowledge. They're not overly confident, and will ring me and say: 'Am I on the right track with this?' And I'll go: 'Yeah or no, or whatever'. [When they go for the role] they get a one-off three-day training. Some SYOs out there haven't even utilised those skills…they haven't verified a charge, or quality-reviewed a juvenile incident. They're still very green.

These reflections were echoed by other participants, all of whom stressed the importance of having 'really good,' well-trained, confident SYOs who can effectively step in when YLOs are unavailable.

Overall, the interviews revealed a fragmentation in the prescribed responsibilities and authority of YLOs and SYOs. As previously noted, the YLO positions were established as a response to the YOA, making them responsible for administering cautions and YJCs referrals within NSW Police. In contrast, SYOs were appointed under the YOA to determine whether a YJC should be held, a caution administered or proceedings to court should commence (YOA, 1997, s. 38). However, in practice, as evidenced by the accounts of those interviewed, SYOs typically function in more of a supporting role regarding determinations. Furthermore, it appears that general duties officers retain much of the authority and responsibility for diversionary decision-making.

Interviewees consistently emphasised the importance of engaging in dialogue with general duties officers to achieve desirable outcomes—regardless of whether SYOs or YLOs are involved. They viewed this dialogue as critical and essential to their effectiveness in the application of diversion. As YLO4 explained:

> I'm here in the office Monday to Friday, and obviously, with juveniles, a lot of the activity will probably be centered around the weekend. So, a juvenile might get picked up on the Friday night, and I won't see that occurrence until I'm back at work on Monday. If I'm not around, there is no conversation [with general duties/arresting officer], no advocacy for diversion. In their minds, they [arresting officers] are wanting to charge. So, by Monday morning that kid's been charged, and they've got a court date. Whereas, if there had been a conversation with me, I'm obviously all about advocating for the YOA, that's my role. So, because that conversation doesn't happen when young person is apprehended, and maybe there's no one else to advocate for it at that time, then diversion doesn't happen. Often, the reason that I'm still seeing as why young people are not being diverted is because they're not making admissions, so they're not wanting to be interviewed, they're not wanting to talk, they're not making those admissions. But in saying that, I don't know whether there's a lot of work that goes on with regards to the way *we* communicate with these kids … sometimes it can be a conversation with the juvenile, their support person and we can change the outcome of how that matter is dealt with.

YLO1 similarly highlighted the importance of educating general duties officers:

> It takes time to explain to general duties, as a lot of them don't know *what a conference is* about. They don't get trained. I'm lucky enough to know in depth what a conference is, about and how the process works. When I can sit down and explain things to them, they get to understand that a conference is actually a better outcome than a charge.

These reflections point to underlying power dynamics and knowledge disparities within the NSW Police Force. While all police officers ostensibly perform the same overarching function, YLOs' roles are distinctly shaped by welfare paradigms, whereas crime control, law enforcement and justice paradigms define the work of other police officers.

YLO4 further articulated the advisory nature of the role, highlighting how their specialised knowledge positions YLOs as advisors with expert authority:

> We are so well informed and should be looking for those opportunities for diversion, and if they haven't been utilised properly. I quality review every event. If I see something that I don't think is right, or that we should divert, then I go straight to the Constable: 'Did you think of this? Did we look into this? What have you done in this space?' There's usually a conversation. But unfortunately, there still are those black holes – because we don't have 24/7 YLO coverage and usually there's only one YLO per command; so, there are going to be gaps. It is because of those gaps that some of those kids who could have been diverted, aren't.

The necessity to address resistance from those preferring a legal response over alternative measures is not unexpected. For instance, YLO3 described their LAC as 'very proactive' when it comes to re-educating officers who tend to favour traditional justice methods:

> We do a lot of proactive stuff here. Every probationer who comes through *our* station does a youth issues training day. That's actually a local initiative. We just talk to them about youth issues; why young offenders offend; what the risk factors are; what the protective factors are; how they could work better with young people; we talk to them about the YOA; and give them a good base to go out there and work as a general duties officer. We do a lot of that kind of stuff *here at this LAC* to try and work with the general duties to help them do their job better.
>
> YLO2 shared a similar experience:
>
> I conduct training for the new police recruits, and I talk about the YOA; we look at warnings, cautions, conferences, PAS. We do some interactive activities; we look at what offences are covered just to make sure that general duties have an understanding of when the YOA can be applied and how important it is that they apply it. As well as, what's required: legal advice, support people – who they can be. We have police from all ranks on our training days. I also assist with training them to be SYO.

These accounts were unique compared to those from other regions where interviews took place, suggesting possible inconsistencies in training across different LACs. This is supported by YLO3's claim that training was implemented primarily as a localised initiative within their specific LAC rather than as part of a standardised approach. The small number of participants limits our ability to generalise from this observation; however, it highlights at minimum, the potential for disparities in how youth justice issues are addressed across different LACs. Notwithstanding, the predominant narrative among interviewees highlighted the existence among general duties of a widespread lack of knowledge about the YOA and a blatant resistance to it due to disinterest or misunderstanding. For example, YLO4 remarked:

> I've had stand-up arguments with sergeants, inspectors, junior police about kids that needed to be diverted, and their mindset was: 'No, they needed to be charged; they needed to go before the court.' … Why? Because that's what police do – catch the baddies and put them before the court; that's what we do. That's as basic as what policing is. Our job is to catch the criminals and put them before the courts for the courts to decide what will happen.

Although this view was vocalised only by one YLO in this study, it aligns with existing research and literature on police culture(s) in Australia and comparable national contexts. Such research generally indicates that despite the broad variety in police roles, the traditional law enforcement approach—focusing on catching criminals and processing them through the judicial system—is still viewed as the priority (Cockcroft, 2013; Cosgrove, 2016; Manning, 1978/2005).

The notion that police are responsible for bringing wrongdoers to court—where justice is ultimately served—is deeply embedded within the institution. This traditional view of policing is also widely held within the broader community. For instance, as YLO4 shared an experience involving community expectations:

> …even in the general community – victims, the victims that we're dealing with – I've had, as an example, a victim ring me after a kid wrote an apology letter as part of a caution. I sent the letter to the victim, obviously without all the details, just the letter… and he [the victim] called me straight away and said: 'I've just received this letter of apology in the mail from a caution'; I said: 'Yes, he's written that, the juvenile's written that so you're entitled to have that'. And he said: 'So you're telling me that this person did this, and they just came and saw you about it, and got a slap on the wrist, wrote an apology letter and that's done?' And I went: 'Yes, that's how that juvenile was diverted', and he said: 'Well, that's not good enough … it might as well have been nothing'. So, I still think that there is a mindset in the community too, that the court is the be-all and end-all as well. That there's nothing else that's going to 'cure' that kid unless they go to court.

Thus, resistance to diversion within the police institution can be seen, in part, as a manifestation of the broader punitive sentiments prevalent in the general public.

As established, YLOs are the most trained officers in matters relating to the YOA. However, as the interviews reveal, the process of diverting young people from court through police referrals extends beyond the formal roles of the SYO and the YLO. While YLOs are by legislation responsible for overseeing cautions and YJC referrals, the decision to charge a young offender, rather than divert, may occur without a YLO's input. The following section focuses on how YLOs navigate this challenge.

YLO's, timing and the limits of gatekeeping

Some YLOs indicated that, for the most part, decision-making and incident logging by general duties were discussed with them. For instance, YLO3 explained:

> I've been here for so long, and they know me, so most officers will come and ask me for advice. Often, there have been situations where I've challenged them on decisions that they've made – and this it's actually more around cautions, rather than charges. I've had a few times where a young person has been put down for a caution, and I've actually spoken to the officer in charge and said: 'You know, actually I think that this is more suitable for a conference, the offence is quite serious, there's quite a degree of violence involved' and all that kind of stuff. And we've actually changed it, so even though they've booked in a kid for a caution, they've done the interview and booked them in, and it is in my folder: Well, we stop that process and have upped-it to a conference instead. So that's happened quite a few times. And to be honest, they [general duties] don't really resist, they are quite happy.

This YLO offered a distinctive perspective on the previously mentioned pockets of resistance and the challenges of persuading certain general duties officers who preferred to 'charge' rather than divert. According to this YLO, there were occasions when she contested decisions to issue 'only a caution,' deeming this as insufficient. The challenge posed by those most trained—the YLOs—that *only a caution* is inadequate fundamentally undermines the YOA. After all, the Act mandates a hierarchical approach, prioritising less intrusive options from warnings to cautions, to conferences and finally court. This scenario highlights how the punitive framework that shapes traditional police practices frequently resurfaces, even within diversion-focused domains.

Moreover, YLO3 diverged from most of her peers by downplaying concerns about the limited availability of YLOs for 24/7 consultation. She expressed strong confidence in the capacity of SYOs to manage decisions in her absence:

> Here, we're very fortunate – we probably have one of the highest numbers of SYOs. We do a lot of training, I deliver training on the SYO course two times a year; so, we have lots of SYOs.
>
> (YLO3)

Further, commenting on decisions made without YLO consultation, the picture painted by YLO3 was, in her own words, 'pretty good':

> A few times, we've stopped a charge and referred it back to a conference instead. That's happened occasionally. Most charges in our area tend to be for things that can't get conferenced – like breach of bail, you can't

> do a conference for breach of bail anyway. Or a breach of an AVO. Or for our very high-risk offenders that have already done time in juvenile detention centres, PCA offences like drink driving, that kind of stuff. So, most of my offences are very black and white – you can't conference them anyway. So, I find they [officers] are *pretty good* here; they *really* are pretty good.

However, characterising the situation as 'pretty good' appears implausible. On the one hand, it acknowledges that many offences fall outside the scope of the YOA, revealing structural limitations in the legislation. On the other hand, presenting the scenario in such benign terms suggests that these YLOs measure success primarily by their ability to maximise diversion within the Act's parameters, rather than their effectiveness in actually helping children—despite the child-centred occupational mission that, as noted earlier in the chapter, YLOs themselves champion.

In contrast, YLO1 acknowledged that not all matters eligible for diversion reach her before decisions are made. However, she emphasised her ability to intervene once cases were identified and viewed by her, at times halting charges if diversion was appropriate:

> I read all disseminations, every day, and if I see something [that should be diverted], I would then be able to put a stop to the charge straight away, if instead it should be a diversion. Most of our guys [general duties] are pretty good in our station because we have very good communication lines.

Similarly, YLO5 noted:

> Any time any police officer enters in the computer 'young person', I get a dissemination. If I read it, and I don't think they've dealt with it the right way, or if they can't deal with it a certain way (and they have) and I need to give them advice, then I can either resubmit the event or I can actually email the officer and, or go to speak to them and discuss, get their options and that sort of stuff.

These assertions highlight a more collaborative and communicative approach, using terms such as 'communication lines' and 'discussion,' indicating mechanisms for addressing decisions made by other officers. It is significantly distinct from YLO3's previous claims noting that she openly *opposed* charges being filed and transformed this into a 'challenge' (a challenge that as illustrated in the anecdote, does not consistently result in the least intrusive intervention for the young person). Collectively, these accounts illustrate varied approaches and perceptions among YLOs concerning the need to train general duties officers, which inevitably, at times, produces varying outcomes.

Adding to this, and presenting another incongruity, some YLOs note that the opportunity to review the process of decisions already made by general duties is not something that is promptly attended to. As YLO2 explained:

> All legal processes on actions with juveniles are reviewed every month. Part of my role is to make sure that young people are being dealt with appropriately and that if they can be diverted through the Act, then they are. Police must outline in their narrative in their reports as to why they haven't dealt with it [under the YOA]. And we had Custody Managers as well, who, if they [general duties] decide to charge a young person, it must be verified by a SYO. Not every officer can accept that charge, so we have police that are gatekeepers –other than myself – and they have to approve that they should be charged and not dealt with under YOA. So, the officer can't just decide: 'I'm going to charge them'; it has to go through a senior SYO as well.

Issues discussed above, including the divergent opinions regarding who gets to be diverted and to what, concerns over training matters and inconsistent availability of trained personnel during certain periods, raise questions about the thoroughness of the review process. Furthermore, it is noteworthy that since the disbandment of the Youth Justice Advisory Committee—which played an important role in monitoring and facilitating the improvement of the Act's operation—in 2007, external oversight of police diversion has been eliminated (Noetic Solutions, 2010). This consequently leads to the necessity for quality assurance via internal reviews around diversion.

Compounding these issues, YLO2 acknowledged a significant delay between incidents and their subsequent review. However, she emphasised that charges are often levied against young people primarily because 'they're [young offenders] refusing to be interviewed,' leaving officers with limited alternatives. This indicates conformity between YLO perspectives and 'the way things are.' This also highlights how the YOA's requirement for admission of guilt potentially undermines the use of diversion, a concern discussed in previous chapters. However, this perspective fails to explain the unexpectedly low diversion rates in *some* LACs documented by Ringland and Smith's study in 2013 (see Chapter 2).

Overall, these accounts reveal a series of contradictions. From some YLOs' perspectives, general duties officers who fail to consult with YLOs may be ill-equipped to consider diversion over charging. These narratives thus highlight the need for a fundamental culture shift within police practices away from entrenched punitive traditions towards more collaborative decision-making. Conversely, other YLOs downplay the significance of this issue, suggesting it has little impact on outcomes. According to these latter accounts, opportunities to divert are not being missed; rather, the only plausible explanation offered for higher court referral rates compared to police referrals is attributed to young offenders' unwillingness to admit guilt while in police custody. This perspective emphasises a strong commitment to notions of individual responsibility wherein blame is allocated to individuals who refuse to cooperate, rather than acknowledging any form of institutional accountability. These issues are further elaborated in the next sections that examine the key decision-making factors influencing the application of the legislation.

Applying the legislation: YLOs' discretionary decision-making in practice

As administrators of the YOA within NSW Police, YLOs are expected to consider five key criteria when making diversionary decisions: the seriousness of the offence, the level of violence, the degree of harm caused and the young person's offending history (YOA, s.37. pt. 3). Unsurprisingly, YLOs frequently refer to these legislative criteria as central to their decision-making. However, the interviews reveal that decision-makers assign various weights to each criterion on a case-by-case basis. Consequently, the high level of discretion afforded by the legislation regarding what and how to apply these criteria permits a degree of subjectivity, potentially resulting in inconsistent or uninformed decisions.

In addition to applying these criteria, YLO3 emphasised the importance of adhering to the hierarchical structure prescribed by the Act, which stipulates that cautions should be considered before a YJC, unless the young person has already received the maximum of three cautions (YOA, pt. 4 s. 20(7)). As YLO3 explained:

> If someone has had three cautions, then obviously, for me, in most cases I'll definitely refer it for a conference rather than going to court for the fourth offence. Unless it's something that I can't do a conference for.

Here, YLO3 is describing a scenario in which a young person, still eligible under the YOA, has exhausted the maximum legal limit of three cautions. In such cases, the next logical step would be to refer the offender to a YJC rather than to court. However, further into the interviews, it was revealed that other criteria, such as the seriousness of the offence and the offender's history, are sometimes prioritised by YLOs. This practice can result in young offenders being referred to a YJC without having exhausted the three cautions. Conversely, there are instances where court referrals will occur without considering the option of referring the young person to a YJC, particularly in cases where the young person had on a previous occasion been diverted to a YJC. This is despite the Act placing no limit on the number of YJC referrals but recommending court referral as *'a last resort.'*

Such practices are not entirely surprising. They align with previous comments made by the Police Association of NSW (PANSW) to the Department of Attorney General in 2011—when, in response to whether the principles of the Act are still valid—PANSW suggested that 'an additional principle that sufficient sanction be taken against offending children to ensure they understand the consequence of their criminal behaviour' should be added to the principles of the YOA (PANSW, 2011, p. 6).

Nevertheless, the YLOs insisted that eligibility is the foremost criterion for determining diversion, as YLO2 remarked:

> Is the offence eligible? If the young person can be cautioned, usually that comes first and that's only because it's a lesser intervention. Here, we have a lot of cautions because we tend to get a lot of shopliftings from Westfield, so ... the young person is eligible to be dealt with by caution first. So, eligibility ... it's really whether the young person is eligible in terms of the offence and whether they make admission.

Overall, while YLOs agreed on adhering to legislative decision-making points, subjective interpretations emerged regarding how much weight should be given to offence seriousness and offender's history. For instance, YLO4 shared an experience of attempting to push for a YJC for an offender without prior cautions due to the offence's perceived gravity, only to be overruled by JJ, highlighting ongoing discussions and relations with JJ managers:

> I wanted to try push it through [to a YJC], the kid hadn't had a caution, but I thought the incident was serious [in nature] and it was more *appropriate* to have it dealt with by YJC rather than caution. JJ disagreed with me on that occasion... that's okay, there was discussion there. So, JJ suggested the case came back to me and we dealt with it by caution. That was fine; sometimes, I feel like it's a little bit subjective with regard to how I'm thinking and then how JJ's thinking. But I have a very good relationship with the Assistant Manager at JJ, which I think is also very important. So, we can have *those* conversations; we can go back and forth and sometimes I win, sometimes I lose.

The quote above clearly emphasises the subjective interpretation of the guidance provided by the YOA. This is not surprising. As discussed in Chapter 2, police attitudes towards diversion and charging are influenced by factors such as rank, age, mental health (Marinos & Innocente, 2008; Shafiq et al., 2016), knowledge about diversion (Foley, 2004; Green et al., 2020), understanding of the YOA (NSWAGJ, 2002) and police officers' prior attendance at YJCs (Stewart & Smith, 2004). The subjective interpretation of the guidance provided by the YOA reflects the diversity of police attitudes towards diversion and charging.

Additionally, YLO4's comments illustrate a belief in the need to treat serious offences in a more 'appropriate' way, suggesting that cautions perhaps should not be seen as suitable for certain behaviours. This view aligns with existing research on police attitudes, which indicates that the seriousness of the offence is one of the most influential factors in diversionary decision-making (Carrington, 1998; Doob & Cesaroni, 2004; Doob & Chan, 1982; Marinos & Innocente, 2008) (see Chapter 2). However, this tendency to place such emphasis on the seriousness of the offence is problematic, as it undermines the purpose of diversion. If the law provides that an offence type is eligible for a caution, then it should be dealt with by a caution, as suggested by JJ in the case described above, and as intended by the YOA.

Before continuing this discussion on discretionary decision-making in diversion, it is essential to set the context using relevant statistical data. The data obtained from BOCSAR (File Reference kf25-24696)[2] for this study allows for a comparison of the number of persons of interest (POIs) aged 10–17 years proceeded against by caution, YJC and court by NSW Police Force from 1998 to 2024. Table 4.1 shows such comparisons from which initial observations can be outlined.

In 1998, when the YOA first came into effect, 25% of POIs were proceeded by way of caution. Over time, cautions peaked at 45% in 2003, making the highest percentage recorded. Aside from 1998, the lowest point occurred in 2023 when cautions accounted for 37%. YJCs had their most significant impact between 2000

Table 4.1 Number of persons of interest (POIs) aged 10–17 years proceeded against by NSW Police under the *Young Offenders Act* 1997.

	Cautions		*YJC*		*Court*	
1998	5,926	25%	444	2%	17,160	73%
1999	8,275	35%	985	4%	14,624	61%
2000	8,779	40%	1,360	6%	11,629	53%
2001	9,800	43%	1,480	6%	11,748	51%
2002	9,697	44%	1,375	6%	11,018	50%
2003	9,446	45%	1,169	6%	10,283	49%
2004	9,015	44%	1,174	6%	10,500	51%
2005	9,056	42%	916	4%	11,821	54%
2006	9,416	42%	758	3%	12,456	55%
2007	10,215	42%	990	4%	13,254	54%
2008	10,892	42%	898	3%	14,205	55%
2009	10,660	42%	1,161	5%	13,846	54%
2010	10,763	43%	902	4%	13,192	53%
2011	9,746	41%	905	4%	12,857	55%
2012	8,379	41%	755	4%	11,488	56%
2013	7,298	38%	785	4%	11,297	58%
2014	6,904	39%	643	4%	10,318	58%
2015	7,149	38%	689	4%	10,874	58%
2016	6,782	39%	519	3%	9,961	58%
2017	7,328	39%	613	3%	10,665	57%
2018	6,977	39%	734	4%	10,140	57%
2019	7,120	40%	792	4%	9,885	56%
2020	6,699	39%	758	4%	9,680	56%
2021	6,750	40%	764	5%	9,315	55%
2022	6,902	39%	649	4%	10,327	58%
2023	7,057	37%	941	5%	11,067	58%
2024	6,360	34%	928	5%	11,451	61%

and 2004, reaching 6%, representing the highest proportion of total POIs proceeded by this method. YJC referrals consistently maintained a low presence, with the fewest recorded at 3% in 2006, 2008, 2016 and 2017.

Court referrals have been the predominant method for processing young people, accounting for the majority of POIs handled. The lowest percentage was observed in 2002 and 2003 when court referrals constituted 50% and 49% of total cases, respectively. In 2024, court referrals reached their highest since 1999 at 61%. For the same year, police cautions are lowest there have ever been since 1999, at 34%. Overall, the data reflects NSW Police's strong reliance on cautions, with YJC playing a minor role and court referrals remaining a major method of processing young offenders.

Taken together, this data suggests significant changes in youth offending trends in NSW in recent years, particularly since 2009. The reasons for these declines are unclear. It is suggested that they are not local to NSW as similar downward trends have been observed internationally (Clancey, 2018).

An overall decline in youth offending is welcome; however, this research focuses on the significant number of young offenders still being sent to court. Despite the drop in youth offending, diversionary decision-making towards cautions and YJC has declined. This trend is evident from the consistently low referral rates to YJC and the increasing number of children proceeding to court annually since 2011, undermining the use of court as 'a last resort,' as stipulated by the YOA.

A plausible explanation for the low number of YJC referrals is the high volume of cautions being used. However, a significant limitation of cautions is the inability to determine whether these young people would have entered the system prior to the YOA, when the option was charging. As noted in Chapter 2, concerns about net-widening have been noted since the introduction of the use of cautions under the Act (Christie, 2009; Polk et al., 2003; Seymour, 1998). Most significantly, given that most young offenders commit the least serious offences, these figures are troubling because they clearly indicate that court as a 'last resort,' as intended by the Act, is not the outcome the system has been able to achieve. From this viewpoint, youth diversion is under-utilised, highlighting the importance of understanding the factors related to NSW Police Force diversionary decision-making.

It is worth noting that the figures discussed so far are limited to police-led diversion. Including court referrals to YJC would more than double the total percentage of YJC for each year. This will be elaborated in Chapter 5. Nonetheless, the overall percentage of young offenders diverted from court remains significantly low compared to those sent to court.

Applying the legislation: further challenges—unlimited YJCs? No way!

Regardless of there being no legislative limit on how many times a young person can be referred to a YJC, YLOs expressed a very conservative approach in their decision-making. For example, YLO2 explained:

> If they have three conferences for the same offence and they're relatively in a short timeframe, I will consider that we need a different intervention. I don't think –having three conferences all for shoplifting, and they've had three

> cautions for shoplifting all in a 12-month period – means that the young person is learning or has put strategies in place to address their criminality. I think we then need to send it to court. Whether this is right or wrong… I'm pretty much a three conference [person]… depending on the timeframe; if they're 13 and get a conference and now they're 17, well that's different because there's been a few years gap.

This quote illustrates that subjective discretionary decision-making will, at times, result in outcomes that do not align with the intentions of the YOA. When legislating for court as the 'last resort,' indeed 'the last resort' is a subjective viewpoint. The most common viewpoint among YLOs interviewed is that two conference referrals are typically sufficient before proceeding to a court referral decision. For example, YLO1 remarked:

> My experience is that when a child hasn't learned their lesson, or realised that they've done the wrong thing by the second conference, what more can you do for them? What more can you put in an outcome plan to help them fix themselves?

Indeed, the figure of two was considered an arbitrary but acceptable maximum for conference referrals by most YLOs. For example, YLO3 remarked:

> I generally wouldn't do more than two conferences…because I kind of think if they've done two and they're not changing – especially if it's the same sorts of offences – then I'll be thinking that they're not changing their behaviour, and we need to step it up… If it had been for an offender that had a conference that they did successfully when they were younger and then another one again and then another one again, then I would contemplate if they had all been successful and they responded well and had done the outcome plan and had shown remorse and that kind of stuff; then yes, I would look at doing another one. But if they're kind of just not showing the greatest attitude at the first conference that they've been to or the second conference that they've been to, I'd be reluctant to use another one. I'd be thinking it's not working; I feel like at some point you've let the courts take charge…we've got to put the responsibility back on the courts to do something about it.

The above quote reflects a common perspective among YLOs interviewed, who see referring a young person twice or three times to YJC as quite generous. This perception is interesting because YLOs claimed to see numerous advantages of YJC over charging. For example, when asked about the strengths of the Act, YLO3 claimed to 'love, love, love conferencing' and explained:

> I'm all for conferencing. I've seen some great conferences over the 15 years that I've been doing this role. I've seen some really good turnarounds and some really good satisfaction for victims. I think, it's the only way that the

> young offender gets to realise the depth of what they've done and how much it's affected others. To me, the court system doesn't allow for that and it's very frustrating for victims and not effective for the young offenders. So, to me, the YOA: I love, love, love conferencing… [long pause]. I like conferencing because obviously you have those additional powers with the outcome plan and the victim being there and all that kind of stuff…Not so big on court.

Most accounts from the interviews suggest that when YLOs and police generally express sentiments like 'I'm not so big on…court' (YLO3), they are indicating their dissatisfaction with what they perceive as the leniency of magistrates towards offenders. Consequently, YLOs sometimes consider opting for a YJC referral as an alternative to court, due to their lack of faith in court outcomes. However, the idea of unlimited conferences does not sit well with them. For example, one respondent remarked:

> Look, there are probably two people in this command who have had about five YJCs. Even then, I question it and think: 'Well, we're looking at five…' because … I see the same faces repeatedly and I know that police might have referred [YJCs] one or two initially and then they've gone to court thinking: 'Well, they are still offending; why are they still offending? Obviously, YJC isn't working even though they are completing the outcome plan. Maybe it needs to be something more serious'. On those occasions then – when those same kids are sent to court – they are referred back to a YJC … and then it's like the process starts again. So, there should be a point where both the court and the police [recognise]: 'Well, look mate you've had … how many chances do you get?'. I think there needs to be some sort of limit on YJC.
>
> (YLO5)

This quote reflects two main perceptions: firstly, that YLOs believe two referrals to conferencing are enough, after which further action should be the responsibility of the courts; and secondly, a dissatisfaction with the courts' perceived lack of a more punitive approach, particularly when magistrates apply the YOA and refer young people to YJC. As discussed in Chapter 2, it is a known fact that since the introduction of the YOA, the majority of the referrals (over 50%) to YJCs originate from the courts (for a comparison from 1998 to 2024 on referrals to YJC by Police and Courts refer to Tables 6.1 and 6.2 (Chapter 6)). However, the data recorded do not specify how many of these cases involve youths who could have been diverted at police level, so this will always be an unknown. Nonetheless, given that the Act covers summary offences and certain indictable offences that may be dealt with summarily under the *Criminal Procedure Act 1986* (NSW), the reality is that most of the re-offenders discussed are engaging in the less serious types of offences.

Despite this, interviewees consistently referenced participation in two or three YJCs as sufficient. As observed by YLO5: 'I think… the fact that it's got three cautions is, you know, good—like three strikes and that sort of thing.' This statement alludes to the US 'three strikes' principle, which has been adopted within policy frameworks based on populist assumptions that such punitive escalation models effectively reduce crime through explicit deterrence messaging. This suggests that YLOs are not immune to the generally punitive culture prevalent within policing institutions. Some officers described themselves as unprepared for 'the innovative thinking' promoted by the YOA legislation. As YLO5 claims:

> I think it needs to go to court, and the magistrate needs to probably decide [what happens next]. I don't know what his parameters are for what he can choose for the young person to do. But I think … the magistrate should be the one thinking: 'Well hang on mate, you had three conferences already, I can see that you've completed them but obviously they are not working. So, we need to look at another avenue' …But…I [as a YLO] don't get paid $500,000 to make those calls, so you'll have to go to somebody higher than me.

This YLO who earlier expressed commitment to preventing young people from making the 'wrong choices', here reveals that such professional dedication is significantly undermined by feelings of occupational rivalry. This rivalry has led the YLO to conclude that their salary is insufficient to justify the decision-making responsibilities expected of them. The legislation explicitly assigns gatekeeper responsibilities to both the police and magistrates, despite the latter's more elite occupational status. However, it seems that this YLO disagrees with this principle, believing that difficult decisions regarding punishment should be left to those in higher-paid roles. This attitude is not unique to policing but reflects a broader issue of professional disengagement—a problematic stance, particularly when it concerns decisions that carry significant implications for young people's lives. Consequently, questions arise about the suitability of police as potentially reluctant, yet primary, gatekeepers to diversion. It is therefore important to determine whether police officers are genuinely committed to acting in the best interests of juveniles, even when *tough decisions* are required, or whether they perceive such responsibilities as being outside their job description.

A prevalent discourse within the NSW Police Force is a lack of faith in the courts. Interestingly, some YLOs use this sentiment to advocate for police-led YJC referrals. YLOs encourage YJC over charging when speaking to general duties officers, particularly those inclined to pursue the proceed-to-court option. As, YLO4 stated:

> I say to police [officers]: 'If you're thinking in your head that something amazingly terrible is going to happen to these kids in a court; do you know what's going to happen? They are going to be referred back to a YJC, so effectively we're doing the YJC the long way around.' That's a conversation I have with the police [officers] who are absolutely adamant that a young person should be charged. I see this happening a lot, a lot of the kids are coming back for YJCs since the court does the referral anyway.

In this context, YJC is promoted not necessarily for its intrinsic merits but as an inevitable outcome that could, ultimately, remain within police discretion rather than being transferred to the courts. Simultaneously, the narratives suggest that such an approach benefits police by saving additional work. Conversations acknowledging that referrals to YJCs can substitute charges—on the basis that courts are likely to divert the case anyway—somewhat contradict the most common account presented by YLOs. They often remarked that many court-referred YJCs 'will just be purely legislative procedural issues where we [the police] haven't got those admissions [of guilt], so we have no choice [but to charge]' (YLO4). According to the YLOs, the failure to obtain admissions of guilt from young people is the most significant factor undermining the use of the YOA.

Legislative constraints to diversion: 'admission of guilt'

The requirement under the YOA for a young person to admit the offence to qualify for diversion to a caution or YJC has posed a significant challenge in the Act's implementation. This requirement has also been a source of considerable tension regarding police accountability (Bargen, 2001, 2005; Noetic Solutions, 2010; NSWDAGJ, 2002; Pearce, 2021). Criticisms in this domain include concerns that young people may feel compelled to make admissions to consent to diversion without having been provided 'sufficient information about diversionary options available and the consequences of withholding consent' (Schetzer & Henderson, 2003, p. 188).

Past criticisms have also highlighted that police subject young people—who may be eligible to be diverted under the YOA—to full interviews, operating under the presumption that the matter might ultimately proceed to court. For instance, in response to the review of the YOA by the NSWDAGJ (2011), the Law Society of NSW (2011) noted:

> Section 10 of the YOA requires only that an adult be present when a child makes an admission for the purposes of the YOA, not that the child be subject to a full interrogation. It is unfair to subject young people to a full interview - young people are immature, usually with low levels of comprehension, are often daunted by the whole process in an unfamiliar environment, where a real power imbalance exists. (p. 8)

This power imbalance has been identified as particularly significant in interactions involving First Nations youth, where there is a danger 'that minority youth will be classified by police as "unsuitable"...particularly if they have prior offending histories or are deemed uncooperative' (Cunneen, 2008, p. 293). Previous research indicates that both police and legal representatives believe First Nations youth may refuse to admit guilt due to unfavourable attitudes towards law enforcement (Little et al., 2011).

As consistently highlighted by research (see Cunneen & White, 2007; Liederbach, 2007; White, 1997, 1998), interactions between police and young people are often characterised by conflict and tension, with high levels of anger, fear and mistrust. Young people's negative perceptions of police have been linked to their feelings of being over-policed without justification (Alder et al., 1992; Collins et al., 2000). Conversely, police perceptions of young people as uncooperative and disrespectful of the law contribute to adverse interactions (Alder et al., 1992; White, 1998). Studies have shown that during encounters with police, young people may experience intimidation, verbal abuse or physical violence (see Alder et al., 1992; Borrero, 2001). Furthermore, young people are reluctant to file complaints, perceiving police harassment and violence as commonplace (Borrero, 2001). Specifically, research highlights that First Nations youth are particularly vulnerable to physical and intimidating treatment by police and may fear reporting such incidents due to the risk of potential retaliation (Cunneen, 2001; White, 1997). These negative interactions perpetuate unfavourable attitudes and perceptions between police and young people, likely contributing to decreased cooperation or compliance, such as an unwillingness to admit guilt (Pearce, 2021).

In response to concerns raised by the Noetic Solutions Review in 2010 regarding the lower number of referrals to YJC by NSW Police compared to court referrals, the NSW Police indicated that the legislative requirement for an offender to admit guilt is the predominant factor contributing to this disparity in referral rates (Police Association of New South Wales, 2011). The YLOs interviewed in the present study agreed with this assessment.

Recognition of the impediments associated with the requirement for an 'admission of guilt' led to the creation of the PAS in 2014. The scheme emerged from collaborative negotiations between the NSW Police Force, the ALS, Legal Aid NSW and the Department of Police and Justice. Under PAS, if an offender is unwilling to admit an offence that could be dealt under the YOA, they can be offered the option to make a 'protected admission.' This provision intends to allow young offenders to make admissions to an offence while safeguarding their right against self-incrimination, ensuring such admissions cannot be used as evidence in court proceedings. When an offender consents to make a protected admission by signing the appropriate document, they receive written assurance from the police that the admission will not be utilised under any circumstances. Following this agreement, the offender may undergo a police interview; however, if the case is neither cautioned nor referred to a YJC and subsequently results in charges being brought before the court, the information collected during the interview cannot be used. Furthermore, the existence of a signed PAS remains undisclosed to the court at any stage.

PAS commenced operation in mid-2014, initially exclusively to facilitate the use of cautions by NSW Police Force. However, in November 2015, the scheme was expanded with the aim of further improving referrals to YJCs. Since the introduction of the PAS, no research or literature has been conducted to evaluate its potential value, leaving its impact largely unexplored. The precise frequency with which PAS is utilised remains unknown. Currently, as the Youth Policy Officer noted during the interviews, 'the police do not have a way to include this information in the Computerised Operational Police System (COPS)' (YLO6). The YLOs' perspectives regarding whether the implementation of the scheme affected the number of referrals to YJC are predominantly negative.

When queried about PAS's impact on the number of guilty admissions, YLOs commonly viewed it as an unwelcome procedure for investigating officers. Overall, there was mixed and sometimes contradictory information regarding how widely used or recommended PAS is. For instance, YLO1 remarked:

> ...we haven't used *that*. I think we've used it once since it's come in...Because it's not very secure. I think it has a hole in it – this is my opinion– I feel that if we're going to offer *that* [PAS] to the young person, we should be able to deliver the caution there and then. It should not be that the young person goes away and then comes back [for the caution], because there is a possibility of them not returning, not coming back for the actual caution to be delivered...and then, what does police have to be able to take them to court? We've got nothing! Because we can't use that admission in court because it was done under the protection: we've got nothing!

When remarking 'I think it has a hole in it,' YLO1 referred to the police perspective that interviews are conducted to gather evidence, including admissions, to secure convictions. As noted, PAS prevents any admissions made by the young persons from being utilised as evidence in court. Thus, police officers harbour culturally embedded reservations regarding an 'admission of guilt' that possesses negligible evidentiary value. The PAS framework does not align with traditional law enforcement-oriented policing practices.

Further elaborating on its use, when asked how often it is employed, YLO1 added:

> We all have to use it [PAS], we have to; every station has to use it.
>
> Police don't have a lot of success using it. A lot of kids don't want to say anything but also, you'll find police might not offer it because they feel that they've got nothing to go to court with. We've got no backup. Where do we go? It's wasted, the kid's free! So, we can't do anything about charging that young person if they don't turn up for the caution.

From these remarks, it becomes clear that YLOs are cautious because PAS usage is mandated, leading them to emphasise (during the interviews) its obligatory nature. Simultaneously, they acknowledge police reluctance due to prosecutorial imperatives, particularly the value of a 'guilty admission' as evidence. This indicates that occupational imperatives often override the young person's best interests, specifically regarding obtaining an admission that allows for diversion.

There are contradictory and implausible claims evident in these discussions. Firstly, it is suggested that PAS is offered consistently because it is required, yet at other times, it is claimed that police officers might not facilitate its use as they feel 'cheated' of the admission. The aversion to PAS seems to stem from the perceived futility of admissions that cannot serve as evidence. This contradicts the traditional policing view of an 'interview' as a tool for evidence collection. Nevertheless, a common account among all YLOs interviewed is that PAS is rarely used—if ever. Resistance from police officers often underlies this lack of use. As YLO3 remarked:

> I think there's a bit of resistance, and I actually quite understand it to be honest. I personally have issues with PAS. There are a few things that I don't like about it. I see lots of issues in the fact that if a young person doesn't turn up for a caution, then you've got nothing. And what do you do with it? ...; I know that has happened ... where they've been put forward for a caution and then the young person doesn't turn up and their statement [PAS] is inadmissible because obviously, we can't use it; and then we haven't got enough to go to Children's Court. So that is one issue.
>
> In general, police see it as somewhat of an inducement, like you really are conning them [children] into making their statement for you; You know it's like; 'you know, if you give us this statement, we're not going to use it in court' like I'm not 100% behind it, so I haven't ... really, to be honest, promoted it and educated other police [officers] as much as other YLO's who would be behind it.

This YLO's opinion reflects the sentiment expressed by all interviewed YLOs, illustrating a shared scepticism about PAS's effectiveness and its fit within existing policing practices.

Additionally, there is a prevailing view among YLOs that young people who are inclined to refuse interviews continue to do so even when offered PAS. For example, when asked whether they always provide the PAS option to offenders not making admissions, YLO1 noted:

> ...if they are eligible for a caution or a conference, we obviously always offer it to them. It gets offered, but it doesn't get taken. Some young kids are just stubborn; the ones that are new to the system and maybe first offenders would be likely to take something like that.

This remark was made in the context of using the PAS for cautions, while YLO1's comments on its use for YJC were:

> Normally if a young person is eligible for the YOA, they would be told that; when we call Legal Aid, we would say that. However, we find that it's a problem, I've been doing this for seven years and for seven years Aboriginal Legal Aid has always advised, the majority of them advised their kids not to interview. To say nothing. It still doesn't work [PAS]...because they don't want to go into the interview process.

The common observation that young people decline PAS when offered continued to emerge during interviews. For example, YLO2 claimed: 'I've had young people, after legal advice, decline Protected Admissions.' When asked about the frequency of using PAS, YLO2 commented: 'Not very much and it is because most people are happy to be interviewed without Protected Admissions. So, we have maybe used it [PAS] twice this year, because they [children] are happy to be interviewed … without Protected Admissions.'

This view—that young offenders are willing to be interviewed—is unique. As previously noted, other YLOs emphasised young people's unwillingness to admit guilt as a significant barrier to referral.

As mentioned earlier in the chapter, the low number of participating YLOs makes it difficult to determine whether their experiences reflect broader trends. However, if First Nations youth and Aboriginal Legal Aid have a reluctance to accept PAS at face value, this would not be surprising given the documented poor relations between police and First Nations young people. As previously noted, such strained relationships likely lead to reduced cooperation—resulting in both officer reluctance to use PAS and young people's unwillingness to be interviewed.

Police interrogations have long been a source of controversy and malpractice, including reports of false confessions, fabricated confessions (often referred to as 'verballing') and instances of violence and torture (Dixon, 1997; Dixon & Travis, 2007). Additionally, research indicates that First Nations people in Australia are over-represented among the wrongfully convicted (Roach, 2015). This history of malpractice justifies the distrust from suspects and Legal Aid regarding promises that 'admissions' to the police under PAS will not be used against them.

The findings discussed in this section so far illustrate several factors constraining the use of diversion. These include, but are not limited to, subjective interpretations of legislation and significant emphasis on the young person's offending history and the seriousness of the offence. Importantly, YLOs have highlighted the admission of guilt as a significant barrier undermining diversion under the YOA. Furthermore, attitudes and concerns regarding PAS suggest that police culture further impedes opportunities for diversion, favouring court processing instead. The next section will explore additional organisational constraints based on YLOs' experiences with the Act.

Interagency consultation and frustration with the legislation

This section presents participants' views on the strengths and weaknesses of the diversion process, including how they interpret and apply the letter of the law, specifically, which offences are covered or not by the Act. Additionally, it explores participants' experiences and their working relationships with other organisations involved in the diversion process.

In describing their overall relationships with these organisations, police generally noted that engagement with the courts is unnecessary. However, collaboration with JJ is frequently unavoidable, as coordination is required to arrange YJC referrals. In this context, YLOs described positive relationships characterised by consultation prior to decision-making to determine the best course of action. This may involve clarifying whether an offence qualifies under the Act or deciding if a caution or YJC is more appropriate for a particular case.

For example, when discussing how much weight to give to a young person's previous history with JJ in making decisions on how to proceed, YLO4 remarked:

> … if it's during the day, I would ring JJ and I would probably say: 'I've got this young person, police want to refer him or her to a conference, but he's had three in the last six months, what do you think?'

This observation exemplifies the predominant narrative among those interviewed regarding working relations with JJ. However, when discussing weaknesses of the Act, several YLOs expressed concerns that YJC is deficient because it does not facilitate the integration of all services that could potentially benefit the young person: 'I think if we work together more with other agencies and make it a more collaborative approach—even inside those conferences—I think we would see stronger conference outcomes' (YLO4).

This view suggests that some YLOs might prefer a more active role in the actual YJC process. At the same time, it indicates scepticism about the current process due to its narrow scope. This lack of faith could influence decision-making, especially regarding young people considered most 'risky' or in need of interventions beyond those available through YJC processes. This is clearly illustrated by YLO2, who while questioning their own approach, observed:

> Am I loading this person up?… he has no accommodation, no support networks. I'm sending him into another conference where he is going to agree to do certain things. He's already got three other plans outstanding – is this right?'

It is well known that First Nations people often face greater challenges in meeting accommodation and support network expectations compared to non-Indigenous communities. The remark prompted the interviewer to ask YLO2 how gender and ethnicity influence diversion. YLO2 replied:

> No, I've never based decisions on other than the criminality component because I find conferencing can be very powerful. I had conferences with varying ethnicities, varying sexualities, varying ages, various support networks, some who were out-of-home, some who are in-home, some who have never been in trouble with police.

The subject of Indigeneity and gender appeared to be somewhat taboo among YLOs, who promptly emphasise that diversion is equally accessible to First Nations and non-Indigenous youth, while asserting that law enforcement maintains an equitable approach towards all individuals. According to the interviewed YLOs, any disparities in outcomes stem primarily from Legal Aid representatives advising First Nations youth to refuse interviews.

When discussing the Act's weaknesses, some YLOs noted concerns about young people feeling pressured to admit guilt for diversion benefits and avoiding a criminal record. As discussed earlier in this chapter, YLOs typically do not favour an unlimited number of YJCs referrals for the same young person. An unofficial consensus among YLOs suggests that, for the most part, a maximum of two or three YJCs will warrant a charge the next time around—a stance more punitive than what the Act intends.

These punitive sentiments are further evidenced in other positions held by YLOs. For example, some respondents argued that cautioning should ideally be limited to those who 'come under the police notice for the first time' (YLO1)—that is, first-time offenders, and used only once, rather than the possible three times as prescribed by the Act. In commenting on YJCs, YLO1 added:

> It works well for those kids who need things put in place. What I'm very interested in is the percentage out of YJCs that have been successful… I think YJC is not doing anything. It's a waste of money…if they [children] are still committing offences, they need to go and do time. Enough is enough – like for young people when do we say: enough is enough? Because if they keep getting [off], they laugh at us at court. We go to court, and they laugh at us as police. They laugh in our face, they go: 'Magistrate will just let me off; I'll get what I want'. So, a lot of police feel dealing with the YOA or young people is a waste of time.

This observation highlights the dilemma YLOs encounter in endorsing the YOA. Within police institutions, the Act is often perceived as a 'soft approach' to juvenile crime, leading to concerns that it undermines police authority and results in young offenders disrespecting or 'laughing at' the police. Further elaborating, YLO1 remarked:

> They [young offenders] think it's a joke. Young kids who have done their three cautions and their conferences, to me, they're far gone. You can't save them because now they're going into the charge process and they've had warning after warning, talk after talk. I've spent each caution, half an hour talking to that person. How much more talking can you do?

Indeed, it appears that some YLOs expect the YOA to be a 'silver bullet,' wherein a single referral to YJC would eliminate further reoffending. Upon discovering this is not the case, YLOs often hastily categorise the process as a failure and abandon their support with minimal persistence. These perspectives reflect high expectations among respondents regarding young people's engagement and/or responsiveness to intervention. There is an implicit belief that repeatedly referring youth to diversionary measures might prevent them from receiving necessary interventions or addressing their criminogenic needs. Consequently, the need for diversion away from the system, as intended by the YOA, is either dismissed or misunderstood. The focus shifts towards a different kind of diversion—early intervention. However, the aims and outcomes of diversion away from the court differ significantly from those of early intervention (Richards, 2014; see Chapter 2). This perceived tension between the two types of diversion during decision-making undermines the YOA diversionary intent, compromising the principle of detention as a 'last resort.' Nevertheless, some YLOs noted that this attitude was not universally shared among police officers and reflects a lack of training or support for diversion among certain LACs.

In discussing the strengths of the Act, some YLOs highlighted the potential for the YJC to repair harm to victims as a positive aspect. However, others were more sceptical about the effectiveness of conferencing in achieving this outcome. For instance, YLO2, who facilitates (as a convenor) YJCs as a secondary role separate from their NSW Police Force employment, explained that convenors must now conduct comprehensive screening of young offenders. This assessment covers various aspects of the young person's life, including sports activities, recreational interests, substance use patterns and home environment, among other factors. The purpose of this thorough screening is to enable more tailored and effective assistance to offenders. The respondent further stated:

> Now that, that system is in place, conferencing is more about restoring the young person – which I am all for – but so much so, that the victim is left in the background… And I've been a victim myself – there is nothing for the victim in a conference. Nothing. Victims don't get anything.
>
> (YLO2)

The remark above highlights significant contradictions in how YLOs perceive the YJC process. Some YLOs value its inclusion of victims, while others believe it mirrors traditional court systems by excluding victim needs.

Another perceived weakness of the Act relates to the scope of offences it covers. Although for the most part, YLOs supported the Act's focus on 'less serious offences,' they also expressed frustration with its practical application. For example, commenting on recent amendments (YOA, s. 8; s. 31) regarding 'graffiti,' YLO2 noted:

> With graffiti, the police now have to charge a young person; however, the courts can refer them for conferencing. There are a few YLOs that are quite frustrated…especially if they are 14-year-olds [who have] never been in trouble, yet, I can head-butt you as a young person and cause an injury and get a caution. So, I think there are some offences that need to be looked at…The offence of intimidation; so, I can threaten to hit you, so I have to be charged; but if I physically hit you, I can get a caution or a conference.

Such scenarios were frequently described by the respondents as 'frustrating' and 'ridiculous.' Furthermore, these perspectives were identified as creating obstacles when advocating for the implementation of the YOA within the police force and when attempting to build community support for the legislation. As YLO4 noted:

> In the minds of some police and even the community, they think: 'That can't be right; we can't be dealing with a full-blown assault under the YOA, but yet we're sending kids off to court for scribbling on a wall with a texta'.

These issues highlight inconsistencies in the types of offences eligible for diversion, rendering the YOA occasionally incoherent and disproportionate, thereby challenging its overall validity. Additionally, frustrations surrounding graffiti cases reflect concerns about the inefficient use of police resources. As YLO4 explained: '...effectively what we're doing is...going around the long way again. Because nine out of ten referrals to court for graffiti will come back for juvenile conference.' This statement highlights YLOs' frustration with a significant procedural inefficiency: officers must complete extensive paperwork to file charges, only to have these cases frequently redirected to YJCs by the court. Moreover, the analysis revealed that police frustrations over the inability to divert such offences themselves stem from the fact that decision-making power lies with the court rather than the police.

Some YLOs also expressed interest in having greater authority to attach conditions to cautions. For example, YLO3 mentioned:

> I would love to see that YLOs could attach conditions to cautions because at the moment all we can do is ask them [the young person] to write an apology letter. I would love to have some sort of thing where I can make them do something; for example, if they've done a shoplifting, that they have to go and reimburse for the damage that was done to the clothing.

Other suggested conditions included drug rehabilitation programs or counselling. These remarks reveal a dual motivation: firstly, an explicit desire among officers to wield greater sanctioning power; and secondly—more significantly—a fundamental resistance to accepting cautions as purely cautionary measures, as originally envisioned by the legislation. Instead, these attitudes reflect an underlying punitive philosophy that seeks to incorporate elements of punishment into what was designed to be a simple warning mechanism. This highlights a central tension explored throughout the chapter: while there is surface-level recognition of the need for less intrusive responses to youth offending, closer analysis reveals entrenched resistance within police culture(s) to embracing non-punitive approaches to youth justice. This fundamental contradiction ultimately undermines effective implementation of the YOA.

Conclusion

This chapter has examined the role of NSW Police Force in the decision-making process that determines whether young people are diverted under the YOA.

Drawing on interviews with representatives from NSW Police, it sheds light on police perspectives regarding various issues. As noted throughout, the limited number of YLOs participating in this research restricts the generalisability of the findings. Nonetheless, significant factors emerge that warrant consideration.

The findings yield several interesting observations. Firstly, the appeal to the YLO role appears gendered, primarily due to the compatibility of working hours with personal responsibilities such as parenting. For some YLOs, this appeal is also tied to a desire to help children and an idealistic belief in early intervention as a means of preventing criminal pathways. Some of these officers have prior professional experience outside the NSW Police Force in roles focused on working with children—or children's welfare—highlighting their passion for supporting young people.

YLOs describe themselves as specialists in the YOA, possessing exclusive in-depth knowledge of the Act, its processes and its rehabilitative potential compared to traditional criminal justice approaches. They note that their expertise surpasses that of general duties police officers or SYOs, attributing this disparity to the lack of education and training received by those officers. However, this perception may also reflect a need to justify their role within the hierarchical structure of their institution. Despite this, interviews suggest that YLOs may share more similarities with general duties officers than they acknowledge, particularly regarding punitive approaches and arbitrary limitations they place on YJCs as a form of restorative practice.

The lack of training emerges as a critical concern, driven by both time constraints and, more fundamentally, insufficient institutional support within the NSW Police Force. Some YLOs report that juvenile justice issues are given low priority within the organisation. At the same time, inadequate education about the YOA contributes to negative attitudes towards the YLO and reinforces the perception that the YOA is a 'soft option' that inappropriately replaces deserved punishment. This further undermines the significance of youth justice matters.

Overcoming resistance from general duties police officers is crucial, as they ultimately decide whether to charge or divert a young person. In this context, the YLOs' power to influence decision-making is limited to offering advice and guidance rather than making final decisions. This dynamic can compromise diversionary outcomes, especially in LACs where engagement and communication between YLOs and general duties officers are minimal. Indeed, some YLOs express awareness of unequal levels of support across different LACs.

The juxtaposition of roles within NSW Police highlights underlying power conflicts and disparities in knowledge. The legislation assigns YLOs a range of responsibilities, including implementing the YOA, providing training, monitoring the use of diversion, acting as SYOs and promoting the Act's provisions. Accordingly, YLOs acknowledge that their role is centred on prevention and rehabilitation rather than punishment. In contrast, traditional police work is more reactive, emphasising and privileging law enforcement—a significant obstacle for YLOs in successfully promoting diversion under the YOA, both within the police force and within the broader community.

Despite these challenges, YLOs play a critical role in implementing the Act by overseeing cautions and YJCs referrals. Thus, their understandings of diversion and attitudes towards it are vital. Interviews reveal that high levels of discretion in applying diversion criteria allow for subjective decision-making, which can lead to inconsistencies.

While YLOs outwardly claim to follow hierarchical order prescribed by legislation—warnings first, followed by cautions, then YJCs, with court as a 'last resort'—closer examination reveals discrepancies between these claims and actual practice. In reality, decisions often prioritise other criteria outlined in the YOA, particularly the 'seriousness' of the offence and the 'young person's offending history.' These factors frequently supersede basic offence eligibility considerations. Moreover, the weight given to these criteria varies and remains open to interpretation. Subjectivity is inherent in discretionary decision-making, particularly given the broad powers vested in police and YLOs by the legislation. However, concerns should be raised when such discretion is influenced by biases embedded in the cultural context of policing. One could argue that the punitive culture within NSW Police Force undermines the use of the YOA to its full potential.

One area where consensus among YLOs emerged—despite not aligning with legislative intent—is the number of times that a young person should be cautioned or conferenced. While the legislation permits up to three cautions and allows for unlimited YJCs, most YLOs view two YJCs as the upper limit, considering any more than two to be excessive, except in rare cases. Concurrently, YLOs express a lack of confidence in the courts' ability to deliver the level of intrusive intervention desired by the NSW Police Force. This scepticism leads them to view YJCs as an alternative for achieving such intervention. This reflects a prevailing philosophy that prioritises *punishment and justice* over *welfare,* with YLO attitudes being heavily influenced by punitive philosophies entrenched within law enforcement cultures. Overcoming these ingrained attitudes proves challenging.

Collectively, these factors contribute to inconsistent views about who should be diverted. When combined with inadequate training and the frequent unavailability of properly trained personnel at critical charging decision points, serious questions arise regarding the NSW Police Force's capacity to implement the YOA as legislatively intended—allowing court proceedings to truly serve as a 'last resort.'

Notably, YLOs appear reluctant to acknowledge institutional and procedural shortcomings as contributing factors to persistently low diversion rates. Instead, YLOs consistently identify two primary obstacles to diversion: the YOA's requirement for an admission of guilt and young offenders' reluctance to make such admissions. Despite the introduction of the PAS, which was specifically designed to address these barriers, YLOs remain sceptical about its potential to meaningfully increase diversion referral rates. Interview findings suggest this scepticism stems partly from police resistance to using a document perceived as an inducement, and partly from the mistrust young people—particularly First Nations youth—harbour towards such documents. Consequently, the ongoing lack of admissions is not only perceived by YLOs as a significant barrier to the effective use of diversion—it continues to function as one in practice.

When discussing the strengths and weaknesses of the YOA, YLOs reveal contradictory perspectives on the capacity of YJCs to deliver victim satisfaction. While some regard the process as beneficial, others criticise it for placing too much emphasis on the rehabilitation of the young person. However, there is broad agreement that the range of precluded offences under the legislation creates fundamental inconsistencies with the Act's overall objectives. This structural incoherence poses a significant barrier to promoting the legislation's adoption and ultimately undermines its broader goal of increasing youth diversion *away* from formal justice processes.

Overall, the findings in this chapter illustrate that within the police bureaucracy, responsibility for the low utilisation of diversion is often attributed to structural 'failings' within the legislation itself, rather than to operational shortcomings. However, a clear discrepancy exists between the Act's legislative intent and its practical application, highlighting underlying tensions in the effective implementation of diversion under the YOA. These tensions are shaped by prevailing cultural norms within policing practices and highlight the need for a more cohesive approach—one that better aligns legislative frameworks with on-the-ground realities to improve diversion referral rates.

Notes

1 Warnings were not examined in this study as the data were not deemed to be reliably recorded by NSW Police prior to January 2010. In addition, BOCSAR advice that while YJC and cautions under the YOA are often given instead of laying a formal charge and proceeding against the young person with a Court Appearance Notice, this is not the case with Warnings. Therefore, warnings are not including when focusing on the use of the YOA.

2 Data file provided by BOCSAR in April 2025 (File Reference: kf25-24637) [extracted from a live database and figures are subject to change].

References

Alder, C., O'Connor, I., Warner, K., & White, R. (1992). *Perceptions of the treatment of juveniles in the legal system: Report to the National Youth Affairs Research Scheme*. National Clearinghouse for Youth Studies, Department of Education, University of Tasmania, at Hobart.

Bargen, J. (2001, October 8—9). *Diverting ATSI young offenders from court and custody in New South Wales: Practices, perspectives and possibilities under the Young Offenders Act 1997* [Paper Presentation]. The Best Practice Interventions in Corrections for Indigenous People Conference, Sydney, Australia. https://rb.gy/469bmz

Bargen, J. (2005, March 3–5). *Regulating police discretion: An assessment of the impact of the NSW Young Offenders Act 1997 Youth Justice Conferencing* [Conference Paper]. "Building a Global Alliance for Restorative Practices and Family Empowerment, Part 3", The International Institute for Restorative Practices Sixth International Conference on Conferencing, Circles and other Restorative Practices, Penrith, NSW, Australia.

Borrero, M. (2001). Perceptions and the police: The widening mistrust between youth and police. *Families in Society: The Journal of Contemporary Human Services*, *82*(4), 399–408.

Carrington, P. J. (1998). *Factors affecting police diversion of young offenders: A statistical analysis*. Solicitor General Canada.

Christie, N. (2009). Restorative justice: Five dangers ahead. In P. Knepper, J. Doak, & J. Shapland (Eds.), *Urban crime prevention, surveillance and restorative justice: Effects of social technologies* (pp. 230–239). CRC Press.

Clancey, G. (2018). *Inquiry into the adequacy of youth diversionary programs in NSW [Submission no 2]*. https://www.parliament.nsw.gov.au/ladocs/submissions/59545/Submission%202.pdf

Cockcroft, T. (2013). *Police culture: Themes and concepts*. Routledge.

Collins, J., Noble, G., Poynting, S., & Taber, P. (2000). *Kebaks, kids, cops and crime: Youth, ethnicity and crime*. Pluto Press.

Cosgrove, F. M. (2016). 'I wannabe a copper': The engagement of Police Community Support Officers with the dominant police occupational culture. *Criminology and Criminal Justice*, *16*(1), 119–138.

Criminal Procedure Act 1986 (NSW)

Cunneen, C. (2001). *Conflict, politics and crime: Aboriginal communities and the police*. Allen & Urwin.

Cunneen, C. (2008). Understanding restorative justice through the lens of critical criminology. In T. Anthony & C. Cunneen (Eds.), *The critical criminology companion* (pp. 290–302). Hawkins Press.

Cunneen, C., & White, R. (2007). *Juvenile justice: Youth and crime in Australia* (3 ed.). Oxford University Press.

Department of Attorney General and Justice (NSW). (2011). *Review of the Young Offenders Act 1997 and the Children (Criminal Proceedings) Act 1987: Consultation Paper*. NSW Government. https://dcj.nsw.gov.au/content/dam/dcj/dcj-website/documents/about-us/engage-with-us/public-consultations/unsorted/consultation_paper_-_yoa_and_ccpa_review.doc

Dixon, D. (1997). *Law in policing: Legal regulation and police practices*. Clarendon Press.

Dixon, D., & Travis, G. (2007). *Interrogating images: Audio-visually recorded police questioning of suspects*. The Sydney Institute of Criminology.

Doob, A. N., & Cesaroni, C. (2004). *Responding to youth crime in Canada*. University of Toronto Press.

Doob, A. N., & Chan, J. (1982). Factors affecting police decision to take juveniles to Court. *Canadian Journal of Criminology and Criminal Justice*, *34*(1), 35–50.

Foley, T. (2004). *"Changed my mode of thinking..." Police Attitudes to the Use of Discretionary Options for Juvenile Drug Offenders*. Report to NSW Police, Australian National University.

Garcia, V. (2005). Constructing the 'other' within police culture: An analysis of a deviant unit within the police organization. *Police Practice and Research*, *6*(1), 65–80.

Green, R., Gray, R. M., Bryant, J., Rance, J., & MacLean, S. (2020). Police decision-making with young offenders: Examining barriers to the use of diversion options. *Australian & New Zealand Journal of Criminology*, *53*(1), 137–154.

Liederbach, J. (2007). Controlling suburban and small-town hoods: An examination of police encounters with juveniles. *Youth Violence and Juvenile Justice*, *5*, 107–124.

Little, S., Allard, T., Chrzanowski, A., & Stewart, A. (2011). *Diverting Young Indigenous People from the Queensland Youth Justice System: The use and impact of police diversionary practices and alternatives for reducing Indigenous over-representation*. Griffith University.

Manning, P. K. (1978/2005). The police: Mandate, strategies and appearances. In T. Newburn (Ed.), *Policing key readings*. Willan.

Marinos, V., & Innocente, N. (2008). Factors influencing police attitudes towards extrajudicial measures under the *Youth Criminal Justice Act*. *Canadian Journal of Criminology and Criminal Justice*, *50*(4), 469–489.

McGovern, A. (2011). Negotiating access to the NSW Police Media Unit: A personal research experience. In L. Bartels & K. M. Richards (Eds.), *Qualitative criminology: Stories from the field* (pp. 58–67). Hawkins Press.

New South Wales Attorney General and Justice. (2002). *Report on the review of the Young Offenders Act 1997*. NSW Government. https://dcj.nsw.gov.au/documents/about-us/engage-with-us/public-consultations/unsorted/young_offenders_act_review.pdf

Noetic Solutions. (2010). *A strategic review of the New South Wales juvenile justice system: Report for the Minister for Juvenile Justice*. New South Wales Department of Human Services.

NSW Police Force. (2016). *Community Issues: Youth*. https://www.police.nsw.gov.au/safety_and_prevention/your_community/young_people_and_youth_issues

Pearce, E. (2021). Why 'admission of guilt' is not working in youth diversionary schemes in NSW – Exploratory findings from interviews with police officers. *Current Issues in Criminal Justice*, *33*(3), 285–299.

Police Association of New South Wales. (2011). *Review of the Young Offenders Act 1997 and the Children (Criminal Proceedings) Act 1987: Police Association of NSW response to the NSW Department of Attorney General and Justice review on laws for child offenders*. NSW Government. https://dcj.nsw.gov.au/documents/about-us/engage-with-us/public-consultations/unsorted/policeassociation.pdf

Polk, K., Alder, C., Muller, D., & Rechtman, K. (2003). *Early intervention: Diversion and youth conferencing, A national profile and review of current approaches to diverting juveniles from the criminal justice system*. Australian Government Attorney-General's Department.

Reiner, R. (2010). *The politics of the police* (4 ed.). Oxford University Press.

Richards, K. (2014). Blurred lines: Reconsidering the concept of 'diversion' in youth justice systems in Australia. *An International Journal*, *14*(2), 122–139.

Ringland, C., & Smith, N. (2013). *Police use of court alternatives for young persons in NSW* (Contemporary Issues in Crime and Criminal Justice, no. 167). NSW Bureau of Crime Statistics and Research.

Roach, K. (2015). The wrongful conviction of Indigenous people in Australia and Canada. *Flinders Law Journal*, *17*, 203–262.

Schetzer, L., & Henderson, J. (2003). *Access to justice and legal needs: A project to identify legal needs, pathways and barriers for disadvantaged people in NSW*. S. L. a. J. F. o. N. S. Wales.

Seymour, J. (1998). *Dealing with juvenile offenders*. Law Book Company.

Shafiq, N., Ohlsson, I., & Mathias, P. (2016). Predictors of punitive attitudes among police officers. *Journal of Forensic Practice*, *18*(1), 76–86.

Silverman, D. (2001). *Interpreting qualitative data: Methods for analysing talk, text and interaction* (2nd ed.). Sage Publications.

Stewart, A. L., & Smith, F. (2004). Youth justice conferencing and police referrals: The gatekeeping role of police in Queensland, Australia. *Journal of Criminal Justice*, *32*, 345–357.

The Law Society of New South Wales. (2011). *Review of the Young Offenders Act 1997 and the Children (Criminal Proceedings) Act 1987*. Submission no. 27 to the Government of NSW. https://www.lawsociety.com.au/sites/default/files/2019-11/Review%20of%20the%20Young%20Offenders%20Act%201997%20and%20the%20Children%20%28Criminal%20Proceedings%29%20Act%201987_Dec_2011.pdf

White, R. (1997). Police practices, punishment and juvenile crime prevention. In A. Borovski & I. O'Connor (Eds.), *Juvenile crime, justice and corrections* (pp. 254–269). Addison Wesley Longman.

White, R. (1998). Contemporary comments: Hassle-free policing and the creation of community space. *Current Issues in Criminal Justice*, *9*(3), 312–324.

Young Offenders Act 1997 (NSW)

5 Judicial Perspectives on Youth Diversion

Introduction

The previous chapter focused on diversionary decision-making under the YOA by the NSW Police Force. This chapter shifts the focus to the Children's Court, offering a nuanced understanding of the judicial decision-making processes that determine whether young people are diverted under the YOA (see Chapter 2 for background). It explores magisterial perceptions and their engagement with diversion processes, drawing primarily on semi-structured qualitative interviews conducted with a diverse and experienced group of magistrates.

The participant sample comprised 13 magistrates: ten *specialist* Children's Court magistrates, two Local Court magistrates, and the President of the Children's Court in NSW. To maintain anonymity, each participant was assigned a numerical identifier (M1–M13), and references to individual courts have been removed from the transcripts. The sample included seven men and six women, with disclosed ages ranging from 46 to 67 years. Several participants chose not to disclose their age, considering it irrelevant to the research. Their experience in the criminal justice system ranged from 17 to 50 years, and their tenure in current roles varied from 2 to 12 years, reflecting a mix of newer appointees and long-serving judicial officers.

At the time of data collection (February 2015 to October 2015), specialist Children's Court magistrates were distributed across NSW, covering both metropolitan and regional areas. These included Parramatta, Bidura (Glebe/Broadmeadow), Campbelltown, Sutherland/Port Kembla and Nowra, Orange, Dubbo/Wellington, Armidale and Woy Woy/Wyong/Hornsby. This sample (n = 13) comprised 11 of 15 specialist Children's Court magistrates (including the President of the Children's Court) appointed at any time, thereby ensuring comprehensive representation in terms of both occupational roles and geographical coverage, as well as two Local Court Magistrates in the rural areas. While the small number in this subset of the sample limits generalisability, their insights offered valuable perspectives on various aspects of youth diversion. Notably, their positions as Local rather than Children's Court specialists, coupled with their rural locations, allowed for meaningful comparisons regarding priorities, resources and the nuances of diversion in both urban and rural settings.

DOI: 10.4324/9781003470366-5

It is important to note that the two Local Court magistrates interviewed—who handle adult cases—deal with children's matters as needed, with these cases comprising 'about 20% or less of their work' (M12). These magistrates' roles are defined by the Local Court and they respond to the Chief Magistrate of the Local Court rather than the President of the Children's Court. Their limited exposure to children's matters appeared to generate a different level of interest in this research compared to their specialist Children's Court colleagues, as evidenced by their relatively lower interest in participating in this study. Additionally, since children's matters are only a secondary focus within the Local Court, notable differences emerged between Local and Children's Court magistrates in their approaches to communication, court processes and decision-making regarding diversion. For instance, interviews revealed concerns about the depth of knowledge regarding the YOA among lawyers and magistrates operating in rural areas. This lack of familiarity could potentially impact their diversionary decision-making.

The interviews were designed to elicit participants' perspectives on a broad range of issues related to diversion. Initial questions explored their career trajectories, and the distinct responsibilities of Children's Court magistrates compared to those in the Local Court. Subsequent questions focused on their involvement with the diversion processes, including cautions and YJCs. Participants also reflected on their interactions with other organisations involved in diversion (under the Act), the factors influencing their decision-making, the strengths and weaknesses of the YOA and recommendations for improving its effectiveness. This comprehensive enquiry provides critical insights into the judicial dimensions of youth justice diversion under the YOA within NSW, an area that remains largely unexplored in the research literature (see Chapter 2).

Attractions to and understandings of the magistrate's role

This section explores the participants' career trajectories leading to their current roles as magistrates, their perceptions of the significance of serving in the Children's Court and their views on their responsibilities regarding diversion under the YOA.

In NSW, magistrates and judges are formally appointed by the Governor in Council. The selection process is guided by a list of professional and personal criteria approved by the NSW Attorney-General (NSW Government, 2024). Vacancies for Local Court magistrates are advertised calling for expressions of interest. However, it has been observed that, at times, appointments are made for individuals who have not applied (Judicial Conference of Australia, 2015). Specialist Children's Court magistrates are selected from among existing Local Court magistrates, based on their expertise, qualifications, skills and experience in dealing with children, young people and their families (NSW Government, 2024).

When explaining their career paths to their current positions, the participants' responses reveal that most had extensive careers within the criminal justice system prior to their appointments, although their career trajectories varied significantly. The most common career trajectory amongst participants involved extensive experience practising criminal law with Legal Aid, followed by several years in the DPP. Additionally, many had careers within the public sector, although a few magistrates also spent some time in private practice. Their areas of practice were diverse, encompassing commercial law, criminal law, coronial enquiries, organised crime, policing and social work. Several participants demonstrated particularly unique career paths, including one magistrate with experience in international criminal law through the International Criminal Tribunal for Yugoslavia, another who combined social work with juvenile justice system expertise before transitioning to law and a former police officer who progressed from police prosecutor to private practice before appointment. Other notable backgrounds included specialised work in Nazi war crime investigations, workers' compensation, family law and commercial litigation. One participant had served as a District Court judge prior to their current appointment, while others brought experience from coronial inquiries and sex crime prosecutions. This variety in professional backgrounds reflects the increasingly representative composition of the magistracy in recent years (see Kiefel & Saunders, 2015).

As previously noted, the selection of Children's Court magistrates takes into account their expertise and experience with children. However, interviews revealed a substantial variation among magistrates concerning their experience working with children, young people and their families. For instance, one participant was appointed as a Children's Magistrate after pursuing investigations into war crimes in Australia and internationally, despite having no prior involvement in children's issues.

Regarding Local Court magistrates in NSW, they are all required to undertake country service during their orientation. This involves working in courts that are part of a rural/regional circuit, where they handle various types of work. As M2 explained:

> When you are a country Magistrate, you do everything! …adult crime, but also do children's crime, civil cases, coronial work. And in the children's jurisdiction I would also do care jurisdiction.

For most magistrates, except for four who had prior involvement with children's issues, country service provided their first substantial exposure to child or family-related matters. Following this experience, some magistrates were invited to take appointments in the Children's Court, while others viewed their exposure to these cases as a pivotal moment that prompted them to express interest in becoming specialist magistrates when opportunities arose.

Speaking on their interest to work on children's matters, one respondent noted:

> This is the most challenging work that I've experienced in my legal career. It's the type of work where you feel as though you have the possibility of making a difference.
>
> (M2)

Similarly, M1 remarked: 'I like being in this jurisdiction because you get an opportunity to turn kids away from what could become a life of crime.' All specialist magistrates in the Children's Court, regardless of their pathway to the role, viewed their positions as opportunities to make a meaningful difference in the lives of young people. These magistrates consistently acknowledged that young people require different judicial approaches compared to adults—an understanding that aligns with evidence-based research (see Johnstone, 2014, 2016; Richards, 2011). They emphasised the Children's Court's focus on rehabilitation over retributive punishment and deterrence, as reflected in Section 6 of the *Children's (Criminal Proceedings) Act 1987* (NSW). Indeed, all interviewed magistrates drew a clear distinction between the Children's Court and adult criminal courts, with the former prioritising rehabilitative outcomes. M1 explained:

> The focus in the children's court is completely different to the other work of the Local Court or the District Court or the Supreme Court in its criminal jurisdiction. The difference is that the focus in the Children's Court is rehabilitation of young people rather than retribution. Retribution and general deterrence are important, but they play a secondary role to rehabilitation. In the Local Court for example, rehabilitation is not the focus; the focus is on looking after the community's interests and ensuring general deterrence and punishment for wrongdoing.

Similarly, M13 noted:

> In the Children's Court we work on the basis that detention, being the most serious of penalties, should only be used as a last resort. That is because we know, all the studies tell us that if a child is put into detention, or a young person is put in detention, the outcomes for that person in later life are quite deleterious, you know, they have less chance of getting suitable work, they are less successful in marital relationships, they generally don't do as well in life as someone who hasn't been in a detention centre.

M13 further explained:

> Firstly, the knowledge that 80% of children under the age of 18 who commit crime stop offending in the very early twenties, and secondly, the knowledge emanating from brain-science research on the development of the adolescent brain that tells us that children commit crimes impulsively and without a lot of thought – are all reasons to advocate for the four pillars of an enlightened youth justice system.

M13 went on to explain these four pillars:

> Prevention: addressing the socio-economic and health issues that lead to crime;

Early intervention: engaging with at-risk youth before criminal patterns develop;

Diversion: Utilising not only the YOA but also other diversionary processes available through the *Mental Health Act 2007* (NSW) and the *Mental Health (Forensics Provisions) Act 1990* (NSW); and

Rehabilitation: following conviction, directing system resources toward rehabilitative programs rather than punitive measures.

These views clearly align, at least in principle, with the framework and objectives of the YOA. The Act provides magistrates with a legislative tool to prioritise the rehabilitation needs of young people rather than focusing solely on their deeds.

The importance of the Children's criminal court as an age-appropriate legal avenue was emphasised by several magistrates, who highlighted the need for communication and court processes to be carried out in ways that recognise children as a vulnerable group requiring specialised treatment under the law. One example frequently cited was the 'closed' nature of the Children's Court, which serves to protect the privacy and vulnerability of young people. Additionally, some magistrates emphasised the importance of effective communication and the creation of an environment tailored to the needs of this demographic. As M4 explained:

> When I sit in the Local Court, there is a sea of people in any courtroom usually, huge numbers of people waiting for their five minutes when their matter is called, and they are dealt with in some way or another. In the children's court of course, it is a *closed* court and there is a lot more personal interaction, perhaps a lot more direct contact with the young person, with his or her family, they are clearly identified, they are in your court and they are *with you*, still could be five minutes sometimes, but they are with you; whereas in the local court it seems more like a distant relationship.

Specialist magistrates emphasised opportunities that such processes afford to positively influence a young person's trajectory away from crime. Practical measures—such as closed courts and increased personal interaction with children and their families—facilitate relationship-building, even if only briefly. This level of engagement is often absent in other criminal court settings.

Conversely, some Local Court magistrates reported challenges in implementing such specialised processes due to the non-exclusive nature of their courtrooms. There were also concerns among some Local Court magistrates about the time-intensive nature of these procedures, which can complicate the management of mixed adult and children's caseloads. The primary concern expressed was the difficulty of safeguarding children within the constraints imposed by the local court environment. For example, M11 expressed frustration:

> I actually find *that* very annoying today because I'm not supposed to have any kids listed on my adult day and the police listed two kids' court charges on an adult day. The reason I find it annoying is that I don't think it's fair for

> kids to wait outside on the list day where, you know, you have a lot of matters coming through court and obviously a lot of adult offenders…And we do have a separately set out day for kids' court, but because the police put the wrong date on the charge, that was the day the kids had to come to court.
>
> So…I don't like because I think is bad for the kids. Also, it means I've got to close the court in the middle of the day which takes time, you know, just to close the court, find the clients, bring them in, et cetera. et cetera. I think it's very distracting for the children because they've just got solicitors coming in and out not realising it is kids' court; they're supposed to put a sign on, but they obviously didn't. And I think it's very distracting for the children whose matters are being dealt with, it really, it really bothers me.

This narrative illustrates how location—whether urban or rural—can significantly affect the operation and effectiveness of the Children's Court. The rural/urban divide has been previously noted by Fernandez et al. (2013), particularly in relation to equitable access to resources in NSW's rural areas. They observed significant differences 'in terms of specialist courtrooms, availability of specialised staff including legal representatives and magistrates and access to training' (Fernandez et al., 2013, p. 31). The participants in this study further illuminate these disparities, particularly in relation to: (1) the contrast between specialist and non-specialist courtrooms practices, and (2) the difference in outcomes when children's matters are heard by a specialised Children's Court magistrate versus a Local Court—especially in relation to diversion.

Another specific concern expressed by participants was the necessity for magistrates who handle both adult and children's matters to effectively shift distinct mindsets. For instance, a Local Court magistrate observed:

> And then, of course, you got to get your head around the fact that you are sentencing in a completely different way. So, the boy today who had a charge of aggravated break and enter and steal – if he was over 18, that would go through to the DPP list and he would then be committed for trial or sentenced in the District Court by a judge. The maximum penalty is, like, 20 years in jail if you're 18. But because he was 16, he doesn't go to the DPP; it stays in the kid's court – the maximum is two years' detention, so it's a completely different mindset and the principles of sentencing are completely different. So, I find it difficult to go from one to the other. But that's the reality of being in a country court sometimes.
>
> (M11)

Specialist magistrates also shared similar experiences. For instance:

> Sometimes you are not needed here, and you will be sent to the Local Court and you have to change your mindset and sometimes it is not easy to do that. Sometimes, initially I forget to do that, and then I realise, oh look I can't or shouldn't be calling the offender by the first name like I do here in the

Children's Court; I've got to look at it more in terms of the adult concepts of punishment, deterrence, retribution, rehabilitation has obviously got a part to play, but you got to give focus, probably a lot of more, to the other concepts of punishment, like retribution, deterrence. So, it is a different mind-set, and you have to remind yourself, sometimes you forget, but you have to remind yourself to do that.

(M6)

M9 speaking on these challenges, elaborated:

After you've been doing the Children's Court for a while, I find it quite difficult to swap back to adults. Because the penalty, it's a completely different regime for the Children's Court. The focus of the Children's Court is pursuant to Section 6 in the Act – *Children's Criminal Procedure Act* - which focuses on rehabilitation rather than retribution. And adult courts don't do that. And so really, the penalties in Children's Court for really quite serious crimes are comparatively minor. Really, they're very light.

These accounts suggest that maintaining a consistent emphasis on rehabilitation—central to the Children's Court—may be more feasible within a specialist court dedicated solely to children's matters. However, not all magistrates agreed. Some argued that a magistrate's approach is shaped by individual experience, attitudes and professional background rather than court structure. As M8 noted:

Well obviously, [in the Local Court] you're dealing with adults, not children, so the mindset is that different stage of life development and of course, different laws and different rules apply. So, that's where the mindset perhaps is different. And obviously, in relation to children, because they are children and youth, depending upon their age, they are treated differently through a number of diversionary programs, such as the YJC and other outcomes under the YOA. But the same diversionary programs apply in the Local Court.

Reflecting on how to adapt to the different mindsets required, M8 added:

It is very much an individual experience as it relates to, not only the judicial officer's background – mine was humanities, always working with people as a behavioural scientist and then coming to law – so I've got the enmeshment of both, if you like – areas of knowledge. Whereas other magistrates may have probably only done law and then, of course, got appointed. So, they haven't had that exposure to persons and working with them. So, I guess for me as an individual I would approach Local Court work similarly to Children's Court work in the sense of using diversionary programs and therapeutic outcomes, not only as required under the law on the appropriate occasion, but also understanding what would fit that particular person best in terms of a therapeutic outcome, or a diversionary outcome.

Given that diversionary options under the YOA necessitate focusing on restorative outcomes, it is crucial for all magistrates handling children's matters to prioritise restorative justice. However, some difficulties highlighted—particularly the challenge of transitioning between adult and child-related matters—raise concerns about the consistency of this focus. While all magistrates acknowledged that the Children's Court emphasises rehabilitation and recognised that legislation such as the YOA provides a framework for diverting young people from punitive sanctions, it remains uncertain whether this rehabilitative focus is consistently applied in practice. The following section explores how magistrates interpret and apply the provisions of the YOA in their decision-making.

Children's Court magistrates and diversion

Some senior magistrates acknowledged that leading the court towards outcomes where detention is used only as a 'last resort' remains a central focus within the current Children's Court in NSW. Respondent M13 noted that discussions within court management often look to international examples such as Sweden, where: 'they don't stigmatise children by labelling them as criminals, they deal with it as a social problem.'

However, M13 also pointed out that this perspective diverges significantly from common-law systems like Australia's, which are deeply rooted in the utilitarian philosophies of Jeremy Bentham. As M13 observed, 'it's only in the last 150–160 years that we've even accepted that people who commit crimes can be rehabilitated' (M13).

Senior magistrates specifically noted that diversionary alternatives often conflict with the foundational ideologies of common law, particularly the adversarial nature of Australian courts. M13 highlighted that while Scandinavian countries embrace a strong welfare ethos, this approach is largely disregarded in Australia. He further added that, instead, prevailing social and cultural pressures tend to push magistrates towards individual attribution of blame, placing responsibility squarely on the child rather than considering broader systemic or social factors.

Despite these challenges, some magistrates expressed optimism that the existing system could be improved by learning from other jurisdictions. One respondent suggested looking at New Zealand as an example. He explained:

> In New Zealand it is compulsory for every child who commits a crime to have what is called family group conferencing, so they are all assessed. And 80% of children in New Zealand don't even go into the criminal justice system, they don't go to court; they are all dealt with in community programs pursuant to a family group plan or family plan that addresses their issues and that's all done by the police under a diversionary process. So, only 20% of children in New Zealand even get into the justice system, so that gives you a bit of an indication of where I think we should be going in NSW.
>
> (M13)

As documented in scholarly literature, New Zealand, which historically relied on adversarial models for social and legal frameworks since colonisation, has recently embraced non-adversarial approaches to justice (Brookbanks, 2015). These include specialised alcohol and drug courts, collaborative family proceedings, transformative mediation, preventative law and family group conferencing. In the context of youth justice, these reforms have led to nearly 80% of young offenders being diverted from court appearances (Becroft, 2003; Cleland, 2016). M13's perspective above is clearly informed by such research. However, this sentiment was not universally shared.

While some magistrates acknowledged the merits of New Zealand's diversionary model, most were reluctant to endorse it fully—particularly the notion of avoiding court proceedings altogether. Nonetheless, a few magistrates recognised the economic rationale behind such an approach. For example, one respondent noted:

> It is much cheaper to use diversion options as they do in New Zealand. There is a whole range of matters that come to this court that shouldn't, that they are a waste of enormously valuable and expensive resources, that could be better devoted to dealing with more serious matters and dealing with the minimum timely matter, so there is an economic rationalist argument for that.
>
> (M10)

According to a study by BOCSAR, YJC is more cost-effective than formal court proceedings (Webber, 2012). Despite this recognition of the economic rationales for diversion, magistrates expressed concerns about the feasibility of implementing such an approach in NSW due to significant resource limitations. For instance, M10 commented:

> It needs to be done with adequate training of those people who are going to be making the decision, it needs to be done with the full level of resources available, and quite frankly, at present the resources available in NSW don't match what is available in New Zealand. It requires even things like, in New Zealand, I know from my attending conferences there, and from talking to their judiciary that the government agencies providing various services are way more cooperative. So it's even those sorts of things, it is not just about the legislation, it is about how things operate in practice, so the people from the education department talk to the people from the child protection area who talk to the people from the juvenile justice area, who talk to the people from the health area. Rather than, in our society [in NSW], where they are treated as a whole bunch, but too often they are separate silos that don't cooperate with each other.

Moreover, one magistrate expressed ambivalence about adopting the New Zealand model:

> I do think that a lot of the offences that come before us shouldn't have been here, and could've been somewhere else, but whether we follow the New Zealand model and have a presumption of diversion over court, I am not at

> that point yet. I think that a lot of what we do, for a lot of young people, does take them off one path and puts them on the path of doing the right thing, obeying the law. So, the seriousness of coming here, to the court, is sometimes important in some young people's lives.
>
> (M4)

This statement reflects a belief that, for some young people, the experience of appearing in court may be more impactful than participation in diversionary programs. However, M4 also acknowledged the potential benefits of diversion:

> I also know in terms of actual rehabilitation, putting them in some type of diversionary program, where they are actually made to confront it, not in front of a magistrate, but confront it personally, talk about it personally, that may have a much greater impact than coming here. So, I don't know about preferences yet, I think [in] Australia, NSW [has] pretty much got it right so far, from what I can see.

There are significant issues with the assumptions underlying these remarks. While the magistracy broadly acknowledges the benefits of diverting children from court appearances and—throughout the interviews, has expressed concern about the under-utilisation of YJC, there remains a notable reluctance to consider more effective models, such as New Zealand's model, which research suggests produces higher rates of diversion and interprets youth conferencing through a less punitive lens. Furthermore, these views reflect a broader Australian societal ethos that emphasises individual responsibility, including the responsibilisation of young people, often at the expense of recognising systemic and structural factors.

M4's assertion that Australia, NSW in particular, has 'pretty much got it right so far,' is particularly concerning in light of youth justice statistics at the time of the interviews. In 2015–2016, on an average day, there were 1,494 young people under youth justice supervision in NSW—accounting for 27% of all supervised youths in Australia (AIHW, 2016). The supervision rate for non-Indigenous young people aged 10–17 in NSW was 10 per 10,000, compared to 167 per 10,000 for First Nations young people (AIHW, 2016). Despite First Nations young people representing only 5% of NSW's population aged between 10 and 17, they represented 47% of those under youth justice supervision on an average day during that period. As discussed in Chapter 3, this over-representation has continued to increase. The latest figures for 2024 indicate that First Nations young people now make up 65.3% of the total youth detention in NSW despite constituting only 6.6% of the population aged 10–17 years (AIHW, 2024).

These views cast doubt on the NSW magistracy's readiness to fully embrace diversionary alternatives for young people. Concerns were further emphasised by approximately one-quarter of the magistrates interviewed, who objected to a model such as New Zealand's due to the perception of 'mandatory referral.' This sentiment was strongly expressed by one of the magistrates:

> There is no magistrate I have ever come across who likes mandatory sentences and what New Zealand has, in my opinion, is a mandatory sentence. I think it's abhorrent. I am so anti any mandatory [approach] – don't bring anything into this court if it has to be a mandated sentence. In other words, if I am being forced to do something, get a computer to do it – don't use my skills and waste my time on something like that. So I am very much against being forced to consider diversionary programs. Where I think there will be a benefit would be to give us more flexibility – open it up. Don't minimise options by forcing us; open it up for all matters so it is my discretion as to whether I will or won't [refer]. I am not going for instance, to refer a sexual assault matter to a conference – I am not going to make ridiculous decisions. But if I had that ability, as I mentioned for the robbery in company, I might consider using it.
> (M3)

The demand for judicial discretion in diversionary decision-making appears to undermine the fundamental principles of the YOA, which clearly positions court appearances as a *last resort*. Despite this contradiction, all interviewed magistrates claimed to be supportive of restorative justice alternatives that divert young people away from formal court processes. However, the remarks presented above suggest that such support does not necessarily translate into embracing diversionary models that challenge the magistracy's traditional role within the adversarial court system.

That said, it is important not to exaggerate the significance of some magistrates' reluctance to embrace a more diversion-focused approach, such as the New Zealand model. Firstly, these concerns appear to stem primarily from resistance to relinquishing the elite decision-making authority traditionally held by the judiciary. Secondly, and more importantly, magistrates expressed support for diversion under the YOA and indicated a favourable view of YJC.

Children's Court magistrates on the YOA and the rural–urban divide

All participants claimed to be supportive of the YOA, describing it overall as a desirable alternative sentencing option. This is consistent with findings from Richards et al. (2017), which highlighted judicial support for restorative justice initiatives, particularly YJCs. However, a disparity exists between *specialist* and local magistrates, particularly in relation to familiarity with the Act.

In rural areas, some Local Court magistrates admitted to having limited knowledge of the Act's provisions. For instance, one magistrate from a rural court expressed uncertainty regarding which offences are excluded from diversion under the YOA, suggesting that their understanding of the legislation falls short of what might be reasonably expected. A Local Court magistrate in a rural location admitted not knowing 'off the top of my head' (M11), which offences are precluded by the Act, adding: 'I think they're sexual offences. But I can always look them up, I just don't use it often enough to know what it is precluded' (M11). This is problematic, as it raises questions about when and why this magistrate would consider it necessary to verify whether an offence is precluded under the Act—a determination critical to whether a case could be diverted.

In contrast, a *specialist* magistrate noted:

> Generally, one of the practitioners who is acting for the child, will say that they get referred to youth justice conferencing, that is usually what happens. I mean that doesn't mean that I don't look at the matter and think, when I read all the material, that it might be an appropriate matter for YJC. But generally, it comes from the practitioner – the solicitor or barrister who is acting for the offender. (M7)

M7's comment clearly indicates that referrals to YJCs are generally expected to be initiated by the young person's legal representatives. This point was consistently echoed by other magistrates. However, in rural areas with non-specialist Children's Courts, some Local Court magistrates expressed doubt about whether legal representatives could appropriately identify opportunities for diversion under the YOA. For instance, M11 noted:

> Really, it is for the lawyers, in my view, to identify for me, that this is the matter that could, say, go to a YJC. But I find that up here [rural area], they don't do that as much as they were doing in Parramatta Children's Court; where a lot of lawyers tend to specialise in children's Court, so they are far *savvier* at knowing what the alternatives are.

This magistrate, who also acknowledged their own limited familiarity with the Act, suggested that responsibility for proposing diversionary options in rural areas, predominantly falls on less experienced lawyers. This indicates that a young person's access to diversion may depend on representation by legal practitioners who lack sufficient expertise. Such dependency raises significant concerns about equality of opportunity, particularly in regions where stakeholders lack the training, knowledge, or experience necessary to fully understand and utilise available diversionary pathways.

The lack of training was acknowledged by some magistrates as a contributing factor to these issues. When asked to elaborate on alternative measures used in their court to prevent children from entering detention—aside from those under the YOA—M11 remarked:

> You know - a caution, a good behaviour bond, probation and then as an alternative to detention, community service order. And only then you go up to a suspended sentence, but yeah, I mean a control order is always the last option.

After a pause, M11 added:

> Certainly, we *could* know more about it [the YOA] and how effective it is, particularly in an area like the country, where you are dealing with a lot of kids, and you are dealing with a lot of very visible crimes that do have a real impact on the community. If there was some, perhaps at the country magistrate's conferences, specific training on those available sentencing options and the YJCs et cetera... Yes, I think it definitely wouldn't hurt.

Overall, these comments suggest that a lack of in-depth understanding among some Local Court magistrates regarding the provisions of the YOA may jeopardise diversion opportunities. This gap in knowledge raises broader questions about the Act's practical utility. For example, another Local Court magistrate remarked:

> The difficulty is that the criminal justice system is not able, in my view, to deal with the underlying social issues for the children who are offending. If the YOA would allow that to occur better, then I would think it was useful. I'm not sure that it does, okay? I'm not sure that it doesn't either. But the children that I see are having inadequate parenting ... From generational problematic issues – largely Aboriginal children down here – and it's an incredibly complex social situation.
>
> So, the YOA – if it's premised on having children who are just being a *bit naughty* and have gone off the rails but have a generally supportive environment, that is not the children that I'm dealing with. They're coming from parents who are mentally ill, drug dependent. There is violent offending in the home; the home is not safe, very commonly. We're talking about the really hard [offenders], the kids that are doing the aggravated break and enters.
>
> (M12)

These accounts raise concerns about whether the Act adequately addresses the complex social and structural needs of many young people who come into contact with the justice system. M12 further noted that a young person's capacity for empathy—or lack thereof—determines the Act's usefulness. From this magistrate's perspective, a young person's ability to empathise is closely linked to a functional and supportive environment. Accordingly, if a young person's socio-economic and familial environment is dysfunctional, it may not foster the development of empathy. Despite all this, M12 acknowledged:

> Because I can't, I would not be able to predict who those kids who have empathy and those kids who don't are, even kids who've had very difficult backgrounds might succeed, so I'd be prepared to give them a go.

Nonetheless, the suggestion remains that the Act fails to address the nexus between 'care' and 'crime.' Undoubtedly, young people who are deeply entrenched in the criminal justice system are likely to have experienced neglect, abuse and mental health problems (Cashmore, 2011, 2013; Indig et al., 2011). Judge Mark Curtis Marien, former President of the Children's Court in NSW, has previously noted that separating the criminal and care and protection jurisdictions within the Children's Court fails to recognise the nexus between care and crime. The Judge specifically noted that the Court 'fails to recognise that with respect to many offenders who come before the Children's Court charged with a criminal offence, the clear underlying cause of the offending behaviour is essentially a welfare issue rather than criminogenic' (Marien, 2012, p. 6).

From this perspective, the justice/care systems collectively fail those most in need, and the YOA—as legislation operating within this broader system—is no exception. It often fails to reach those most deeply entrenched in the system. This stands in contrast to New Zealand, where the 'Youth Court cannot impose any measure or sanction unless a family group conference has been tried' (Walgrave, 2004, p. 566). In Australia, however, YJC and other diversionary programs typically serve as alternatives for the less serious offences, leaving more serious matters to be dealt with in court (Walgrave, 2004). Moreover, the discretionary nature of diversionary decision-making means that outcomes depend heavily on the magistrate's training, knowledge and experience with the YOA. Consequently, young people appearing before non-specialist courts may be disadvantaged due to the judiciary's lack of familiarity with available diversionary options.

As M12's comments suggest, some non-specialist magistrates view the YOA as inadequate because it merely diverts cases from court towards a perceived "soft option"—suitable only for those who are 'a bit naughty' (M12). Similarly, M1, a non-specialist magistrate in a rural location, shared:

> If I'm not asked for it and it's a very serious charge and it does have a very big impact on the community – here and also on my circuit courts – so, I am highly unlikely to make the referral [to YJC] myself…If it's a less serious charge, like if it's a shoplifting or maybe even a drug charge or you know, a fight with a girl – 'Because she slagged me off on Facebook', that sort of thing, then I might say: Well, why can't this go to a YJC? Has anyone thought about that? Go and have a word to the client, you know, the young person about that. So, yeah if it's a less serious charge I'd certainly think about it but probably not for break and enter, just because of the effect on the community.

In reality, restorative justice initiatives such as YJC should not be considered 'a soft option'; they offer varying levels of engagement and accountability (Bottoms & Dignan, 2004). This perspective is more commonly appreciated by magistrates who specialise in the Children's Court. For example, M4 explained:

> If it's a first or a second offence for a fairly low level crime or low level objective seriousness, our choices are, for sentencing, if we don't go down the YJC route, there are bond – a33, 1b bond for it to be a good behaviour; it seems to me that that puts something over the head for a little while but

> it doesn't get them to do very much, to understand what they've done, why they've done it, so it seems to me that a YJC– while it appears as a dismissal after they've completed the work on the record– they personally are required to do more than a bond, so it seems to be potentially more effective.

This view was shared by most specialist magistrates, who also suggested that dismissing offences upon YJC completion aligns with the court's rehabilitative function and acknowledges that young offenders 'are foolish at times' (M4). In contrast, Local Court magistrates—those without Children's Court specialisation—did not emphasise these perspectives.

The discussion above illustrates a clear gap between specialist and Local Court magistrates regarding their knowledge and understanding of the YOA. Some of the most senior specialist magistrates expressed concern, suggesting that all child-related matters should be handled by specialists. For instance, M13 described the ideal scenario for the Children's Court:

> In its crime jurisdiction, for all children in NSW to be dealt with by specialist Children's magistrates who have become more proficient in understanding brain development and all the issues that I've just been discussing, so that we can get a more consistent outcome across the whole of the state. So, that means that what I want to see is the Children's Court better resourced and separated away from the Local Court and have the capacity to deal with young offenders at every location in NSW… that means having a Children's Court which extends across the whole of the state.

The importance of establishing a separate, specialist jurisdiction—independent from the Local Court—to address children's matters across the entire state as a solution for handling inequalities was also highlighted by participants in Fernandez et al.'s study of the Children's Court in NSW in 2013. In the current study, concerning diversion, senior magistrates from the specialist Children's Court suggested that such independence would facilitate specialised training and education aimed at 'keeping children out of detention' (M13), potentially increasing the use of the YOA, and referrals to YJC.

Currently, as part of their statutory duties, the President of the Children's Court is responsible for ensuring that Children's Court magistrates possess the necessary expertise and skills to perform their roles effectively. Specialist magistrates explained that they meet biannually for a full day 'to discuss mutual issues of interest, problems and have people present to us [the magistrates] on particular topics that are relevant to the jurisdiction' (M13). However, these meetings do not include magistrates from the Local Court. This lack of participation potentially impacts both the processes and outcomes in rural areas, including opportunities for diversion. One specialist magistrate observed:

> In relation to diversion, it's my perception that the opportunity to divert children under the YOA by the police and by the courts, is under-utilised. So, if

> for example, Children's Court magistrates are usually good at diverting kids under the YOA, either by way of a reprimand or caution or to a YJC. Some of the Local Court magistrates aren't as good and mainly some of them don't fully understand and appreciate that opportunity is available or that process is available to them. So, that's an issue.
>
> (M13)

Adopting the current view noted above—that all children's matters across NSW should be handled by specialist magistrates—would help ensure that all judicial officers working with young people are equally trained and skilled. If lack of training is a factor undermining diversion, then expanding the specialist Children's Court could potentially increase the use of the YOA and referrals to YJC. However, this study found the factors undermining diversion extent beyond training and expertise. As the focus shifted to decision-making processes and the legislation itself, findings indicated that diversion is also undermined by magistrates' attitudes, unrealistic expectations of diversion as a 'quick fix' and limitations inherent in the legislation.

Magistrates' approach to YOA diversion: decision-making, judicial attitudes and perspectives on the legislation

When considering whether it is appropriate to refer a young person to a YJC under the YOA, magistrates reported that they primarily focus on the type of offence, following the hierarchical order prescribed by the legislation. They also emphasised that factors such as the young person's age, prior record, the young offender's needs and their willingness and capacity to engage in YJC may influence their decision. For example, M9 remarked:

> If it's an offence that falls within a conferrable matter, and it's *their first offence* and they've got some other, you know, indicators that think it might work, I would definitely try that first.

As noted in previous chapters, the YOA established a framework for responding to certain offences through alternative processes to court, through the use of warnings, cautions and YJCs (YOA, s. 3). The legislation also mandates that the investigating official must determine whether the offence is covered by the Act before proceeding (YOA, s. 9, pt. 2). Thus, the magistracy's first focus on the nature of the offence and its eligibility for diversion is expected. However, challenges arise when an eligible offence is considered alongside other factors.

The YOA provides guidance on decision-making by noting important considerations such as the seriousness of the offence, the level of violence involved, the degree of harm caused to any victim, the offending history and 'any other matter the official thinks appropriate' (YOA, s. 37, pt. 3). Regarding offending history, the Act allows for consideration of 'the number and nature of any offences committed by the child and the number of times the child has been dealt with under' (YOA,

s. 20, pt. 3; s. 37, pt. 3; s. 40, pt. 5). At the same time, the Act stipulates that 'the less restrictive form of sanction is to be applied' (YOA, s. 7, pt. 2) and notes that a child should not be precluded from receiving a warning, caution or YJC 'merely because the child has previously committed offences or being dealt' with under the Act (YOA, s. 14 (3), pt. 3; s. 20 (6), pt. 4; and s. 37 (5), pt. 4). These provisions illustrate flexibility afforded to the judiciary to consider contextual and mitigating factors in their decisions.

Interviews in this study clearly indicated that magistrates generally place a substantial weight on the young person's offending history, and particularly on the number of times they have been dealt with under the YOA—especially in relation to YJC. For example, M6 noted:

> If they've [young offenders] been involved before [in YJC] that might persuade me not to go that way, because you do not want to set up kids to fail.

This emphasises recidivism, which suggests that diversion through YJC for repeat offenders may be undermined, thus contradicting the legislative intent.

As discussed in previous chapters, the legislation specifies that an offender can be dealt with by way of caution up to three times (YOA, s. 20 (7), pt. 3). However, there is no statutory limit on the number of referrals a young offender may receive to YJCs. While magistrates acknowledged that it is difficult to generalise how often they would refer the same young person to a YJC, most indicated that one or two referrals are generally considered appropriate. For example, M1 stated:

> From time to time, I had a young person appearing where they had conferences before, and I'm prepared to give them another conference if the circumstances are appropriate. So, I have referred young persons to more than one conference but it's not common. There is no sort of clear-cut rule that you don't send anyone to a second or third conference. I don't think I have sent anyone to a third conference, but I have sent people off for a second conference.

Similarly, M13 observed:

> No, I would really only ever refer once to a YJC. In my view, a young person really only gets one opportunity, if you like, to use the YOA, sometimes two, depending on the nature of the crime. But if they haven't learnt from the first time around, then they need a more serious penalty the next time around.

These remarks reflect a common sentiment among magistrates that if a young person reappears for the same type of offence, they are unlikely to be referred to a YJC again. However, one magistrate emphasised that the time lapse between similar offences was an important consideration:

> A young person had received a YOA caution and been given the benefit of a conference in 2012. And here we are, in 2015, prosecution said *'no, this*

> *young person clearly has not learned from it'*. I end up referring to a YJC – because in 2012 this young person was 12, nearly 13, he is now 15 nearly, [PAUSE] yes 15 and half, it seems to me there're insights to be gained as a 12–13-year-old versus 15-16. I can't assume that there will be no further insight gained. I think YJC is more onerous, sometimes what they have to do is a more positive and active thing, rather than just sitting back and saying: well I've done wrong and now I have to wait for 6 months or 9 months or 12 months for the bond to expire, you know, with JYC, they actually have to do something.
>
> (M4)

The relevance of time between offences was a contentious issue among magistrates. Some did not believe it significantly influenced their decision-making. For instance, when asked if YJC would be considered for a young offender returning two years later with the same charge, one specialist magistrate noted:

> No, probably not so much, if they have been 15 and they have been through a conference for an identical offence, and they are back before me for an identical type of offence, I will be disinclined to do conferencing again. So, I will see that as a failure of conferencing – but I have never turned my mind to the issues of development of children.
>
> (M7)

Although young people have occasionally received additional referrals, the majority of magistrates clearly viewed two YJC referrals as sufficient opportunities for desistance from offending. M9 echoed this view:

> Look, frankly, if they are coming back before me, I might give them two conferences, maybe, just maybe. After that, forget it – because they are not participating. And particularly, and if they fail to participate in the conference, I won't consider it again. Because there is obviously something else going wrong; they are not amenable to that.

For some magistrates, this decision appeared to be driven by a focus on recidivism, reflecting an emphasis on individual responsibilisation over the social and structural circumstances contributing to youth offending. As M3 stated: 'If they have already been diverted, I have a strong question mark in whether there is any benefit at all in repeating the process.'

Furthermore, M13 explained:

> Well, the thing we need to measure, I think is, what is the recidivism rate for children who go on those things? How often do they reoffend? And if it's been only, if after the first time they're sent to a YJC and that's all that happens, and they don't learn from that, well they come back, well the next time a round you don't, as I've said, I'll only use it, myself, once; more often than not

> I won't send them back a second time under the YOA, I'll give them a more serious sentence.

This expectation of a quick fix was pervasive in magistrates' decision-making processes. If one YJC did not deter further offending, many questioned the value of a second YJC referral. This viewpoint was widely shared among those interviewed, suggesting that YJC is primarily reserved for first-time offenders, despite the absence of any legal limit on the number of referrals a young person may receive.

Additionally, the efficiency imperative through which diversion is viewed by the magistracy imposes serious limitations on youth justice measures, often with less-than-positive implications. As noted in Chapter 2, studies have reported mixed results regarding the effect of YJC on recidivism. Some research suggests that YJC can be more effective than court proceedings in reducing re-offending (see Bergseth & Bouffard, 2007; KPMG, 2010; Luke & Lind, 2002). However, other studies indicate that YJC is not significantly more effective than court in mitigating the risk of offending (Smith & Weatherburn, 2012). Nonetheless, reducing the risk of re-offending is not the sole justification for YJC. Victim satisfaction and economic efficiency also support its use (see Moore, 2012). Moreover, diversion to YJC is preferable to any entry into the formal justice system, which can contribute to a 'revolving door' effect.

Despite this, magistrates placed considerable weight on whether a first YJC referral resulted in desistance when considering further referrals. It can therefore be argued that they are constraining the scope of the legislation based on their perceptions of the importance of recidivism in relation to diversion via YJC.

Community expectations also emerged as a factor influencing decision-making. Some magistrates expressed awareness of the public's perceptions of diversion, acknowledging that YJC is often viewed as a 'soft option.' For instance, M1 observed:

> What can be learned this time from a conference that wasn't achieved last time? What hasn't he learned? Because if they keep on offending, the time arrives in my view where you just can't keep on dismissing charges, *the community expects* that the court will take a little bit more serious intervention.

Similarly, community expectations were mentioned by a Local Court magistrate in a rural area:

> People have got to realise, in the country, every time someone's house is broken into – in the country people leave their houses unlocked– people start locking their doors. And that might seem weird to people in the city: 'Oh, well why wouldn't you lock your door?' But that's the mindset of people who live in the country: That it's so safe here, we don't have to. So, when there is a break and enter, that changes people's mindset in

> how they live in their own homes. So even: 'Gosh, even if I'm at home, I've got to have the front door locked'. And it really does affect people. It affects, yeah, how safe they feel in their own home. And a YJC people might just think: 'Well, what's that? Like, what, they had to write a letter of apology? I mean, big deal, what is that?' And it would be seen as being far too lenient, compared to the effect that the crime has had on the local community.
>
> (M11)

Magistrate 11 further explained various factors that must be considered in such cases and described scenarios where diversion may *not* occur:

> Look, it just depends on how old they are, is it the first offence, is it the second? What's their background like? I mean… most of the kids I deal with in kids Court … are kids who have been removed from their parents, they've had significant drug and alcohol issues and domestic violence they've had to encounter as they've been growing up. But I don't know… I probably, if it was their first offence, give them a bond or probation under the supervision of JJ. And then, if there was another offence…I might consider …if they got a bond first, then probation, or if they breach probation, then another control order.

Similarly, M4 raised concerns about how the community perceives the suitability of YJCs for more serious offences:

> I think it [YJC] can send that message [not suitable for serious offences] because it ultimately results in a dismissal of the charge, under the YOA, so it's seen as a first level or low-level intervention and punishment. And for some young people, at least initially, I think they see it as a less serious outcome for them. My view is that it involves them doing more, so that the ultimate punishment, what they are required to do is greater, than what they are often required to do just by having a bond. However, the perception is that [it] is, perhaps for less serious crimes, and I don't want domestic violence to ever be seen as a less serious crime…I guess is because is one of our first level interventions, is a low level intervention [YJC] for the court, it only applies for less serious offences, so there is a general impression [within the community] that even if you are refer to a YJC for a serious offence, the court sees it perhaps as less serious, and the outcome is less serious.

While this view does not represent all magistrates, it highlights the influence of community expectations on judicial decision-making. M4's comments reflect a broader sentiment among many interviewed magistrates: that restorative justice processes like YJC can encourage young offenders to take greater responsibility for their actions than traditional sentencing, even if it is not always recognised by the public.

However, recognising that YJC may be more demanding for the young person does not necessarily equate to satisfaction with the process. While magistrates generally expressed support for YJC, opinions varied—particularly regarding the adequacy of outcomes plans. Some magistrates expressed confidence in these plans:

> From my perspective, by and large, I always think that the action plans produced are appropriate and adequate. I have heard some magistrates complain that there is insufficient, if you like, action required of some young people who have quite serious offences, and they reject the plans and insist on them being a bit more onerous or requiring something more, particularly in some of the sexual offending type cases. But from my perspective they're usually very good.
> (M13)

Conversely, one local magistrate felt that outcome plans in regional areas lack the robustness of those in urban settings:

> Some of them up here are a little bit light, in my view, like, writing a letter of apology and I don't know, some of them only say that. But certainly, in Parramatta I found it was far more [silence] I don't know, I think there was just a lot more meat to the plans up there. I think maybe up here; people aren't as creative, if I can use that term? In you know, suggesting different outcome plans. Having said that, I've never said no to an outcome plan. My view is, if that's something the victim has agreed to, then, you know, who am I to interfere with that when I haven't been part of it? So, I'm unlikely to change it, but I think the ones here [in the rural area] are probably a little bit lacking in substance.
> (M11)

This suggests that geographic location may influence the quality of outcome plans, potentially due to disparities in resources, access to trained staff and availability of specialised staff, including legal representatives.

Even in metropolitan areas, some specialist magistrates expressed dissatisfaction. M4 noted:

> I am trying not to be too difficult, but sometimes I have a very strong feeling that perhaps that [the outcome plan] is not enough, so maybe that's a weakness, in that maybe there should be some further guidelines about minimum outcome plans.

This view indicates support for more structured requirements in outcome plans. Interestingly, despite resistance to mandatory sentencing in the context of YJC referrals (previously discussed), magistrates advocate for establishing baseline mandates in outcome plans.

Currently, the YOA provides recommendations but lacks specific minimum requirements for outcome plans. Section 52 (1) of the YOA states that 'the participants at a conference may agree to make such recommendations or decisions as they think fit.' However, Section 52 (5) offers no binding requirements. Some magistrates argue that common components—such as apology letters or Police Citizens Youth Club (PCYC) attendance—do not sufficiently hold young offenders accountable. As M7 commented:

> It will be useful to include community service work, up to a certain number of hours. I know that sometimes they are required to do some sort of community work, but not a lot. If they can actually incorporate up to say 20 hours of community work, that would be advantageous. Because, when I do see the outcome plan, there is a letter of apology and they are going to go to the PCYC on a number of occasions [but] that is the extent of the plan. Often, I think that is a little bit on the low side in terms of what the individual should be [doing]… but I understand that there is a restriction in terms of what can be required of the outcome plan.
>
> (M7)

Such concerns suggest that, from the magistrates' perspective, outcome plans may fall short in imposing meaningful accountability, potentially undermining the legitimacy of diversion for more serious offences. M7 elaborated:

> I will be more inclined to refer more serious offences to YJC if there was an ability to impose some community service requirement, because I will see that as an alternative to a control order, and an appropriate punishment for the offence… at the moment, the limited options are the things I normally look [at], as well when deciding to refer, and that is why serious offences generally don't get a referral. Whereas if there was…as part of conferencing, that they might need juvenile justice supervision. Of course, if I refer them to YJC. But that cannot happen, and that is something that is in the back of my mind, because I am thinking I want to make sure they are properly rehabilitated. I want to make sure that someone is looking, that there is an oversight of them [young people] for a period of time.

In Australia, responsibilisation often involves balancing punitive and restorative justice practices (Cunneen & White, 2007). Youth offenders are seen as responsible for their actions and must be served with their *just deserts* (White & Wyn, 2008). The shift from punishment to repairing harm, typical of restorative justice, does not minimise the emphasis placed on holding the young offender responsible (White and Wyn, 2008). The magistrates' comments suggest that outcome plans often lack sufficient depth and fail to adequately hold individuals accountable or address their specific needs. Despite the stated focus on rehabilitation, for persistent offenders, these interventions can resemble ongoing surveillance, further entrenching them within the justice system.

In expressing their dissatisfaction with outcome plans, magistrates lament the 'McDonaldization' (see Bohm, 2006; Umbreit, 1999) of YJC, where outcome plans become overly standardised and fail to address individual needs. Consequently,

YJC may not effectively address young people's criminogenic needs due to the lack of varied interventions. Similar concerns were raised in a study by Richards et al. (2017). However, research by Taussig (2012) indicates that 80% of young offenders in NSW are required to undertake at least two additional tasks beyond writing an apology letter. This discrepancy highlights a tension between magistrates' perceptions (or recollections) and empirical findings, emphasising the scepticism and the gap between perceived practice and research findings regarding the content of outcome plans. Nonetheless, magistrates' perceptions of insufficient intervention with outcome plans compromise the utility of YJC as a diversionary tool.

At times, magistrates appear to overlook how restorative justice and YJC extend responsibility and accountability beyond the individual. This oversight can lead to misconceptions about the broader aims of restorative justice. As Braithwaite (2006, p. 35) notes, 'from a restorative justice perspective, justice is always unfinished business until an account has been accepted by the stakeholders in the injustice.' Yet, the potential of restorative justice—and in this case, YJC—to hold the courts and criminal law accountable is largely absent from the magistrates' reflections. For instance, the magistracy could be held accountable for prematurely relinquishing its procedural commitment to restorative justice. Instead, the magistrates' focus appears to centre on enhancing youth accountability through responsibilisation processes. Consequently, they advocate that outcome plans should encompass more substantive measures than merely requiring an apology. Nevertheless, magistrates generally acknowledge the value of YJC, recognising that it can facilitate more meaningful interventions than those available through court proceedings. Accordingly, there was a general desire among magistrates for the expansion of YJC to encompass additional categories of offences.

Magistrates largely agree on the need to include, under the YOA, offences such as assault in company, travelling without a ticket, traffic offences and robbery in company. These types of offences are precluded from the YOA, yet many magistrates find this exclusion illogical. M3 illustrated this point:

> The robbery in company, which is precluded is one of the major charges we deal with, but there is a whole range of what comes under robbery in company which has a maximum penalty of 20 years jail. They can be the really nasty ones, and of course, I will never consider those for conferences, but almost, the typical one, I get a little bit cranky with the police for charging, because it is two or three kids, pick on someone and say: *'give me your cigarettes, give me your phone'*, and that is definitely a 'robbery in company' if the child is the one saying 'give me', but it is the lower end of the scale. Those sorts of matters, I would like to refer a child to a conference, because it is one thing me saying: *'you and your mates surrounding this poor boy/girl adds fear because of the numbers, how do you think the victim would feel?'* That is just me posing the question. [As opposed to] Having the victim said: *'I was scared to death, every time I see someone with red hair, or wearing clothes like you I'm in fear it's going to happen again'*, that has a lot more impact than me trying to get the child to consider that [in court].

M9 echoed this sentiment:

> A lot of offences in company are precluded [from the Act], but that's exactly what kids do! It's ridiculous to preclude kids from youth diversion: they're up charged… like it sounds really bad – a 'robbery in company', but really what they've done is in a group, you know, nicked a few packets of chips or something, you know. I know that's minimising it, but you know, the fact that it's *in company* doesn't mean it shouldn't be conferrable.

These comments raise important issues. Firstly, it has long been recognised that young people have a tendency to commit crimes in groups to a greater degree than adults (Cunneen & White, 2007; McVie, 2009; Shaw & McKay, 1969 [1942]) because they are more gregarious and peer-oriented (Carrington, 2002; Warr, 1996). Secondly, while the law assumes, as it does for adults, that people who commit crimes in groups are more dangerous, this might not apply to young people.

Instead, research suggests that youth who commit crime alone tend to demonstrate greater responsibility, temperance and perspective, with their actions often involving more deliberate planning rather than being spontaneous acts (Goldweber et al., 2011). In contrast, co-offending among youth often stems from poor impulse control and a lack of self-discipline. Therefore, collectively, co-offenders tend to be less reactive and less strategic in their criminal behaviour. This suggests that group offending reflects adolescence as a developmental stage more than it does the individual characteristics of offenders (Goldweber et al., 2011). Therefore, while the law views offences committed in company as more serious, simply because this is the norm for adult offenders, it fails to account for the developmental differences between youth and adult offenders.

Nevertheless, as M3 noted, 'robbery in company' offences are legally classified as aggravated because they involve multiple offenders. As such, these 'in company' offences have been precluded from the YOA. Most magistrates find this illogical, as it prevents the use of YJC at times when it could be effective. M10 expressed frustration with this limitation, reflecting the views of most participants:

> An aggravated break/entrance/steal offence, so if the young person broke into somebody's house by themselves that could be diverted to a YJC. But, if they are with a friend and they break in, it can't be diverted, now that is crazy to me… because I don't think in reality the offending is any more serious because [it] is done in company. I can see why for adults [it] is an aggravating feature, but for the perspective of the young person, um, it's probably more serious if they do it by themselves rather than being egged on a bit, or having some sort of mutual courage raising from having a friend with them, so I think it just doesn't recognise the dynamics of the way young people think.

The exclusion of traffic offences from diversion under the YOA was also a source of disappointment for some magistrates, as reflected in this observation:

> For minor traffic offences, I don't see why a caution under the YOA – say, for driving whilst unlicensed – wouldn't be an appropriate outcome. Police should be able to deal with it directly. I don't think it should have to come to court. I think the real issue is when there might be a need for license disqualification or something like that because of the nature and seriousness of the offence, or drink driving offences or driving under the influence of drugs, or dangerous driving is sufficiently serious that a court should deal with it.
>
> But [for things like] driving whilst unlicensed or speeding over a certain speed limit, as long as it is not one of the more extreme versions of speeding…I would have thought they should be able to be dealt with under the YOA. Even if they come to a magistrate…a referral to a conference, why wouldn't that be an appropriate outcome for a dangerous driving offence; again you got to treat the seriousness of the offence as a critical factor, but I don't quite understand why diversion is categorically unavailable.
>
> (M10).

Magistrates' frustrations with the exclusion of traffic offences extended to other infringement matters. For instance, 'travelling without a ticket,' M3 remarked:

> Certain categories I think scream out for it [the need to be included in the Act], for instance travelling on a train without a ticket. That comes with a very hefty fine that I will find it an *ouch* factor: a child cannot afford $400… It should be more about trying to get them to accept that what they did was incorrect and how to avoid it in the future.

Infringement notices are among the most common penalties issued by criminal justice systems in Australia (NSWLRC, 2012). The penalty under an infringement notice is fixed. For example, under the *Fines Act 1996* (NSW), unlicensed-driving-offences carry a penalty notice of $1045, a maximum court imposed fine of $3300 if first-time offence, or $5500 for subsequent offences, as well as mandatory disqualification (NSW Government, 2025). The imposition of monetary penalties has faced criticisms for disproportionately impacting individuals from low socio-economic backgrounds, including young people (DAGJ, 2011).

The impact of infringement penalties is further heightening for First Nations young people. This is due to their over-representation in low socio-economic demographics and within the criminal justice system. Additionally, many First Nations people live in remote rural areas where mail delivery may be unreliable, increasing the risk of accruing fines (NSW Law Reform, 2012). Furthermore, First Nations people are more likely than their non-Indigenous counterparts to receive 'criminal infringement notices' for offences such as offensive language (NSW Ombudsman, 2009). A significant concern is that defaults on fines can escalate from a financial penalty to court proceedings or even imprisonment. Given that these fines often relate to minor offences, such outcomes contradict diversionary principles of using court as a last resort and are counterproductive to the objectives of the YOA—a point emphasised by specialist magistrates during the interviews.

Additionally, several magistrates expressed frustration over graffiti offences being ineligible for *police* diversion under the Act. M10 illustrated this concern:

> There is absolutely no logic in the current arrangement. The current law actually even makes it more cumbersome to get a young person to do clean-up work than when it was possible to refer graffiti matters under the YOA (by police). Police should be able to refer those matters directly. Look in fact, [it] is counterproductive, because anyone who has even a small clue about youth offending realises that even bringing young people to court is a negative thing, because it makes them associate with other offenders and runs the risk of, what people call the contamination effect of coming to court, the risk of the young person forming a criminal association by coming to court is much higher that the benefit of a tongue lashing from some crusty old magistrate like me.
>
> (M10)

The *Graffiti Legislation Amendment Act 2012* (NSW) removed the power of police to divert graffiti offences. Instead, a person charged with graffiti must now appear in court. While courts may still issue cautions or refer graffiti matters to a YJC under the YOA, the legislative change has reduced the flexibility of early intervention. As a transgressive act of property crime, graffiti has become a highly emotive issue in public discourse (Fitzgerald, 2000; White, 2001), and community pressure has shaped policy objectives aimed at reducing its prevalence.

Contrary to public perceptions linking graffiti with violence and fear—perceptions that research has deemed baseless (White, 2001)—studies demonstrate that those within graffiti culture who engage in high-risk criminal activities represent a minority of all graffiti offenders (Jones, 2003). Most magistrates interviewed expressed concern that mandating court proceedings for all graffiti offences increases financial costs for both offenders and the broader community. This procedural approach contradicts the YOA's principle of emphasising pre-court diversion.

A prevailing view among magistrates was that the YOA itself undermines diversion opportunities through the nonsensical exclusion of certain offences, such as those discussed above. However, opinions varied regarding whether domestic violence offences should be eligible for YJC. In support of extending YJC to such cases, M13 stated:

> The YOA is limited in its application, and we tend to only utilise it for the lesser crimes. I'd love to have the Victorian system, where they have used diversion for even more serious crimes. I think a large proportion of youth crime in Victoria goes through the youth diversion process. And it's a much better system, as far as I'm concerned, because it involves restorative justice as opposed to traditional adversarial processes.

Similarly, M10 supported the inclusion of domestic violence offences:

> A lot of the domestic violence offending by young people is within the family and usually is the young person over a parent, most commonly a mother. I can see why you will not provide that sort of option for adults, where the more usual dynamic will be partner to partner violence. But, some reconciliation process between a young person and a parent, I would have thought that'd be a smart option, rather than something excluded for blinkered, shallow ideological reasons.

M9 provided further insight into the nature of these offences:

> Mum says: 'You can't do X', so they are cranky, and they might have been using drugs. So, they kick a hole in the wall. Or they threaten Mum or Dad with a knife; they call them every name they can lay their tongue to, and they think that that's okay – most of the time it's Mum or it's Dad. Sometimes it extends to a girlfriend; that really worries me, and I do jump on that. But I think they need training. I would like them to have the opportunity for a lot of these offences to go through YJC, to have the opportunity of a creative outcome plan that would involve counselling. You can at least order it [counselling]. Or as part of the outcome plan it becomes something that they have to do.

In contrast, M4 expressed concerns about referring domestic violence offences to YJC. According to this magistrate, the YOA ultimately results in dismissals or 'it's seen as a first level or low-level intervention, a first level, low-level punishment and for some young people, at least initially, I think they see it as a less serious outcome.' Thus, referring domestic violence offences to YJC risks conveying the *wrong* message that such behaviour is not serious.

The legal meaning of domestic violence is very broad and includes physical assault (ranging from punching, hitting, kicking, pushing, to use of weapons), emotional abuse, verbal abuse (e.g., shouting, name-calling, swearing), property damage and financial abuse (see *Crimes Act 1900* (NSW); *Crimes (Domestic and Personal Violence) Act 2007* (NSW)).

Magistrates' views on YJC for domestic violence offences reflect the internal tensions they face—balancing the need to protect victims and uphold justice with the opportunity to rehabilitate young offenders in less serious cases, while ensuring that serious offenders are appropriately sanctioned within a justice framework that unequivocally condemns domestic violence.

Similar concerns were raised regarding sexual offences. Some magistrates expressed apprehension that referring such cases to YJC could send the wrong message. M9 stated:

> There's a real weirdness when a young person is charged with a sexual offence. I don't like it at all, and I think they need specialist treatment somewhere else. I wouldn't support YJC for a number [of sexual offences], I don't even want to have it as an option due to potential community outrage.

M8 added:

> Sexual offences, that's very, very tricky because I think we have to look at crimes within the gender disempowerment in the community. Yeah, the disempowerment issues in relation to men and women, gender inequality in society, you'd have to be looking at the victim's willingness to participate, which I think in most cases would be absolute zero.

However, as with domestic violence, other magistrates noted that certain sexual offence charges involving young people are less serious than the legal terminology suggests. M10 explained:

> I will think that where any sexual assault involves the overcoming or disregarding of the victim's will, it's sufficiently serious that YJC – the most serious part of the YOA– is not suitable. I do, however, think that there are some offences, say, where let's say both of the participants engaged in underage but consensual sex, so where their capacity to consent is irrelevant, should be able to be a minimal to a YJC. So, I think that it depends on issues of consent, it depends on issues of power, it depends on knowledge, it depends on the need, the therapeutic need that might be involved in dealing with the offence.

Once again, the findings signal differences in perspectives and attitudes among magistrates regarding specific offences. Although domestic violence and sexual offences are currently excluded from the YOA, the underlying attitudes remain relevant, as they highlight variations in judicial decision-making. This is particularly significant because several magistrates interviewed suggested that increased flexibility and greater discretion could enhance opportunities for additional YJCs referrals.

For example, M13 noted:

> I think that we need to have total discretion; we shouldn't be limited by statute from being able to use the YOA because of certain types of offence. We should have full discretion to utilise the diversionary process where we think it's appropriate.

Additionally, M10 observed:

> There has got to be some trust in the fact that magistrates will deal with these matters appropriately and not make ridiculous referrals. I can see why there is a concern about the extent of matters that police can refer, and there should be much more significant limits on that; but I don't see a problem with having magistrates with a much greater scope of matters that they can refer.

It is also important to note that when discussing First Nations referrals to YJC, most magistrates claimed that First Nations youth have the same access opportunities to diversion as their non-Indigenous counterparts. Only two magistrates deviated from this position, expressing concern that the YOA is not equipped to address First Nations' social issues. One magistrate, in a rural area noted:

> We often get a lot of Aboriginal kids, in particular that I see, that the family are not really interested in this process, and often you get the child back after they have been diverted, say that they go to a police caution, for example, and they can't even tell me what's happened. Diversion is very important if the people around that person are supportive of the process and reinforce the process.
>
> (M5)

M5's comment reflects a discourse that positions First Nations Australians as responsible for their own disadvantage, externalising blame and placing responsibility for failure squarely on the families, while absolving policymakers, or in this case, the institutional gatekeepers of accountability.

As discussed in Chapter 2, research shows a clear discrepancy between diversion rates for First Nations and non-Indigenous youth, with First Nations youth less likely to be diverted. The most recent trends in police and court diversion by Indigenous status are included in Chapter 6, and show that the pattern of under-representation for First Nations young people in diversionary alternatives continues to be evident in the most recent data (see Tables 6.3 and 6.4). The flexibility and lack of specific guidance within the Act—such as the provision allowing for 'any other matter the official thinks appropriate' (YOA, s. 37, pt. 3)—can contribute to inconsistent application. It could be argued that magistrates who believe the YOA is not suited to addressing the social issues faced by First Nations communities, or who perceive a lack of a supportive family network (as in M5's comment), may be less inclined to divert First Nations youth. Such attitudes risk further undermining the use of YJC for an already disproportionately disadvantaged population.

Conclusion

The findings presented in this chapter offer valuable insights into the magistracy's perspective on restorative justice versus adversarial justice, particularly in relation to YJC. This research reveals that magistrates in the NSW Children's Court generally support the YJC model. However, numerous concerns raised throughout the chapter cast doubt on their readiness to fully embrace diversionary alternatives. This is evident not only in discussions about the 'informally and arbitrarily imposed' limited number of referrals to YJC but also in objections to adopting a more inclusive model—such as New Zealand's—which some magistrates argue amounts to 'mandatory referral.'

Diversionary options under the YOA emphasise restorative justice and rehabilitation, the latter being a prescribed priority of the Children's Court. Some findings suggest that the challenges of transitioning between adult and youth paradigms, along with disparities in access to training and resources, contribute to inconsistencies between rural and urban jurisdictions, thereby undermining diversion in rural areas.

The discussion on judicial decision-making and the magistrates' perspectives on the legislation reveals that diversion is sometimes further compromised by judicial attitudes and high expectations of diversionary practices. Firstly, the discretion afforded to magistrates to consider contextual and mitigating factors can result in inconsistencies in diversion decisions across the judiciary. Secondly, a strong emphasis on recidivism has fostered the perception that if one or two YJCs fail to deter a young person from reoffending, further referrals are futile. Consequently, YJCs are viewed more as sentencing tools rather than *true* alternatives aimed at diverting children away from the criminal justice system. This perception undermines the core intent of the YOA, which positions court intervention as a measure of *last resort*.

Thirdly, community expectations exert considerable influence. A common view among magistrates is that the public perceives YJC as a lenient or 'soft' approach. For some, this perception renders YJC inappropriate for certain offences, as it may appear to condone the behaviour. This concern was particularly evident in discussions surrounding sexual and domestic violence offences.

While the magistracy generally supports restorative justice and YJC—often viewing it as more onerous for the young person and more effective (than the court) in fostering accountability—opinions vary regarding the adequacy of outcomes plans. Some magistrates believe that these plans lack sufficient substance, suggesting that individual views on their rigour may influence decisions to refer cases to YJC, especially for more serious offences. Outcome plans that go beyond a letter of apology are seen as more appropriate, as they better hold young offenders more accountable. Thus, perceptions of insufficiently demanding outcome plans may deter referrals to YJC.

Magistrates also expressed frustration over the statutory exclusion of certain offences from YJC eligibility. There was broad consensus that offences committed in *company*—such as robbery or break and enter—should be eligible for diversion. Magistrates argued that the involvement of peers does not inherently increase the seriousness of the offence, particularly given that youth offending often occurs with peers. In these cases, judicial willingness to refer to YJC is constrained by legislative limitations.

The discussion surrounding domestic and sexual offences—currently excluded from the YOA—revealed clear divisions among magistrates. Some viewed these offences as too serious for diversion, arguing that referring such behaviour to YJC could send the wrong message to the community by implying that the conduct is acceptable. In contrast, others contended that many of these offences, when committed by young people, are relatively minor in nature and that those individuals could benefit from restorative interventions. Nonetheless, the statutory exclusion of these offences prevents young people from accessing the potential benefits of YJC. These different perspectives highlight variations in judicial perceptions—and ultimately, decision-making—and signal the complexity of applying the law in this area. While discretion is essential to avoid a one-size fits-all approach, particularly for vulnerable groups, it also introduces the risk of inconsistent referral practices. This issue is further exacerbated across different geographical regions, where disparities in resources and access to specialised expertise deepen the divide between rural and urban jurisdictions.

Overall, the findings in this chapter indicate that magistrates of the NSW Children's Court advocate for increased judicial flexibility and broader discretion to apply the diversionary processes where deemed appropriate—particularly with fewer legislative restrictions on offence eligibility—as a means to enhance YJC referrals. However, tensions between individual judicial approaches, combined with broader social forces such as efficiency demands, political considerations, the need to maintain public confidence in the courts, moral performance and structural factors including court location, contribute to a complex, messy and inconsistent landscape of diversionary decision-making. A significant concern is that many decisions are guided by high-risk factors, which often result in the exclusion of repeat offenders or those classified as serious. This practice ultimately undermines the principle of using court as a 'last resort,' as envisioned in the YOA's hierarchical approach to intervention.

References

Australia Institute of Health and Welfare. (2016). *Youth justice orders and supervision in 2015–2016*. (Youth Justice Fact sheet no. 64. Cat. No JUV 85). Australian Government. http://www.aihw.gov.au/publication-detail/?id=60129556330

Australian Institute of Health and Welfare. (2024). *Youth justice in Australia 2022–23*. https://www.aihw.gov.au/reports/youth-justice/youth-justice-in-australia-annual-report-2022-23

Becroft, A. (2003). *Youth Justice: The New Zealand Experience Past Lessons and Future Challenges*. The Juvenile Justice: From Lessons of the Past to a Road for the Future Conference convened by the Australian Institute of Criminology in conjunction with the NSW Department of Juvenile Justice, Sydney.

Bergseth, K. J., & Bouffard, J. A. (2007). The long-term impact of restorative justice programming for juvenile offenders. *Journal of Criminal Justice*, *35*, 433–451.

Bohm, R. M. (2006). "McJustice": On the McDonaldization of criminal justice. *Justice Quarterly*, *23*(1), 127–146.

Bottoms, A., & Dignan, J. (2004). Youth justice in Great Britain. In M. Tonry & A. Doob (Eds.), *Crime and justice, a review of research, volume 31: Youth crime and youth justice: Comparative and cross-national perspectives* (pp. 21–183). University of Chicago Press.

Braithwaite, J. (2006). Accountability and responsibility through restorative justice. In M. W. Dowdle (Ed.), *Public accountability: Designs, dilemmas and experiences*. Cambridge University Press.

Brookbanks, W. (2015). *Therapeutic jurisprudence: New Zealand perspectives*. Thomson Reuters New Zealand Ltd.

Carrington, P. J. (2002). Group crime in Canada. *Canadian Journal of Criminology and Criminal Justice*, *44*, 277–316.

Cashmore, J. (2011). The link between child maltreatment and adolescent offending: System neglect of adolescents. *Family Matters*, *89*, 31–41.

Cashmore, J. (2013). Juvenile justice: Australian court responses situated in the international context. In R. Sheehan & A. Borowski (Eds.), *Australia's Children's Courts today and tomorrow* (pp. 197–207). Springer.

Children's (Criminal Proceedings) Act 1987 (NSW).
Cleland, A. (2016). Portrait of the accused as a young man: New Zealand's harsh treatment of young people who commit serious crimes. *The Round Table, 105*(4), 377–387.
Crimes Act 1900 (NSW)
Crimes (Domestic and Personal Violence) Act 2007 (NSW)
Cunneen, C., & White, R. (2007). *Juvenile justice: Youth and crime in Australia* (3 ed.). Oxford University Press.
Department of Attorney General and Justice (NSW). (2011). *A fairer fine system for disadvantaged people: An evaluation of time to pay, cautions, internal review and the work development order scheme*. NSW Government. https://dcj.nsw.gov.au/documents/about-us/engage-with-us/public-consultations/unsorted/a_fairer_fine_system.pdf
Fernandez, E., Bolitho, J., Hansen, P., & Hudson, M. (2013). The Children's Court in New South Wales. In R. Sheehan & A. Borowski (Eds.), *Australia's Children's Court today and tomorrow* (pp. 27–44). Springer.
Fines Act 1996. (NSW).
Fitzgerald, J. (2000). *Graffiti in New South Wales* (Bureau Brief Issue no. 5). NSW Bureau of Crime Statistics and Research.
Goldweber, A., Dmitireva, J., Cauffman, E., Piquero, A. R., & Steinberg, L. (2011). The development of criminal style in adolescence and young adulthood: Separating the lemmings from the loners. *Journal of Youth and Adolescence, 40*(3), 332–346.
Graffiti Legislation Amendment Act 2012 (NSW)
Indig, D., Vecchiato, C., Haysom, L., Beilby, R., Carter, J., Champion, U., Gaskin, C., Heller, E., Kumar, S., Mamone, N., Muir, P., van den Dolder, P., & Whitton, G. (2011). *2009 NSW young people in custody health survey: Full report*. Justice Health and Juvenile Justice. https://www.nsw.gov.au/sites/default/files/2022-05/2009_NSW_YPiCHS_Full_report.pdf?contentOnly=true
Johnstone, P. (2014, March 25). *Emerging developments in juvenile justice*. The 5th Annual Juvenile Justice Summit, Melbourne. https://childrenscourt.nsw.gov.au/documents/other/paper%20for%20jj%20summit%2020.3.14.pdf
Johnstone, P. (2016, August 5). *Cross-over Kids – The Drift of Children from the Child Protection System into the Criminal Justice System* [Paper presentation]. Aboriginal Legal Service Conference, Newcastle. https://childrenscourt.nsw.gov.au/documents/other/ALS%20CONFERENCE%202016%20CROSS%20OVER%20KIDS%20JULY%203.pdf
Jones, M. (2003, August 18–19). *Graffiti culture and Hip Hop: Working from within*. The Graffiti and Disorder Conference, Brisbane.
Judicial Conference of Australia. (2015). *Judicial appointments: A comparative study* [Research Paper]. The Judicial Conference of Australia. https://www.ajoa.asn.au/wp-content/uploads/2013/10/P17_02_42-RESEARCH-PAPER-final.pdf
Kiefel, S., & Saunders, C. (2015). Concepts of representations in their application of the judiciary in Australia. In S. Turenne (Ed.), *Fair reflection of society in judicial systems - A comparative study* (pp. 41–63). Springer International Publishing.
KPMG. (2010). *Review of the Youth Justice Group Conferencing Program – Final Report*. V. Department of Human Services, Melbourne.
Luke, G., & Lind, B. (2002). *Reducing Juvenile Crime: Conferencing versus Court* (Contemporary Issues in Crime and Justice, no.69). NSW Bureau of Crime Statistics and Research.
Marien, M. C. (2012, March 26–27). *"Cross-over kids" – Childhood and adolescent abuse and neglect and juvenile offending*. National Juvenile Justice Summit, Melbourne. https://childrenscourt.nsw.gov.au/documents/news/2012%20clnv%20cross_over_kids_2012.pdf
McVie, S. (2009). Criminal careers and young people. In M. Barry & F. McNeill (Eds.), *Youth offending and youth justice: Research highlights in social work* (pp. 38–55). Jessica Kingsley Publishers.

Moore, E. (2012). *Restorative justice initiatives: Public opinion and support in NSW* (Criminal Justice and Statistics Bureau Brief 77). NSW Bureau of Crime Statistics and Research.

New South Wales Law Reform Commission. (2012). *Penalty Notices* (Report no 132). NSW Law Reform Commission. https://lawreform.nsw.gov.au/documents/Publications/Reports/Report-132.pdf

New South Wales Ombudsman. (2009). *Review of the Impact of Criminal Infringement Notices on Aboriginal Communities*. NSW Ombudsman. https://cmsassets.ombo.nsw.gov.au/assets/Reports/FR_CINs_ATSI_review_Aug09.pdf.pdf

NSW Government. (2024, March 8). *Judicial Careers*. [Community and Justice]. https://dcj.nsw.gov.au/about-us/careers-at-dcj/pathways/judicial-careers.html#judicial

NSW Government. (2025). Licence and registration offences and penalties. https://www.nsw.gov.au/driving-boating-and-transport/demerits-penalties-and-offences/offences/licence-and-registration-offences-and-penalties

Richards, K. (2011). *What makes juvenile offenders different from adult offenders?* (Trends and Issues in Crime and Criminal Justice, No. 409). Australian Institute of Criminology.

Richards, K., Bartels, L., & Bolitho, J. (2017). Children's Court magistrates' views of restorative justice and therapeutic jurisprudence measures for young offenders. *Youth Justice, 17*(1), 22–40.

Shaw, C. R., & McKay, H. D. (1969 [1942]). *Juvenile delinquency and urban areas*. University of Chicago Press.

Smith, N., & Weatherburn, D. (2012). *Youth Justice Conferences versus Children's Court: A comparison of re-offending* (Contemporary Issues in Crime and Justice no. 160). NSW Bureau of Crime Statistics and Research.

Taussig, I. (2012). *Youth justice conferences: Participant profile and conference characteristics* (Crime and Justice Statistics Bureau Brief No. 73). NSW Bureau of Crime Statistics and Research.

Umbreit, M. (1999). Avoiding the marginalization and 'McDonaldization' of victim-offender mediation: A case study in moving toward the mainstream. In G. Bazemore & L. Walgrave (Eds.), *Restorative juvenile justice: Repairing the harm of youth crime* (pp. 213–234). Criminal Justice Press.

Walgrave, L. (2004). Restoration in youth justice: Youth crime and youth justice: Comparative and cross-national perspectives. *Crime and Justice, 31*, 543–597.

Warr, M. (1996). Organisation and instigation in delinquent groups. *Criminology, 34*, 11–37.

Webber, A. (2012). *Youth justice conferences versus children's court: A comparison of cost effectiveness* (Crime and Justice Bulletin no 164). NSW Bureau of Crime Statistics and Research.

White, R. (2001). Graffiti, crime prevention and cultural space. *Current Issues in Criminal Justice, 12*(3), 253–266.

White, R., & Wyn, J. (2008). Doing bad: Juvenile justice. In R. White & J. Wyn (Eds.), *Youth and society: Exploring the social dynamics of youth experience* (pp. 155–169). Oxford University Press.

6 Perspectives from Juvenile Justice Professionals on Youth Diversion

Introduction

Juvenile Justice NSW (JJ) is responsible for supervising young offenders in community settings and juvenile justice centres. Formerly known as the Department of Juvenile Justice (DJJ), JJ was assigned administrative responsibility for conferencing programmes under the YOA. This includes managing referrals to YJCs from both the police and the Children's Court. Aboriginal Legal Services (ALS) is a specialist legal organisation for First Nations people established in NSW to address racism and to promote self-determination. ALS solicitors typically encounter YOA matters primarily through custody notification services or when representing young people in court.

This chapter draws primarily on interview data with ALS solicitors and JJ assistant managers, triangulated with data from other interview respondents from this study, to examine institutional perspectives on diversionary processes under the YOA. Understanding JJ's perspectives on diversion practices is essential for identifying systemic factors that could enhance YJC referral rates across NSW. Correspondingly, insights from ALS are critical for understanding barriers to diversion, particularly those pertaining to criminal responsibility and admission protocols. As established in previous chapters, both police cautions and YJC eligibility require that young people admit to the offence in the presence of an appropriate adult. Chapter 4 demonstrated that police officers identified children's reluctance to make admissions of guilt—often attributed to ALS counsel advising against admissions—as a primary impediment to diversion for First Nations youth. ALS practitioners offer important perspectives on these admission-related challenges from a position grounded in advocacy and legal protection for First Nations young people.

The respondents were recruited by contacting the organisations and inviting participation in the study. Interviews with ALS occurred in May 2015, while those with JJ assistant managers took place between October and December 2015. Although small, the interview cohort included ALS respondents (n = 1) located in the metropolitan area and JJ Assistant Managers (n = 5) across areas ranging from metropolitan to outer rural NSW. The respondents will be referred to as 'solicitor' (S) for ALS solicitors and 'Assistant Managers' (AM); collectively, they are termed 'youth justice personnel.'

DOI: 10.4324/9781003470366-6

The participant group was predominantly female (a ratio of 5:1), with ages ranging from 32 to 55 years. Only one participant identified as an Indigenous Australian. The solicitor brought valuable insights to the study despite her junior status and being the only representative from ALS. With six years of experience advising domestic violence victims in the criminal justice system and four years as an ALS solicitor, she provided essential perspectives on the administrative and policy aspects of youth diversion processes, including specific insights on the failure to divert. ALS solicitors engage with issues related to the YOA in two primary ways: first, through the Custody Notification Service, and second, by representing young people in court. At the time of the interviews, this participant handled court matters across several metropolitan areas in Sydney and offered advice via the NSW-wide custody notification service.

Assistant manager positions within JJ represented a recent organisational restructuring. The participants had experience in current or similar roles within JJ, varying from 3 to 17 years, and had a total career span ranging from 14 to 23 years. They demonstrated substantial experience within the criminal justice system or related fields. Their professional backgrounds were varied, with mediation and community corrections being common pathways into JJ. Three respondents had previously served as YJC 'convenors' in NSW, with one continuing to convene conferences while working for JJ temporarily. However, recent policy changes by JJ curtailed this practice due to a perceived conflict of interest.

The JJ respondents collectively covered extensive regions across NSW, including metropolitan areas, regional centres, and rural locations spanning from the Far South Coast to Newcastle District, ensuring representation of diverse operational contexts across the state's youth justice system. Their coverage extended to Woy Woy and Wyong; Newcastle District; the Far South Coast, including Batemans Bay, Bega, and Eden Courts; Griffith, Deniliquin, Aubrey, Wagga Wagga, and Cootamundra; and Fairfield District, comprising Fairfield, Bonnyrigg, Cabramatta, Revesby, Merrylands, and Holroyd. For anonymity purposes, the specific area names for each respondent have been deleted from the transcript records. The diverse geographical experience of each participant contributed to a broad understanding of diversionary options in NSW. As will be discussed throughout the chapter, JJ respondents often indicated that acceptance levels of diversionary options vary across different institutions and are often dependent on geographical locations. This finding is consistent with the Noetic report in 2010 and the DAGJ (2011), which highlighted that diversionary options are not being used uniformly and equitably across NSW. Insights from youth justice personnel help elucidate potential institutionally driven factors behind these discrepancies.

This participant profile reflects a highly experienced cohort with deep institutional knowledge and varied professional backgrounds, well-positioned to provide comprehensive insights into diversionary processes under the YOA. This chapter examines qualitative interview findings, beginning with an analysis of their roles within the diversion process. It subsequently explores their contributions to diversionary decision-making in NSW by examining their experiences working within the system, particularly in collaboration with police and magistrates who function as gatekeepers to diversion. Additionally, it considers their perspectives on systemic failures within the current framework. The findings indicate the relationship quality between youth justice personnel and institutional actors varies significantly across police LACs and court jurisdictions. Internal strategic discussions focused on strengthening stakeholder relationships are essential to maximise the use of diversion. Furthermore, the findings presented in this chapter corroborate conclusions from previous chapters by illustrating competing tensions between welfare and justice approaches within diversionary decision-making.

Aboriginal legal services—the solicitor's role in diversion under the YOA

ALS was established in the 1970s in response to the lack of representation for Indigenous defendants in the criminal justice system. ALS solicitors engage with matters under the YOA primarily through two avenues: by providing legal advice via the Custody Notification Service and by representing young people in court proceedings.

The Custody Notification Service is a 24-hour legal advice phone line for First Nations people, established in 2000, following recommendations from the Royal Commission into Aboriginal Deaths in Custody (ALRC, 2017). Under NSW law, police must contact ALS when a First Nations person is taken into custody to ensure timely legal advice and uphold the protection of fundamental rights. Through this service, ALS solicitors provide immediate legal guidance and assess the health and welfare of detainees, addressing concerns like self-harm (including suicide) and access to medication (Aboriginal Legal Services (NSW/ACT), n.d.). Solicitors also verify that appropriate standards of care are met, including medical treatment access, contact with family or friends, access to clothing and other basic necessities (ALRC, 2017).

All ALS solicitors participate in the Custody Notification Service on a rotating basis, handling calls from any police station across NSW. At the time this call is made, police are often offering the young person an opportunity to admit guilt to the offence, which would make the young person eligible for diversion under the YOA. The suggestion is that they could participate in a caution or YJC without the matter being referred to court. At this juncture, the solicitor's advice can significantly influence the referral process.

The solicitor respondent explained that providing counsel over the phone is complex and time-consuming. First, there is the challenge of explaining the provisions of the YOA to a young person and their support person. Second, as S1 noted, at times these provisions also need to be explained to the police officer. However, S1 further explained that there is no guarantee that an admission of guilt will result in diversion, as police are often unwilling to commit to it at this stage. Consequently, according to S1, the advice to the young person is frequently not to participate in an interview, answer questions, or make admissions—even at times when a PAS is offered (see Chapter 4). This further highlights the legislative constraints—discussed in Chapter 4—imposed by requiring admissions of guilt for diversion under the YOA and supports arguments for removing such requirements.

An alternative approach could follow New Zealand's model, where young people are not required to admit the offence; instead, they simply 'not deny' the offence (see Becroft & Norrie, 2015 for an overview of New Zealand's model). In New Zealand, a 'not denied' is considered a useful mechanism to trigger a Family Group Conference—the equivalent of a YJC in NSW—without requiring a formal admission of guilt (O'Driscoll, 2008).

The second avenue through which the ALS solicitors engage with the YOA is in court, when young people appear before a magistrate. In these instances, magistrates have the discretion to refer the young person to a caution or a YJC under the Act. Solicitors can advocate for diversion under the YOA rather than having the young person processed under the *Children (Criminal Proceedings) Act* 1987. Although some magistrates report that young people occasionally change their minds (having not made admissions to the police) and admit to the offence during court appearances, this is not always the case. Therefore, the limitations on access to diversionary alternatives remain a concern, particularly as they stem from the YOA's requirement for an admission of guilt. The respondent's observations on these issues are discussed throughout the remainder of the chapter.

Institutional framework for JJ personnel

JJ in NSW has undergone several administrative transformations over the years. Initially managed by the Department of Youth and Community Services until 1987, it transitioned into Juvenile Justice Service and became part of the Department of Family and Community Services. In July 1991, control was transferred to the Department of Corrective Services, where it functioned as a division. By November 1991, it was proclaimed an independent department known as the Department of Juvenile Justice (DJJ) (New South Wales Government, 1991). In 2009 DJJ merged into the newly formed principal department, the Department of Human Services (see *Public Sector Employment and Management (Departmental Amalgamations) Order* 2009, no. 352, cls. 28). Later, in 2011, DJJ was integrated into the NSW Department of Attorney General and Justice and subsequently renamed the Department of Justice. As a consequence, what was formerly known as DJJ—at the time of this study was referred to as Juvenile Justice NSW (JJ)—is known now as Youth Justice (see Chapter 1)—an agency of the New South Wales Government and an administrative division within the Department of Justice of NSW (see *Public Sector Employment and Management (Departments) Order 2011*, no. 184, cl. 4).

Operating under various legislative frameworks—including the *Children (Detention Centres) Act 1987* (NSW), the *Children (Community Service Orders) Act 1987* (NSW), the *Young Offenders Act 1997* (NSW), and the *Children (Interstate Transfer of Offenders) Act 1988* (NSW)—JJ is responsible for a comprehensive range of functions, as outlined by the Department of Justice (2016):

- Supervising young people sentenced to community-based or custodial orders and on conditional bail.

- Supporting and supervising young people to meet the conditions of bail.
- Supervising young people remanded in custody pending court hearings.
- Preparing reports to assist judicial officers in determining sentences.
- Administering the Work and Development Order scheme targeting young offenders
- Managing the Youth on Track early intervention scheme.
- Delivering interventions aimed at reducing juvenile reoffending rates.
- Providing funding to communities to support young offenders and their families.
- Administering the YJC scheme, as previously noted.

The role of JJ assistant managers in diversion under the YOA

Traditionally, YJC was managed by a 'YJC Assistant Manager' within JJ, with specific community officers recruited to administer YJC and oversee conference convenors. However, following organisational restructuring within JJ, this responsibility transitioned to a generalist role shared amongst all assistant managers within JJ. According to JJ, this change 'streamlined a number of practices and provided professional opportunities for staff' (Department of Justice, 2016, p. 19). While the chapter does not aim to evaluate the organisation, it is important to note that restructuring within JJ was raised by interviewees as a concern, particularly regarding its impact on the diversionary decision-making process.

Interviewees expressed a lack of confidence in the current structure's ability to manage YJC diversion effectively. A common concern was that under the current structure, the Assistant Manager role, as it currently stands, lacks the specialisation required for YJC and its associated legislation. As a result, individuals in these positions may not possess the same depth of knowledge regarding the various aspects of youth justice they are expected to manage. This lack of specialisation was viewed as a negative factor with potential adverse effects on diversionary practices. For example, police officers occasionally seek advice or confirmation from assistant managers regarding diversion options for specific cases. Many interviewees argued that such advice would be better provided by specialists with in-depth knowledge of diversionary practices. They highlighted the now-defunct role of 'Assistant Manager of Youth Conferencing' as having previously fulfilled this function. The responsibilities once held by those in that specialised role have now been absorbed into the broader, generalist 'Assistant Manager' role, occupied by all current interviewees. This shift has raised concerns about the dilution of expertise in managing YJC diversion, as the new structure lacks the focused specialisation that previously characterised the role.

Oversight and management of YJC referrals now constitute just one aspect of a broader set of responsibilities assigned to assistant managers. These include managing community caseworkers and overseeing community-based orders such as probation, bonds or community service. Interviewees indicated that while some assistant managers have prior experience in the specialised YJC role and therefore possess deeper insights into diversion under the YOA, others may be more familiar with other aspects of youth justice, such as community-based supervision, and lack specific experience with YJC.

It is important to acknowledge that, at the time participants were recruited for this study, the restructuring within JJ was still relatively recent. Consequently, JJ agreed to provide access only to assistant managers who had previously managed YJC under the old structure. Therefore, caution should be exercised when interpreting participants' views on the current lack of specialisation and its potential to undermine diversion efforts, as these perspectives are shaped by their prior experience in *specialised* roles that have since been removed. Yet it is precisely this background that enabled all interviewed Assistant Managers to possess extensive knowledge of YJC and the diversion process, positioning them exceptionally well to contextualise their current roles in relation to the YOA.

The 'gatekeeping' role of youth justice personnel

Assistant Managers oversee all aspects of YJC, from the referral point—whether originating from the police or court—to the final notifications regarding completion. At the referral stage, determinations are made as to the appropriateness of the referral. Interviewees noted that they occasionally receive referrals from both police and court that either cannot be conferenced (due to legislative preclusions) or require additional information to assess whether a YJC is appropriate. For instance, AM2 explained:

> Occasionally, we get a referral of offences that can't be conferenced. Our guiding tool is the YOA… [for example] sometimes we might get something from police where a young person is only 12 or 13 and we need to make sure that they've asked the *doli incapax* questions…[also] is it conferrable? … Have all the legal processes been covered?

Once a referral is deemed appropriate, assistant managers work to match a convenor to 'not only the young person but also the victims and the circumstance' (AM1). Factors such as gender, location, demographics of potential attendees, cultural needs and disability considerations are taken into account. For example, AM1 highlighted that a screening disability tool is used to assess whether a young person can participate in a YJC and whether they have an adequate support network. She further explained that the Assistant Manager 'liaises with the convener over that; where the Assistant Manager is the only contact that the convener has with JJ' (AM1).

After considering all relevant factors, approval is given to proceed with the YJC and its outcome plan. Upon completion, a caseworker monitors the implementation of the outcome plan and notifies participants—of the YJC—of whether it has been successfully completed. Finally, notifications are sent to the referring authority—either the police or the court.

If the outcome plan is not completed, the referring agent is informed. This notification influences subsequent actions. Regarding police referrals, AM1 explained that failure to complete an outcome is akin to non-participation in the YJC, effectively nullifying it. The police must then decide whether to extend the time for completion or refer the matter to another resolution method, typically the court. Conversely, if a YJC was referred by a court and not completed, the court is notified and may issue a warrant requiring the young person's appearance.

Assistant managers interact with various actors throughout this administrative process, including police and court magistrates. In their administrative roles, they contribute significantly to understanding decision-making and practices surrounding diversion, despite not being directly involved with making the referral.

Overall, all interviewed youth justice personnel—JJ Assistant Managers and the ALS solicitor—asserted that the utilisation of YJC as a form of diversion under the YOA is suboptimal. They argued that the YOA's goal of using detention as a last resort is compromised by several factors: the legislative preclusion of specific offences; insufficient training and knowledge regarding diversion; misinterpretation or incorrect application of the legislation; and inconsistencies in practice, access to resources, and training for managing diversion.

Challenges to YJC diversion

All interviewed assistant managers expressed positive attitudes towards diversionary alternatives and the restorative justice process—attitudes that were not uniformly held across the broader JJ division. For instance, one participant who had previously worked as a convenor in a community youth conferencing pilot programme from 1995 to 1996 (prior to the establishment of the YOA) remarked:

> It is the social aspect of YJC outcomes that appeals to me. I think that at heart I am kind of a bit of a peacemaker; and I was attracted to the possibility for people to make amends and move on in their lives after making mistakes.
>
> (AM4)

Similarly, another participant noted her motivation to pursue a professional position in JJ stemmed from a desire to help and support young people. Having previously worked in community corrections with offenders aged 19–20 years old on parole, she remarked:

> I saw young people who had come into the system, who hadn't had a chance to divert out of it [offending]...I heard about family group conferencing in New Zealand and read a book about it and it just seemed to make a lot of sense to me that it would help, particularly for young people.
>
> (AM5)

This participant began her career with JJ in the early days of YJC and, at one point, held the position of Director of Youth Justice Conferencing, a role that, during its existence, was responsible for ensuring statewide adherence to proper YJC practices.

Three participants had previously served as YJC convenors, with one continuing to convene conferences while temporarily working for JJ. However, recent policy changes within JJ curtailed this practice due to a perceived conflict of interest:

> I was one of the first convenors in NSW and conferenced hundreds of YJCs. About four years ago, the Department said it was a conflict of interest to work for JJ full-time and run YJCs at the same time, so they stopped us from doing that as secondary employment.
>
> (AM2)

Convenors are contractors to JJ responsible for coordinating and facilitating YJCs. After serving as convenors, some respondents transitioned into part-time or full-time roles within JJ. For instance, one participant credited her part-time position as a project policy officer to frequently filling in as an assistant manager. As she explained, while working as a convenor, 'she began to be asked to backfill on the Assistant Manager YJC positions in the metropolitan area' (AM3). The experience gained from facilitating at YJCs created opportunities for these individuals to join JJ in management roles. She elaborated:

> If you were going to backfill a manager who was going on leave, you really needed to know something about YJC… they didn't go to the rest of JJ [for filling these roles] because YJC was just a division on its own. That's how myself and others [convenors] would have got into this [current role as Assistant Manager].
>
> (AM3)

This remark highlights that knowledge of YJC practices and related legislation is not universally held among broader JJ staff, which is not surprising given the division's large size, diverse functions and long history of administrative restructuring.

Collectively, these examples highlight that some assistant managers possess in-depth knowledge of the complexities and logistics of diversion under the Act. This is significant in light of the administrative decisions that have seen the specialist manager role within JJ amalgamated, potentially undermining the focus on diversionary alternatives and, consequently, the outcomes of diversion. All interviewees expressed concerns to this effect, as illustrated by this remark:

> When there is a specialist role that people become knowledgeable, and they become skilled, and their attention is solely directed towards particular aims… and the YJCs outcome [plans] are more substantial… With combined responsibilities in the [new] role, the attention to YJC will be diluted [across various tasks].
>
> (AM4)

Concerns were also raised regarding the inadequate training provided to new assistant managers. For example, AM4 remarked:

> They've been trained on how to check whether the referral is covered under the YOA, but my understanding is that the training hasn't really addressed the principles and the objectives of the Act.

Further elaborating on this point, AM4 noted that the lack of training reflects a broader issue of limited resources being stretched too thin. The sentiment expressed was that, under current constraints within JJ, diversion is not a priority. This concern was illustrated by the following observation: 'When we have team meetings, and we had training for our regional area – like we had two days of training earlier this year – not one agenda item was a YJC agenda item' (AM4).

These comments reflect the prevailing sentiment at the time of this research. With JJ undergoing significant structural changes, several interviewees expressed concern that JJ—and the government more broadly—were failing to prioritise essential training, resources and a sustained focus on diversionary practices and processes. The following sections will explore these issues in more detail, including the offences precluded by the Act, training and knowledge related to diversion, the interpretation and application of the legislation and the lack of consistent practices in the management of diversion. According to the assistant managers, these factors collectively undermine the use of the YOA and the diversion of young people *away* from court, contributing to a broader and increasingly punitive political agenda towards youth offenders.

The need for consistent practices within JJ

One of the key issues raised by most participants was the absence of a policy guiding practices within JJ, particularly in recent years. According to interviewees, this has led to localised approaches, where different solutions result in varied outcomes. For instance, one participant noted:

> The Assistant Managers for YJC – specialist role prior to re-structuring– used to get together twice a year and have a conference and meeting about what's working, what's not, what they could do better, and what were the challenges? So, there was a core effective practice of a group of people from YJC [division] and I was in the committee. I think it would be helpful for all Assistant Managers to talk about things like that; because we're working in silo; we very rarely talk to each other [paused], hence the lack of consistency.
>
> (AM1)

Overall, the consensus among interviewees is that additional resources are necessary to facilitate dialogue, training and knowledge sharing—thereby highlighting successful practices and integrating them into standard procedures. The inconsistency in managing YJC referrals within JJ was identified as a persistent issue since the inception of the YOA undermining the promotion of diversionary alternatives—particularly YJC referrals—both within and outside JJ. For instance, AM5 noted:

> One of the limiting factors in the first five years of operation of the Act was that we thought very much about our partners the police, our partners the courts, our partners the legal profession. But we didn't think a lot about our partners in JJ… where particularly JJ officers are writing back to the courts and making recommendations or providing advice to the court that could influence diversion, but also put it front-and-centre… I think we forgot about that a little bit.

A more robust forum for internal and external discussions around diversion was highlighted as essential for increasing the overall use of the YOA and boosting referrals to YJC. This relationship was observed to vary across jurisdictions and LACs due to inconsistent practices. Some participants expressed concerns that recent restructuring in JJ, which, as discussed earlier, turned the administration of YJC into a generalist role, might weaken relationships with police officers specifically:

> In each LAC, the police have a YLO who is the contact point. For much of the last 15-17 years, that has been a one-on-one [relationship] between the conference manager and the YLO, so you do build quite a strong peer support. Whereas under the new structure that may or may not continue. In some areas it will continue, like for me it's the South Coast, I still have a command that I'm responsible for. But I think in other locations there'll be more than one person dealing with the police. So, it remains to be seen what will happen.
>
> (AM5)

This quote highlights concerns regarding the potential weakening of relationships between police and JJ due to the loss of established rapport that previously facilitated informal consultations. As indicated by AM5, such consultations often relied on pre-existing relationships. Moreover, the outcomes of these consultations could significantly influence diversionary decisions, as the choice to divert or not may be shaped by the nature of these discussions. This challenge is further compounded by the lack of specialist training provided to all stakeholders involved—particularly within JJ, as well as among other key criminal justice actors such as police and magistrates (see Chapters 4 and 5).

Training deficits

The YJC Directorate, responsible for the overall operation of YJCs in NSW since the scheme's inception, was abolished in 2007. Subsequently, this responsibility shifted to JJ. As a result, however, the interviewees argued that YJC is not prioritised due to resource constraints, as previously noted.

Participants noted that there has been insufficient capacity to address training and education for stakeholders, as much of their time is instead consumed by administrative tasks. This challenge has become even more pronounced over the last two years. Regarding internal JJ personnel training, one assistant manager remarked:

> Eight years ago, there was a Youth Justice Conferencing Directorate that looked after the Youth Justice Conferencing Managers, and they guided and supported the work of the managers. Then…in 2007, the directorate was dissolved, and the broader department looked after [us], so we were just looked after by regions, and our capacity to do that kind of community consultation and stakeholder support and focus diminished.
>
> (AM4)

The focus here is not on whether outcomes or the use of diversion improved or declined post-dissolution, but rather on the diminished capacity—due to resource constraints—to address community consultation, stakeholder support needs and training. For instance, some participants noted that co-training with police has diminished over time:

> We used to do joint training with police for SYO training and it was agreed that JJ would participate in the two days of that training and that we would sign off individuals' accreditation. But over the years, that's kind of been diluted too… and over time, police will do the SYO training without the co-facilitation of JJ. I can see why they would take advantage of having those police in training and want to ensure that their other youth targets were met, but I think that JJ had a lot to contribute around some checks and balances that perhaps aren't there now.
>
> (AM4)

Participants' perceptions regarding the adequacy of police training on diversion align with concerns raised by the YLOs in this study (see Chapter 4). The significance of training issues is two-fold. Firstly, a lack of adequate training focusing on the rationale for prioritising diversion may undermine its use. Reflecting on the early days of the Act, one assistant manager noted:

> When the SYO training was first developed, I ran a pilot with my YLOs. Police became aware of it. I worked with the senior tutor to enhance the program which was then rolled-out state-wide. A big part of that was talking about youth offending, the reasons why we should divert young people, some of the research about it, et cetera. Part of the deal with the police was that over the years, JJ would have an active [role], like we'd continue to develop the training together. But that's kind of fallen off a little bit as well, so the last iteration of the training has not had as much JJ involvement, and I think the training is a bit more [focusing on] –how they [the police] do the paperwork for their charges and stuff.
>
> (AM5)

The sentiment here is that the importance of treating young people differently from adults—and diverting them away from the court system (see Richards, 2011)—needs to be more strongly emphasised to those making diversionary decisions. This principle should also be consistently reinforced in training sessions.

Secondly, the lack of co-training between JJ and police YLOs can undermine diversion by failing to foster strong relationships among stakeholders involved in the process. AM3 noted:

> With the police, we used to do all that [YLO training] locally and that used to really help you get to know the new police officers. But now, they do it centrally…and I feel that's a great pity because we are not getting to know our *local* police officers in the same way.

The importance of ongoing and strong rapport—built on trust and peer-consultation between decision-makers like JJ personnel, police and magistrates—cannot be underestimated. As will be further illustrated, the decision-making around referrals to YJCs presents opportunities for dialogue between JJ staff and YLOs. These conversations typically focus on identifying the best outcomes for the young person, with an emphasis on diversion and treating court as a 'last resort.' However, open dialogue is more likely to occur when strong, established relationships exist between involved parties. Such communication has the potential to increase the number of youth referrals to diversionary alternatives.

Institutional cultures and attitudes affecting diversion to YJC

> I think with the police it's the entrenched culture… I think if the crime managers [within police] and the top [management] have this view that conferencing is a load of rubbish, and that it just trickles through, I don't think anyone else (other officers) – even if they did believe conferencing was going to work – I don't believe that they will be speaking up about it when you've got your hierarchy within the police system.
>
> (AM1)

These sentiments were echoed by all youth justice personnel interviewed—from solicitors to JJ's assistant managers. Their perspectives are shaped by direct exchanges and experiences with police officers. One participant illustrated this point:

> I used to encourage the YLOs to come to convenor's training [sessions] and they never did. But I used to say: 'Is there any feedback you want me to give to them? Is there anything we can be doing better? Are there any gaps in conferencing?' And their [the police area of command] feedback to me was always like: 'The outcomes are too soft. The outcomes are too wishy-washy. They are always the same; an apology letter, what's an apology letter going to do?' And so, I always say: 'Well, it might be the first time the kids ever verbalised that they are sorry, and it might be, what might seem an easy task

> for you, it might be enormous for a 15-year-old'. But, I think, even the YLOs have that view, the problem is at a higher level. At the last YLO meeting I had, I said to the part-time YLO: 'Is everything okay because you really seem like something's wrong?' She said: 'I'm sick of having these meetings saying the same things and nothing changes in our station'. And she said: 'It needs to go to a higher level'. She said: 'We all know at this table know what needs to happen; it's up above that they need to know'.
>
> (AM1)

The entrenched police culture(s) and resistance to diversionary alternatives have been documented before (see Chan, 2005) and discussed in the early chapters. Culture is analogous to a group as personality is to an individual (Schein, 2010). Police culture has often been described as monolithic, homogenous, authoritarian, suspicious, distrustful, socially isolated and highly resistant to change (see Chan, 1997; Kingshott et al., 2004; Reiner, 2010). Typically, it is regarded as a byproduct of modern police work focusing on street danger, officer discretion and authority to use violence– highlighting conflicts between frontline officers and managers (see Reiner, 2010). Police culture(s) is frequently characterised by shared beliefs—amongst officers—largely influenced by the conditions of their work (Reiner, 2010). Within this cultural framework, attitudes tend to align with punitive and law-enforcement-orientated approaches, reflecting a strong adherence to traditional policing methods and a reluctance to move away from such approaches. This resistance to reform is exemplified by a comment made by one of the assistant managers interviewed:

> In the last training session I did, I think I had about 24 male officers and 2 female officers. At the beginning, they were very upfront; they thought it [YJC] was a load of crap, it was a very soft option, juvenile justice is soft, and they told me: 'we want these kids to have consequences and if we hit them hard, they are less likely to reoffend'.
>
> (AM1)

As noted in earlier chapters, there is no evidence supporting the notion that punitive approaches reduce youth recidivism (see Chen et al., 2005; Richards & Lee, 2013; Weatherburn et al., 2012). Conversely, significant research indicates that young people typically grow out of crime (Mukherjee, 1983; Richards, 2011), with early contact with the criminal justice system increasing the likelihood of entrenchment within it (Chen et al., 2005; McAra & McVie, 2007, 2010).

Despite these findings, 'tough on crime' attitudes are deeply ingrained in institutions such as the police. According to youth justice personnel interviewed, police have consistently displayed disapproval of diversionary options for not aligning with a tough-on-crime approach. However, participants noted that since the enactment of the YOA, police attitudes have gradually become more accepting—albeit slowly.

While a study by Chan et al. (2005) highlighted this shift in police attitudes towards the Act. Empirical analysis of YJC referral data in this research reveals no corresponding increase in police-initiated referrals to YJC. As illustrated in Table 6.1[1], which presents data from 1998–2017, court-initiated referrals consistently predominated, with a median percentage of 54.5%. Only during the initial two years following the YOA implementation—1998–1999 and 1999–2000—did police referrals exceed court referrals by percentage. Subsequently, police referral rates declined significantly, reaching their lowest points at 41% in 2015–2016 and 42% in 2016–2017. Conversely, court-initiated YJC referrals increased during these same periods to 59% and 58%, respectively. This absence of sustained change suggests that documented shifts in police attitudes towards diversion have either failed to materialise in practice or have exerted minimal influence on actual YJC referral patterns.

Table 6.1 Referrals to a YJC by police and courts from 1998 to 2017.

Year	*YJC referrals by police (%)*	*YJC referrals by court (%)*
1998–1999	53	47
1999–2000	51	49
2000–2001	44	56
2001–2002	43	57
2002–2003	43	57
2003–2004	42	58
2004–2005	41	59
2005–2006	48	52
2006–2007	49	51
2007–2008	44	56
2008–2009	43	57
2009–2010	47	53
2010–2011	46	54
2011–2012	46	54
2012–2013	49	51
2013–2014	45	55
2014–2015	48	52
2015–2016	41	59
2016–2017	42	58

Table 6.2 Referrals to a YJC by police and courts from 2019–2020 to 2023–2024.

Year	*YJC referrals by police (%)*	*YJC referrals by court (%)*
2019–2020	56	44
2020–2021	52	48
2021–2022	56	44
2022–2023	52	48
2023–2024	54	46

Interestingly, more recent data presented in Table 6.2[2], which provides a year-by-year comparison for the periods 2019–2020 to 2023–2024, indicate that for the first time since 1999–2000, the percentage of referrals to YJCs by police slightly exceeded those made by the courts during 2019–2020. However, these findings should be interpreted with caution due to other potential factors that could explain this change in pattern. For instance, this coincides with the COVID-19 pandemic—which has had substantial impacts on the operations of the youth justice sector, including custody, policing and the courts—and as a result, the COVID-19 pandemic may have affected the trend over time for the most recent years. Nonetheless, the shift in referral patterns remains minimal. Moreover, data indicate a subsequent decline in YJC diversion referrals by the police for the years 2022–2023 and 2023–2024 compared to the immediately preceding years.

Despite recent trends, it is important to note that when the majority of referrals to YJC come from courts rather than police—or, in the best-case scenario seen so far, even when police refer a slightly higher percentage than courts—a significant number of young people continue to be exposed to the criminal justice system. This undermines the principles of the YOA. Further attention needs to be placed on how police, as the first point of contact for young people, apply the YOA to ensure it meets its original intention of effectively and consistently diverting youth *away* from the criminal justice system, rather than requiring them to proceed to court before being referred to diversion.

Youth justice personnel interviewed for this study believe that cynical attitudes towards diversionary options among police still prevail and have resulted in differential referrals across different LACs. Some LACs embrace diversionary alternatives more than others. As one assistant manager pointed out:

> Different LACs have different attitudes. I've got a couple who are excellent and a couple who you never hear anything from and some who are in between. We've got one LAC where they are just not interested in YJC at all: nothing. I haven't had a referral from them for so long, I can't remember; they just don't even think about it.
>
> (AM3)

These observations are consistent with Noetic Solutions' 2010 review of youth justice in NSW, which highlighted significant variability in police diversion rates to YJCs across LACs. Similarly, Ringland and Smith (2013) found that while 85% of LACs diverted at least 70% of eligible cases, some LACs had diversion rates as low as 30%. Several potential explanations for these disparities have been discussed in earlier chapters. Diversion under the YOA is complex, applying only under specific conditions such as an admission of guilt and the eligibility of the offence. Additionally, both police and magistrates must consider five factors in their decision-making: the seriousness of the offence; the degree of violence in the offence; harm caused to any victim; the young person's criminal history and previous dealings under the YOA; and 'any other matter the official thinks appropriate' (see Chapter 2). The legislation offers great leeway for interpretation on the weight of such factors.

Moreover, offender profiles can differ across LACs, influencing referral rates. Ringland and Smith's study (2013) identified characteristics such as being older at the time of referral, male gender, First Nations identity, multiple charges and prior cautions or YJCs as associated with reduced diversion likelihood. Despite adjustment for case-specific and individual-level factors, some LACs exhibit unexpectedly low diversion rates, warranting further attention.

Youth justice personnel interviewed believe that in some LACs, the underutilisation of diversion results from a lack of support within LAC management and its police community. For example, one participant noted:

> If the Superintendent – the local area commander, promotes the YOA within their LAC, then it does quite well…If you have a YLO who has a significant level of on-the-ground experience and that YLO is respected by their colleagues, then, there are better outcomes under the YOA, both in the way of cautioning and in the way of YJC.
>
> (AM4)

Additionally, interviewees highlighted that some YLOs choose their role for reasons unrelated to a passion for promoting diversion. JJ personnel's frustration is not so much with the individual YLOs; rather, the real frustration lies with the failures of a broader system within a particular social and political context. According to some youth justice personnel, the administrative nature of the YLO's role 'sometimes attracts people who are less enthusiastic and do not promote it [diversion] to the same degree as others do' (AM4).

Chapter 4 discusses how several YLOs were drawn to their roles due to their compatibility with personal commitment, largely because they typically involve a Monday-to-Friday, nine-to-five schedule—unusual for police positions. Some of the youth justice personnel interviewed noted that this administrative aspect makes the role attractive for those prioritising work-life balance, rather than necessarily because of its focus on diversion. For instance, AM3 observed that at times, 'there is not a lot of enthusiasm with a lot of police officers about learning about YJC,' suggesting that this may be partly due to a high turnover of YLOs:

> They always have different YLOs...there's no one, sort of, permanently in the position. They seem to have a lot of women who are pregnant go into the YLO role, and they are only there for six months, maybe, and then they move onto maternity leave.
>
> (AM3)

According to youth justice personnel, YLOs play a crucial gatekeeper role in promoting diversionary practices. Their enthusiasm for the values underpinning these alternatives encourages engagement with training and stakeholder collaboration, thereby enhancing the Act's promotion within institutions and maximising diversion potential. The youth justice personnel interviewed suggested that an enthusiastic—or lacklustre—approach to diversionary alternatives could account for the variations in referral numbers to YJC.

Similarly, youth justice interviewees suggested that significant discrepancies exist in how courts across various locations use the Act. They highlighted differences in the number and frequency of referrals to YJC. While there are many possible explanations for these referral disparities, no specific research has been conducted on this issue.

Youth justice personnel who have worked with both local magistrates and the specialist Children's Court magistrates believe that 'outside of the specialist Children's Court, it's very difficult to get magistrates on board' (AM2). An example illustrating the difference in interest across court jurisdictions—Children's Courts versus Local Courts—was pointed out during the interviews:

> The magistrate in Newcastle has been great. We've had three different magistrates here over the last ten years and all three of them have been terrific, with regular referrals to YJC. They see the value in it because they see the direct results. The outcome plans and the YJC report go back to the magistrate, so they directly get to see the impact of the conference on the young person, on the victims and on the families. In contrast, I worked in Campsie for 12 months… and the Campsie magistrate at the time would not refer, just did not refer to conferencing at all. And I took it upon myself to find out why; so, I set up meetings and that sort of stuff. Basically, [I was told] that it was a *soft option*. He told me: 'No, no, no! by the time these kids get to court, they should be punished'.
>
> (AM2)

According to the interviewee, differing attitudes towards using the Act between the two magistrates in Newcastle and Campsie can be attributed directly to structural differences. In Newcastle, the presence of a dedicated Children's Court facilitates diversionary practices. Conversely, at Campsie, juvenile matters are interspersed with regular adult cases, making it challenging for local courts to adopt a non-punitive approach:

> Somewhere like Campsie, they're just at the Local Court and they empty the court and have the juvenile matters heard. And then it's back to Local Court again, the gallery is full. So, you know, it's very difficult for them to take a punitive hat off and put on a diversionary hat.
>
> (AM2)

These observations corroborate claims made by some magistrates—noted in Chapter 5—regarding challenges faced by non-specialist Children's Courts. Furthermore, AM2's perception that certain magistrates are less supportive of diversion under the Act is significant, as it undermines these efforts in multiple ways. If accurate, such perceptions result in fewer referrals to YJC for young people. Even if these perceptions are incorrect, they may still lead to reduced diversion due to reactions from other legal practitioners. For instance, an ALS solicitor highlighted how awareness of a magistrate's attitudes influences their recommendations:

> Like with any situation, as a solicitor you're conscious of who your audience is when you're addressing them. Some magistrates are a lot more willing to use the YOA than others. But if it were that typical situation of a less serious offence with no criminal history, I would always suggest having the matter dealt with by the YOA. But, there are some magistrates who, even if the child does have a criminal history, they might think it's appropriate, and of course in that situation I'd be suggesting it. Then, there are some magistrates to whom I may not even suggest it because I know it's out of the question.
>
> (S1)

Findings in Chapter 5 showed that some local court magistrates in regional communities—those who are non-specialists in youth court—are often unaware 'off the top of their heads'—of all matters eligible for referral under the Act. Additionally, some magistrates expect recommendations regarding the YOA to come from counsel. However, as highlighted by the solicitor's testimony, such suggestions are sometimes withheld due to perceptions that certain magistrates are unwilling to use the YOA. Thus, negative attitudes or perceived negative attitudes towards diversion can clearly undermine opportunities for young people.

Youth justice personnel interviewed believed that some of the less favourable attitudes held by local court magistrates towards diversionary alternatives could be mitigated through further education and training. However, this approach was also acknowledged as 'very difficult' (AM2). The significance of education and training in broadening the application of the YOA and increasing referrals to YJC has been emphasised by Chan et al. (2003) and further supported by the Youth Justice Coalition in their 2011 submission to the Department of Attorney General Justice on the Review of the YOA and *Children (Criminal Proceedings) Act 1987*. Drawing from Hart's concept of 'open texture' (Hart, 1961), Chan et al. (2003) argue that legislative rules require interpretation for application, necessitating an informed audience familiar with both the context and objectives of such legislation. Consequently, promotion and education are critical to minimising disparities in law application.

Observations from JJ assistant managers regarding the benefits of additional training align with similar views expressed by the YLOs, as discussed in Chapter 4. Concerns about whether insufficient training might limit diversion opportunities—especially for non-specialist magistrates in rural areas—were also raised by the magistracy in this study (see Chapter 5).

Furthermore, a JJ assistant manager who primarily interacts with local court magistrates observed that these officials were generally more receptive to discussions during the early years following the Act's implementation. However, she noted a shift and claimed:

> I work with local magistrates, and there are some magistrates across the state who just don't believe in it [YOA] and won't refer to YJC. And, they're not really interested in having [training]... they don't think there's anything to learn about it. But it does depend on the magistrate.
>
> (AM5)

It could be argued that local court magistrates have lost interest because the act has not received sufficient support to reach its full potential. Alternatively, as discussed in Chapter 5, this may stem from an overall lack of training, particularly for non-specialist magistrates. Youth justice personnel noted occasional invitations for JJ to address magistrate forums once or twice a year. However, no official diversion training for magistrates exists, and these forums are primarily attended by specialist children's court magistrates, leaving local court magistrates—the group most in need of such information—without access.

Aside from the lack of official training, JJ assistant managers highlighted the value of informal discussion with courts regarding diversion. Depending on their relationship with the court, they noted opportunities for dialogue about conferencing between magistrates and JJ personnel, namely the assistant managers or their administrative assistant. Youth justice personnel reported that such conversations did not occur uniformly across different areas since it is not an official management practice. Nevertheless, some assistant managers have successfully built rapport with courts, allowing them to gain insights into why certain magistrates may under-utilise diversion.

Youth justice personnel indicated that some magistrates, particularly in 'small country communities' (AM4), felt their role was to support police decisions. For instance, one assistant manager interviewed noted:

> I've also had magistrates who've said that they won't refer to conference because the police obviously think that it should go to court, [and have told

me]: 'If the police wanted to refer, they would have referred [to YJC] and so they should. Because the police have decided [to] send it to court, well [paused], then, it's obviously more serious'.

(AM4)

Building on this theme, some youth justice personnel observed that magistrates' decisions are occasionally influenced by efforts to appease communities that hold more punitive attitudes. An assistant manager illustrated:

> Once a magistrate had referred a case to YJC for a young person riding their bike on the footpath, without a helmet…I got in touch with the magistrate and I said: 'Look, with respect, this isn't something that we would deal with by way of YJC because there's no victim and it's not very serious'... The young person could have been in trouble before, I think that they've been, it wasn't the first time they'd been to court. And the magistrate said to me: 'Look, you know, this is a small community and people take this kind of thing really seriously, so I referred it to a conference, for a conference'. So, we did the conference because the magistrate said so.
>
> (AM4)

These accounts corroborate the findings presented in Chapter 5 from the magistracy interviews, which indicated that community expectations influence judicial decision-making.

A focus on occupational cultures, training and education issues, and interagency relations has highlighted several areas requiring attention to enhance the implementation of diversion, particularly in increasing referral numbers. The long-term failure to apply the YOA to its full potential appears attributable partly to insufficient investment in necessary resources, including comprehensive training across all involved agencies and enhanced interagency cooperation. Youth justice personnel interviews revealed additional implementation barriers during their discussion of challenges faced in the implementation process.

Barriers to implementation

This section examines key impediments to the effective implementation of diversion under the Act, highlighting the complexities encountered by decision-makers. Central issues include determining appropriate levels of intervention, legislative ambiguity, the requirement for admissions of guilt, and specific challenges related to First Nations young people. Similar concerns were also raised during interviews with the magistracy and the NSW Police Force, as discussed in Chapters 4 and 5.

PAS does not solve the 'admission of guilt problem'

> When you say to a young Aboriginal boy who has heard his parents, his uncles, his aunties all saying: 'Don't trust the white fellas, don't trust the

> white fellas, they're a bunch of ass holes, they're going to get ya'. You know you're behind the eight-ball already… you know? They're all out to 'punish ya'.
>
> Kid is in the police station after having committed several offences, they're sitting there in the 'police station', and the police say: 'Do you admit to the offences?'…
>
> The kid: 'No. Wasn't me'.
>
> Any chance of a conference gone out the window.
>
> (AM2)

The YOA requires an admission of guilt for eligibility for a caution or YJC (see YOA, s. 19(b), s. 36(b)). As discussed in Chapters 4 and 5, both NSW Police and magistrates noted that children cannot be referred because they do not admit guilt. There are no records kept on this; nonetheless, the lack of admission equals no referral.

As discussed in Chapter 4, this issue has long been recognised as a fundamental barrier to diversion since the Act's inception. To address this, the Protected Admission Scheme (PAS) was introduced (see Chapter 4), yet there are concerns regarding its appropriateness. The PAS presents significant challenges in relation to due process and the extent to which it effectively protects the rights and interests of young people (Pearce, 2021). An assistant manager observed:

> The idea is that a young person can admit the offence and gain the advantage of being referred to a conference, but not have that admission held against them: How do you explain that to a young person? How do you explain that to a 14-year-old, at 2 o'clock in the morning when they're being charged for break and enter; their mates all done a runner on them; they're the only one that's got picked up? They've got a very tired and very angry father sitting there, who is continually saying to them: 'What the hell were you doing? You told us …' And then the father is saying to the police officer: 'We thought he was at a mate's place; I don't know what's got into him, we can't handle him anymore. He's being disrespectful' blah, blah, blah, blah, blah.
>
> So, as a young person you're sitting there being hammered by absolutely everyone and then the police say to you: 'If you admit the offences, you won't really be admitting them'. That, for a young person, that's not going to wash.
>
> (AM2)

PAS has been designed to operate in cases where a young person has declined to make an admission, but a court alternative under the YOA is appropriate. It is understood that by signing the PAS, the young offender can maintain their right to silence in relation to admissions that could be used as evidence in court. However, this assumes an unrealistic level of autonomy in decision-making by youths, detached from real-world pressures and complexities.

According to the ALS Solicitor, the PAS is a hard scheme to explain to minors, particularly when a quick look at the form shows that this is a record of admission to offences for them to sign. The policy has been developed without sufficient consideration of the lived experiences of young offenders. Additionally, S1 noted that while the PAS prevents police from making enquiries about unlisted offences on the form, it does not prevent self-incrimination through disclosure, nor does it eliminate the possibility of new investigations based on such disclosures. Thus, 'PAS is not necessarily something designed with the best interest of the young person in mind' (S1).

As documented in Chapter 4, YLOs frequently observed that Legal Aid commonly advises young people, while in police custody, not to admit to the offence. This observation is reinforced by youth justice personnel:

> The first thing they'll do is, they'll be offered their phone call to the Legal Aid or the Aboriginal Legal Aid hotline, and the hotline's first piece of advice has always been, and to this day is: 'Don't say anything'.
>
> Because remember, the Aboriginal Legal Aid's first responsibility is to protect the person, their client, regardless of their age.
>
> (AM2)

According to the ALS solicitor interviewed, while the advice to 'say nothing' is often given, it is not universally applied. Nonetheless, she acknowledged that this is a likely scenario for several reasons. Firstly, when the call comes through the 24-hour hotline, the ALS solicitor usually does not get to speak directly with the YLO but 'rather with the custody manager or the officer in charge at the station' (S1). This means that although the option to divert may exist and suggestions may be made, there is no certainty that they will be pursued. S1 further explained:

> The young person is under arrest at the police station, so they're not free to leave. And the custody manager is there but hasn't been able to confirm that they're eligible to be dealt with under the YOA. Normally, in that situation before giving advice to the young person I would ask the police to find out and to make a decision – are they dealing with them under the YOA? Or are they going to be charged?
>
> Because then, obviously, it drastically changes the nature of the advice that we give to the young person. So, I'll make them make the call first and commit before I give the young person advice. Because, first of all, if I'm giving a child advice about two different possibilities it's going to be overwhelmingly confusing; it's already a confusing process for them, they don't need more information than it is necessary. So, if I can make the police go and find out, ring me back and then answer me: 'Are you going to offer him diversion? Or are you going to charge him?' And then, I will give [the young person] advice.

Moreover, according to the ALS Solicitor, the problem is that there are no guarantees regarding what a young person might disclose during police questioning.

The ALS solicitor elaborates that often, details about the incident remain unclear because their conversation with the young person occurs while the police officer listens in. This setup restricts thorough discussions with the young person about their involvement:

> Normally I just say to them: 'If you agree with what the police say you did, then it's fine to talk to them about it'. But that can be problematic because you can get a kid who then admits to other things in the process of the interview. (S1)

The ALS solicitor further explains that advising on pursuing a YJC or caution does not always align with the young person's best interests. For instance:

> I would also explain to them, if it's relevant – *doli incapax*. If they are under 14, I explain to them that they do have the opportunity, if they wish, to elect to go to court because they may be able to defend the charge based on the *doli incapax*; rather than having them, you know, take the option of the caution or the conference. Another thing we need to give advice to young people on is the consequences of having a caution or a conference and that it is recorded on the police system, that they only get a certain number of them, that they're not something that you can get over and over. And, also that it shows up on a Working with Children check; so if, for example, when they get older they want to work in childcare or be a police officer or something that involves working with kids and they go through that process, their employer may be notified about the fact that they were cautioned or conferenced as a juvenile. (S1)

These remarks highlight the necessity of in-person legal advice due to the complexities inherent in remote consultations. As noted by the ALS Solicitor: 'you might be 800 kms away from what's happening. So, they can say one thing to us on the phone…hang up and then do something entirely different' (S1). The difficulties of providing legal advice remotely, especially to young children, have been well-documented (see Chan et al., 2003; O'Sullivan, 2003), with the additional challenge now of having to explain the PAS to young people.

According to the youth justice personnel interviewed, PAS is, in most cases, not utilised by NSW police. While no official records are available to confirm this, the assistant managers noted that such paperwork would typically be included in youth justice case files, making its absence notable: 'I've never seen one. And everything, every conference in the Hunter would come through this office, and I've never yet seen a Protected Admissions form [included in the documentation]' (AM2).

While AM1 noted: 'in all my meetings with YLOs every single one has said: "we have never used this in our station; we have never used PAS".'

Interviews with YLOs discussed in Chapter 4 revealed their unwillingness to acknowledge their under-utilisation of PAS. However, evidence of strong resistance to PAS and reluctance to employ it was apparent throughout their responses.

Youth justice personnel interviews confirm that police largely do not use PAS. Thus, PAS—designed to address the 'non-admission' issue that undermines diversion practices—is not being implemented as intended. Consequently, the YOA's requirement for admissions of guilt continues to impede diversion.

Legislative ambiguity and intervention decision-making

> You just never know when something is going to change for a young person, and you never know how they're going to react to a situation. But…wrongly, people think: 'They've had two conferences, it hasn't worked'.
>
> So, bloody hell, they're on their next line-up to, they need bonds, they need this and that.
>
> (AM1)

As previously noted, under the YOA, a young person can receive a maximum of three cautions upon repeat offending. However, the legislation does not impose a limit on the number of YJC referrals a young person may receive. It does, however, prescribe that the number of times the young person has been dealt with under the YOA should be taken into account. This results in a high degree of variability in diversion-related decision-making.

Youth justice personnel expressed frustration over legislative ambiguities that lead to misinterpretations. From the perspective of some, the absence of a cap on YJC referrals is intentional, allowing flexibility to be able to rely on this option as many times as needed to keep court as a 'last resort': 'Maybe at 13 they were too immature to get it and maybe at 17 they're at a good place in their life to actually have a conference, you know, after having two failed ones' (AM1). However, this perspective varies among decision-makers, resulting in inconsistent outcomes based on individual practitioner perspectives.

For instance, one assistant manager quoted YLOs as saying: 'you've had your three cautions, you've had your two conferences, you're to the big house now. You're going to court' (AM1). Disagreements about referral limits also exist within JJ. AM1 recalled a contentious meeting where an area manager argued against further conferencing after two attempts:

> One of the area managers was saying: 'Once our kids have had two conferences, we don't have them for conferencing after that'.
>
> This was controversial with some executive staff saying: 'Well, that's not right, you know, there is no limit on it'.
>
> And he was saying: 'Bad luck, I don't think they should be conferenced after two'.

The legislation's lack of specificity regarding the number of allowable YJC referrals becomes problematic for two reasons. Firstly, as illustrated above, there is a possibility that some police officers or magistrates may be less inclined than others to offer further YJC referrals to a young person with a history of previous participation. This, in turn, undermines diversion in an *inequitable* manner, as the alternative is chosen based on personal opinions that vary across the state. Secondly, the absence of a specified maximum number for YJCs leads decision-makers to impose arbitrary limits on what they consider an appropriate number. This undermines the purpose of the Act. While the legislation clearly sets a maximum of three cautions, it does not specify a limit for YCJ referrals. Therefore, it appears illogical to assume that a fixed number should guide such decisions. Nevertheless, interviews with all participants—police, magistrates and youth justice personnel—indicate that most youth justice actors have informally decided that two YJC referrals is the optimal limit. As a result, most young people are rarely given the opportunity for more than two YJC referrals. Some viewed this positively; for example, AM4 noted:

> The majority of young people would not have more than two conferences, if known to the police for several years perhaps three, but this is rare. [Consequently], they [the young people] don't view conferencing as a revolving door.

The implication here is that limiting the number of YJC referrals signals to young people that reoffending will result in more serious consequences. This reflects a tendency among some youth justice personnel to adopt a punitive approach. Such approaches can also lead to decisions to divert young people to a YJC even when they have no prior criminal history—situations in which others in gatekeeping roles might consider a caution more appropriate. One assistant manager provided an example of a 'break and enter' at a school where items were taken and some mess was left behind, leading police to generate a YJC referral. Reflecting on this case, AM4 observed:

> The YOA legislates for the less restrictive sanction in all cases…So, I would say that in that instance, yes, it is kind of serious that a young person would break into a building and make a mess but if you compare that to, say, if they broke into somebody's house and made a mess; it's less serious. There was no violence caused and let's say the clean-up for the school, you know it's not very good for the school to have to clean up any mess or whatever but it's less onerous for a school to clean up something like that than what it would be to an individual person. So, I would say that, that criteria [harm to the victim] would not be strongly met either…or then if a young person has no criminal history, I would say said that criteria hasn't been met either. So out of those four criteria, only one, being the seriousness, has been met… So, I would say to the police that quite possibly the young person should be issued a caution. And if they did something similar again, then we could certainly … look seriously about accepting a YJC.
>
> (AM4)

Other youth justice personnel cited similar examples, claiming that the ambiguity of the legislation enables criminal justice actors in this area to interpret and apply the YOA in ways that align with their own agendas.

'Everyone is equal under the law': the reality of discretionary bias in diversion

The YOA allows for broad discretionary decision-making by criminal justice actors, which can lead to varied outcomes even in similar cases. Some youth justice personnel interviewed believed that certain actors exploit this discretion to advance specific agendas. For instance, AM4 highlighted a typical scenario—more common in smaller rural communities than in densely populated cities—explaining that, 'in a smaller LAC where, perhaps, the populations are less, and the community expectations are higher,' police may choose to focus on one of the five decision-making criteria from the Act over others to justify an outcome that aligns with a 'tough on crime' community stance. As a result, a young person who might be eligible for a caution could instead receive a YJC diversion, or someone eligible for a YJC might end up being charged and sent to court. This observation indicates that diversionary opportunities for rural youth may be constrained by heightened community expectations for punitive responses. This finding corroborates the analysis presented in Chapter 5.

Additionally, youth justice personnel highlighted that First Nations young people are disproportionately affected by these practices compared to non-Indigenous populations. Several interviewees observed a 'massive difference' (AM2) in the treatment of First Nations juveniles between urban and rural communities. AM 2 explained:

> This is because in the city, they are treated as children across the board; so, there's a much more level playing field. And the Aboriginal communities in these areas [city] are less active, certainly less noticeable; whereas they are very militant in the country because First Nations young people are more visible.

First Nations communities' visibility makes them vulnerable to 'moral panics' (Cunneen, 1987, 2008; White, 2009), which typically precipitate calls for punitive criminal justice responses to perceived threats to social order. M2 shared her understanding of the issue:

> Those [rural] Aboriginal communities are more visible. There are more issues related to their behaviour. So, magistrates are reacting to community opinion; and if community opinion is poor, their decision-making process will be a reflection of that.

Youth justice personnel identified a perceived overall need for greater cultural awareness and sensitivity among magistrates, police and JJ staff. Interviewees noted that all new employees participate in a two-day 'cultural respect training' as part of the introductory JJ programme. One assistant manager, who identified himself as being of First Nations descent, remarked:

> Knowledge around my culture is limited. Therefore, the ability to influence people's decision-making is also limited. Unfortunately, the same thing happens with the magistrates. I can honestly say in the last 18 months, no magistrate in NSW has received cultural awareness training from JJ.
>
> (AM2)

Indeed, cultural awareness training would benefit all actors in the criminal justice system. Such training should be framed around what First Nations youth have internalised about themselves due to the broader colonial system (see Fischer, 2010 for the effects of internalised racism and the self-fulfilling prophecy phenomenon, and Gorringe et al., 2011, on deficit language echoed in Aboriginal people's descriptions of themselves and lateral violence as a consequence of the internalised negative perceptions of Aboriginality).

As argued throughout this book, the over-representation of First Nations young people (aged 10–17 years) in the criminal justice system represents one of Australia's most pressing social injustices. Data from 2022–2023 reveal that, while First Nations youth constitute only 5.8% of the Australian youth population aged 10 to 17 years, they accounted for 63% of those in detention on an average day nationally (AIHW, 2024). In NSW during the same period, First Nations young people aged 10–17 years represented 65% of the youth in custody on an average day, despite comprising only 7.5% of the state's youth population (AIHW, 2024). Historically, First Nations young people have not been afforded the same opportunities for diversion as their non-Aboriginal counterparts (see Allard et al., 2010; Ringland & Smith, 2013).

Data obtained from BOCSAR (File Reference kf25-24637)[3] provided in Table 6.3 compares POI aged 10 to 17 years proceeded against via a caution, YJC and court by NSW Police by Indigenous status between 2010 and 2017. These data illustrate that First Nations young people are diverted at a lower rate than their non-Indigenous

Table 6.3 Number of persons of interest (POIs) aged 10–17 years proceeded against via a caution, YJC and to court by NSW Police by Indigenous status in NSW between 2010 and 2017.

Year	*2010*	*2011*	*2012*	*2013*	*2014*	*2015*	*2016*	*2017*
Proceeded against by way of YJC								
Aboriginal	236	204	200	253	240	281	157	190
Non-Aboriginal	665	700	555	532	403	406	362	419
Unknown	1	1	0	0	0	2	0	4
Proceeded against by way of a caution								
Aboriginal	2,058	1,773	1,639	1,630	1,630	1,725	1,598	1,775
Non-Aboriginal	8,679	7,955	6,714	5,641	5,247	5,400	5,124	5,438
Unknown	26	18	26	27	27	24	60	115
Proceeded against to court								
Aboriginal	4,421	4,072	4,041	4,188	4,291	4,037	4,423	4,258
Non-Aboriginal	8,405	7,377	7,221	6,098	6,556	5,899	6,210	5,839
Unknown	31	39	35	32	27	25	32	43

Source: BOCSAR (File Reference kf25-24637) live dataset.

counterparts, with little change over time in the likelihood of diversion for these groups. In 2017—two years after the interviews for the study—68.4% of First Nations young people who became POIs to the NSW Police Force were proceeded to court, 28.5% received a caution, and 3% were referred to a YJC. In contrast, during the same period, 49% of non-Indigenous youth were proceeded to court, 46% received cautions and 3.5% were referred to a YJC.

The pattern of First Nations young people being under-represented in diversionary alternatives continues in the most recent data. Table 6.4 illustrates the processing of POI by police through cautions, YJC and court proceedings from 2018 to 2024. These data, obtained from BOCSAR (File Reference kf25-24637)[3], indicate that in 2024, 70.4% of First Nations young people who became POIs were proceeded against in court rather than diverted. This percentage represents the highest rate of court proceedings for First Nations youth since 2000.

Interviewee AM2, who identifies as being of First Nations descent, shared insights from his long-term career within JJ, working with the NSW Police Force and the courts on matters related to the YOA. He maintained opportunities to reduce First Nations youth engagement with the criminal justice system will remain constrained by flawed decision-making as long as 'cultural ignorance prevails.' This participant was unique amongst interviewees in both his identification as First Nations and his willingness to acknowledge systemic bias. As established in preceding chapters, the extent to which Indigeneity affects diversion opportunities constituted a taboo subject (during the interviews), with both magistrates and NSW

Table 6.4 Number of persons of interest (POIs) aged 10–17 years proceeded against via a caution, YJC and to court by NSW Police by Indigenous status in NSW between 2018 and 2024.

Year	*2018*	*2019*	*2020*	*2021*	*2022*	*2023*	*2024*
Proceeded against by way of YJC							
Aboriginal	300	289	332	403	369	495	507
Non-Aboriginal	432	502	426	356	278	444	418
Unknown	2	1	0	5	2	2	3
Proceeded against by way of a caution							
Aboriginal	1,765	1,838	1,769	2,016	2,415	2,467	2,201
Non-Aboriginal	5,134	5,147	4,796	4,572	4,413	4,549	4,125
Unknown	78	135	134	162	74	41	34
Proceeded against to court							
Aboriginal	4,258	4,097	4,007	4,362	5,840	6,330	6,453
Non-Aboriginal	5,839	5,751	5,618	4,906	4,443	4,669	4,878
Unknown	43	37	55	47	44	68	120

Source: BOCSAR (File Reference kf25-24637) live dataset.

Police Force personnel invoking the principle that *'everyone is equal under the law'* while maintaining that Indigenous status bears no relevance. This egalitarian rhetoric reflects a deeply concerning disregard for the structural inequalities faced by First Nations youth, reveals a troubling lack of engagement with the realities of institutional racism, and is fundamentally predicated upon white colonialist assumptions.

Resource constraints and perceptions of YJC outcome plans

Beyond the previously examined factors, youth justice personnel observed that resource constraints affecting 'outcome plans' formulation generated both barriers to successful diversion and hesitancy among *gatekeepers* to initiate diversionary pathways. The scope and adequacy of outcome plans in YJCs have emerged as a judicial concern for certain magistrates (see Chapter 5). Youth justice personnel reported that police-initiated referrals to YJC permit JJ to proceed autonomously without seeking approval for proposed outcome plans. Conversely, court-initiated referrals necessitate judicial endorsement of the proposed outcome plan. Interviewed participants noted that this procedural requirement has, at times, led to magistrates rejecting outcome plans perceived as lacking sufficient substance. JJ personnel find this frustrating, asserting that plans are complex and thoroughly considered—often constrained by available resources but crafted to address core issues positively for the young person. One respondent elaborated:

> For example, we had a young person who stole a car and damaged it. The outcome plan involved him participating in a program where they fix up cars; so, he did some repairs on the car. He was also asked to do a snorkelling course. And then, some clean-up along the littoral zone of the beach; so, it was a bit of community work, a bit of skills, and something for the victim.
>
> (AM5)

This example illustrates the proactive approach to outcome plan development that characterises practice when resources permit. However, the insufficiency and uneven distribution of resources within government and community services systematically limit the provision of comprehensive outcome plan alternatives. Youth justice personnel reported that these resource constraints have been exacerbated in recent years by organisational shifts towards risk assessment methodologies:

> These days everything is risk assessed out; we do very little voluntary community work, just simply because you can't let the young person go and do it on their own, they've got to be supervised. Hardly anyone has resources that can give one-on-one supervision to a young person. So, the kind of things they might do is, they might go to a youth centre and, maybe the youth centre is having a clean-up; they might help hand out brochures for a community event. We can't do barbecues anymore because it's *too dangerous* … They

> can't really do lawn mowing anymore because you have to make sure the lawnmower is safe to use, that it has been serviced, that they [young people] have the proper clothing– like boots and goggles and earmuffs. So, it's harder and harder because we're such a risk averse society.
>
> (AM3)

The foregoing accounts illuminate a systemic preoccupation with risk assessment and management. Contemporary anxieties regarding pervasive risks—characteristic of Beck's (1992) 'risk society' (see Chapter 3)—have systematically narrowed the repertoire of options available for outcome plan development. Health and safety imperatives governing young people's participation have become primary determinants of permissible activities. Nevertheless, the critical source of frustration among JJ managers relates to judicial rejection of YJC outcomes plans. While JJ personnel acknowledge that such rejections may be relatively uncommon, the phenomenon of magistrates withholding approval constitutes a persistent source of professional dissatisfaction.

All youth justice personnel interviewed expressed frustration regarding the prevailing perception among YLOs and magistrates that outcome plans are 'soft'—too lenient or simplistic—especially when reduced to mere 'letters of apology.' This viewpoint corresponds with judicial and police perspectives examined in preceding chapters, reflecting entrenched institutional cultures that have traditionally emphasised punitive intervention methodologies (see Chapter 2). Furthermore, such attitudes embody the punitive framework that pervades youth justice administration. Rather than representing a coherent, monolithic ideology deliberately implemented throughout the system, this punitive approach operates as part of the underlying cultural context that, as demonstrated in previous chapters, shapes decisions that systematically *exclude* certain young people from diversionary opportunities.

Nevertheless, as discussed, resource factors—including availability, quality, geographical distribution and adequacy—fundamentally determine both the accessibility of diversionary pathways for young people and the substantive quality of alternative diversionary measures. Achieving the policy objectives articulated within the YOA requires strategic funding commitments to develop support services that can satisfy the expectations inherent in diversionary alternatives, particularly YJC outcome plans. This resource-contingent reality reinforces the magistrate and police perspectives discussed in previous chapters while reflecting the underlying punitive orientation that shapes youth justice administrative practices.

Conclusion

This chapter's findings substantiate the conclusions drawn in the two preceding chapters. Despite widespread practitioner support for the YOA, interviews with youth justice personnel confirm persistent institutional resistance among police personnel and some magistrates. The successful implementation of diversion within each LAC is fundamentally contingent upon senior management advocacy for diversionary alternatives. Additionally, success depends further on

YLOs' philosophical alignment with, and commitment to, the YOA principles. The evidence indicates significant disparities in YLO engagement levels. Participants further suggested that formal, systematic training initiatives are necessary to further educate police and magistrates, as well as other stakeholders, on the importance of prioritising diversionary alternatives and enhancing procedural effectiveness.

Moreover, findings suggest that localised approaches to diversion management within JJ generate differential patterns of consultation with police and magistrates across localities. Consultation and information-sharing mechanisms have consistently been identified as effective informal training tools through which JJ can promote diversionary practices to courts and police. Yet, the research reveals substantial variation in the quality of inter-agency relationships between JJ and institutional stakeholders across LACs and court jurisdictions. Strategic internal deliberations aimed at strengthening these relationships are essential for optimising the implementation of diversion.

Court referrals to diversionary alternatives also appear to be influenced by geographical location. Interviews with youth justice personnel indicate that *specialist* Children's Court magistrates demonstrate significantly more favourable attitudes towards diversion compared to regional Local Court magistrates, who tend to adopt more restrictive approaches. The absence of exposure to the specialised training received by specialist magistrates of the Children's Court places Local Court magistrates at a disadvantage, often leaving them reliant on legal counsel for guidance regarding the YOA matters. Additionally, in small rural communities, local court magistrates are more likely to prioritise public or community confidence in the courts, which may further constrain access to diversion—particularly for First Nations youth, for whom the latest trends in diversion presented in this chapter reveal an increasingly adverse outlook.

The YOA requirement of an admission of guilt as a prerequisite for diversion continues to present systematic challenges that undermine diversionary objectives, with practitioners expressing concern about the restrictive nature of this provision. As established in preceding chapters, the PAS, introduced to address this issue, is not being utilised by NSW Police. Furthermore, the PAS has complicated the provision of legal advice to young people. Most critically, it has been highlighted that PAS may not constitute an effective solution to the admission requirement, as it still necessitates a signed admission of guilt, placing young offenders in a vulnerable position given their limited understanding of the scheme's implications.

Lastly, legislative ambiguity gives rise to varied interpretations of appropriate intervention levels among police, magistrates and JJ personnel, resulting in inconsistent treatment often shaped by individual discretion and personal beliefs. This variability enables institutions to advance their own operational preferences. A significant point of contention amongst practitioners is the lack of commitment by decision-makers to the legislated provision allowing an unlimited number of YJCs for young offenders. In practice, most actors have unilaterally imposed a limit of two referrals—a practice widely regarded by youth justice personnel as undermining the objectives and principles of the Act. Broader institutional and occupational cultures, along with the individuals operating within them, tend to favour punitive responses—shaped in part by prevailing social and political contexts. As a result, the Act, in its current form, fails to effectively fulfil its intended purpose. This disjunction is a key reason why diversionary efforts are failing, and the findings presented in this chapter—when triangulated with the interviews conducted with police and magistrates—corroborate these conclusions.

Notes

1 The data presented in Table 6.1 were compiled from the Department of Attorney General and Justice/Department of Juvenile Justice/Justice Juveniles Strategic Information System (a live database subject to ongoing modifications).
2 Data in Table 6.2 was adapted from NSW Government. (2024, July 6). *Youth Justice Conferencing*. https://www.nsw.gov.au/legal-and-justice/youth-justice/about/statistics/conferencing
3 The file is from a live dataset; consequently, all figures remain subject to modification. Please note: In January 2022, NSW Police implemented mandatory identification protocols requiring officers to enquire about Aboriginal status for all offenders. This procedural change has resulted in increases in both the absolute number and proportional representation of Aboriginal offenders recorded in official statistics. Within this dataset, records are classified as relating to an Aboriginal or Torres Strait Islander person when at least 20% of an individual's police reports indicate Aboriginal and/or Torres Strait Islander identity. Due to these methodological changes, Aboriginality data reported here are not comparable with data generated prior to 2023.

References

Aboriginal Legal Services (NSW/ACT Limited). (n.d.). *Custody notification service*. Aboriginal Legal Services (NSW/ACT Limited). Retrieved March 12, 2025 from https://www.alsnswact.org.au/our-work/custody-notification-service/

Allard, T., Stewart, A., Chrzanowski, A., Ogilvie, J., Birks, D. J., & Little, S. (2010). *Police diversion of young offenders and Indigenous over-representations* (Trends and Issues in Crime and Criminal Justice, No. 390). Australian Institute of Criminology.

Australian Institute of Health and Welfare. (2024). *Youth justice in Australia 2022–23*. https://www.aihw.gov.au/reports/youth-justice/youth-justice-in-australia-annual-report-2022-23

Australian Law Reform Commission (ALRC). (2017). *Incarceration rates of Aboriginal and Torres Strait Islander peoples* (Discussion Paper No. 84). https://www.alrc.gov.au/wp-content/uploads/2019/08/discussion_paper_84_compressed_cover2.pdf

Beck, U. (1992). *Risk society: Towards a new modernity*. Sage.

Becroft, A., & Norrie, S. (2015, May 1). *Out of court (and sometimes in) – Playing to win: Restorative practices and processes of the New Zealand Youth Justice System*. [Paper Presentation]. Journal Released at the Restorative Practices in Action: A Conference for School and Justice Practitioners, New York State Permanent Judicial Commission on Justice for Children. https://www.nycourts.gov/ip/justiceforchildren/PDF/RestorativePracticeConf/RP_Journal.pdf

Chan, J. (1997). *Changing police culture: Policing in a multicultural society*. Cambridge University Press.

Chan, J., Doran, S., Maloney, E., Pekovska, N., Bargen, J., Luke, G., & Clancey, G. (2003). *Reshaping juvenile justice: A study of the NSW Young Offenders Act 1997* [Final report to the Department of Juvenile Justice and Aboriginal Justice Advisory Council]. UNSW.

Chan, J. B. L. (2005). *Reshaping juvenile justice: The NSW Young Offenders Act 1997*. The Sydney Institute of Criminology.

Chen, S., Matruglio, T., Weatherburn, D., & Hua, J. (2005). The transition from juvenile to adult criminal careers. *Crime and Justice Bulletin, 86*, 1–12.

Children (Community Service Orders) Act 1987 (NSW). (1987). https://legislation.nsw.gov.au/view/html/inforce/current/act-1987-056

Children (Detention Centres) Act 1987 (NSW). (1987). https://legislation.nsw.gov.au/view/html/inforce/current/act-1987-057

Children (Interstate Transfer of Offenders) Act 1988 (NSW). (1988). https://legislation.nsw.gov.au/view/html/inforce/current/act-1988-074

Cunneen, C. (1987). Newspaper reporting of crime, law and order in North-West NSW. *Journal for Social Justice Studies, 2*, 14–32.

Cunneen, C. (2008). Understanding restorative justice through the lens of critical criminology. In T. Anthony & C. Cunneen (Eds.), *The critical criminology companion* (pp. 290–302). Hawkins Press.

Department of Attorney General and Justice (NSW). (2011). *Review of the Young Offenders Act 1997 and the Children (Criminal Proceedings) Act 1987: Consultation Paper*. NSW Government. https://dcj.nsw.gov.au/content/dam/dcj/dcj-website/documents/about-us/engage-with-us/public-consultations/unsorted/consultation_paper_-_yoa_and_ccpa_review.doc

Department of Justice (NSW). (2016). *Juvenile justice year in review 2015–16 annual report*. NSW Government. https://www.parliament.nsw.gov.au/tp/files/69964/DJAG%20Annual%20Report-2015-16.pdf

Fischer, M. (2010). A longitudinal examination of the role of stereotype threat and racial climate on college outcomes for minorities at elite institutions. *Social Psychology of Education, 13*(1), 19–40.

Gorringe, S., Ross, J., & Fforde, C. (2011). *'Will the real aborigine please stand up': Strategies for breaking the stereotypes and changing the conversation* (AIATSIS Research Discussion Paper no. 28). Australian Institute of Aboriginal and Torres Strait Islander Studies. https://aiatsis.gov.au/sites/default/files/research_pub/gorringe-ross-fforde-dp28-real-aborigines-stereotypes_0_2.pdf

Hart, H. L. A. (1961). *The Concept of Law*. Oxford University Press.

Kingshott, B. F., Bailey, K., & Wolfe, S. E. (2004). Police culture, ethics and entitlement theory. *Criminal Justice Studies: A Critical Journal of Crime, Law and Society, 17*(2), 187–202.

McAra, L., & McVie, S. (2007). Youth justice? The impact of system contact on patterns of desistance from offending. *European Journal of Criminology, 4*, 315–345.

McAra, L., & McVie, S. (2010). Youth crime and justice: Key messages from the Edinburgh study of youth transitions and crime. *Criminology and Criminal Justice, 10*(2), 179–209.

Mukherjee, S. K. (1983). *Youth and crime project part 1: Age and crime* (Archive). Australian Institute of Criminology.

New South Wales Government. (1991). *Government Gazette* (p. 9207). New South Wales Government Printing Office.

Noetic Solutions. (2010). *A strategic review of the New South Wales juvenile justice system: Report for the Minister for Juvenile Justice*. New South Wales Department of Human Services.

NSW Government. (2024, July 6). *Youth justice conferencing*. https://www.nsw.gov.au/legal-and-justice/youth-justice/about/statistics/conferencing

O'Driscoll, S. J. (2008). Youth Justice in New Zealand: A restorative justice approach to reduce youth offending. In Grace Lord (Ed.), *From UNAFEI: Annual Report for 2007 and Resource Material Series No. 75* (pp. 55–80). See NCJ-229038. https://www.unafei.or.jp/publications/pdf/RS_No75/No75_00All.pdf

O'Sullivan, T. (2003, 7 May 2003). *Provision of legal advice and the legal aid commission's youth hotline*. Paper presented to the Institute of Criminology.

Pearce, E. (2021). Why 'admission of guilt' is not working in youth diversionary schemes in NSW – Exploratory findings from interviews with police officers. *Current Issues in Criminal Justice*, *33*(3), 285–299.
Public Sector Employment and Management (Departmental Amalgamations) Order 2009 (NSW). (2011; cl 28).
Public Sector Employment and Management (Departments) Order 2011 *(NSW)*. (2011 No 184; cl. 4).
Reiner, R. (2010). *The politics of the police* (4 ed.). Oxford University Press.
Richards, K. (2011). *What makes juvenile offenders different from adult offenders?* (Trends and Issues in Crime and Criminal Justice, No. 409). Australian Institute of Criminology.
Richards, K., & Lee, M. (2013). Beyond the 'three dogmas of juvenile justice': A response to Weatherburn, McGrath and Bartels. *University of New South Wales Law Journal*, *36*(3), 839–862.
Ringland, C., & Smith, N. (2013). *Police use of court alternatives for young persons in NSW* (Contemporary Issues in Crime and Criminal Justice, no. 167). NSW Bureau of Crime Statistics and Research.
Schein, E. (2010). *Organizational culture and leadership* (4 ed.). Jossey-Bass.
Weatherburn, D., McGrath, A., & Bartels, L. (2012). Three dogmas of juvenile justice. *University of New South Wales Journal*, *35*(3), 781–809.
White, R. (2009). Ethnic diversity and differential policing in Australia: The Good, the Bad and the Ugly. *Journal of International Migration and Integration*, *10*(4), 359–375.
Young Offenders Act 1997 (NSW).

7 Conclusion

Overcoming the Constraints to Youth Diversion

The arrest, detention or imprisonment of a child shall be in conformity with the law and shall be used only as a measure of last resort and for the shortest appropriate period of time.

—United Nations Convention on the Rights of the Child, Article 37(b)

Despite this clear international standard, the routine use of detention for children remains a persistent issue in many jurisdictions. In New South Wales (NSW), Australia, the *Young Offenders Act 1997* (YOA) was introduced to embed the principle of detention as a last resort into youth justice practice. Yet, more than two decades later, diversion remains under-utilised, and detention continues to be imposed in circumstances that contradict both the spirit and the letter of the law.

This book has provided insight into the minutiae of the workings of pre-court diversion in the youth justice system through an examination of an Australian case study on discretionary decision-making processes in youth diversion under the YOA. In doing so, it focused on the institutional and individual actors directly involved in the application of the Act to explain the wide failure to divert in NSW. Using a mix of quantitative and qualitative data—but relying heavily on qualitative material from in-depth interviews with experienced NSW police, magistrates and youth justice personnel—the study has analysed the decision-making processes surrounding diversion, presenting rival perspectives on the under-utilisation of youth diversion under the YOA.

The book addressed one overarching question: why has there been a failure to refer young people to diversion in NSW? The implementation of diversionary practices away from court under the YOA rests heavily on the various criminal justice actors that trade in youth justice, namely the NSW Police Force and the Children's Court magistrates. Therefore, the study first sought to explore how these institutional and individual actors perform a gatekeeping function to diversionary practices. It examined their attitudes and understandings of diversion within the frameworks of their roles in institutions such as the police, the courts and juvenile justice personnel. Second, the study moved from exploring individual attitudes—which at times both reproduced and departed from prevailing institutional cultures—to identifying broader political and policy constraints and opportunities

DOI: 10.4324/9781003470366-7

surrounding the pursuit of existing forms of youth diversion. This research was particularly concerned with understanding the factors that have limited the YOA's implementation to its full potential. Lastly, the study sought to utilise the information gathered from participants and supporting research to propose what the researcher believes are the necessary reforms to juvenile justice in order to address the failure to refer young people to diversion in NSW.

The research adopted a critical perspective to explore the nuances and inherent contradictions of decision-making by examining the inner workings of the system, with a focus on the divided sectors of state policing, the magistracy and the juvenile justice bureaucracy. Aspects of social control, the dichotomy between punitivism and welfarism, risk management theories, police culture(s) and other occupational/professional cultures were integrated to critically analyse the findings. In doing so, the study has aimed to enrich current understandings of youth justice by examining the array and intersection of factors influencing youth justice decision-making and the broader law and order landscape in NSW.

This book argues that the persistent failure to divert young people from court demonstrates that the diversion system in NSW has failed to achieve the Act's core objectives of making court and detention last resorts. The study identified a number of co-existing factors that, alone or in combination, undermine diversionary decision-making under the YOA. These factors can be grouped into two broad categories: internal challenges and external/structural factors. The individual/institutional and structural practices are inseparable in shaping decision-making. While individual decision-makers can influence diversionary practices, they do so within the constraints of institutional and broader socio-political frameworks.

Internal challenges refer to those that emerge from within the institutions. These include organisational and bureaucratic structures, occupational status or rank, specialisation (e.g., specialist Children's Court magistrates versus non-specialists, or Youth Liaison Officers (YLOs) versus general duties police), and a lack of internal training or education on the YOA, as well as the norms and micro-politics of institutionalised cultures within those institutions. Co-existing with these are external challenges; namely, the broader political law and order issues such as legislative constraints and public attitudes. The findings indicate that all diversionary decision-making occurs within the framework of rules/guidance of the policy, that is, the YOA. However, the negotiated order of such legislative rules/guidance is fluid and continually shaped in relation to these internal and external pressures, which limit when and how diversion is possible.

Overall, the findings suggest that individuals in positions to make decisions regarding whether to divert young people away from the system have internalised the cultures, politics and institutional practices of their respective organisations, and therefore reproduce them. While they always have a choice to divert and are individually responsible in part, they are not wholly responsible because they are compelled to do things the way they are always done within their organisations and in line with broader political moods. This is evident in magistrates' desire to both balance the factors presented to them in individual youth offender cases and maintain public confidence in the courts within a particular social context. Similarly, police officers make decisions based on their expertise, attitudes and interpretation of the legislation while responding to a combination of institutional/occupational, social and political forces. Thus, diversionary decisions under the YOA are made in micro worlds situated within a macro social/political context. Most of the time, this undermines the utilisation of youth diversion under the YOA.

There is a failure to divert under the YOA in NSW. The remainder of this chapter presents the reasons for this failure. Police, magistrates and juvenile justice personnel were examined through the lens of how their micro-institutional worlds (organisational structures, cultures and politics) interact with broader cultural, social and political contexts—contexts that vary geographically within NSW—to significantly influence individual decision-making. The implications of those decisions for youth and society are considered. The chapter concludes by proposing an alternative to the diversionary framework for NSW to address the limitations of the current system. Finally, should such an alternative not be embraced, the chapter outlines factors that ought to be addressed and practice changes needed to increase diversionary referrals under the YOA.

The failure to divert

In 1997, the YOA introduced a hierarchical diversionary response to juvenile offending, aiming to keep children and young people out of the criminal justice system by reducing the number of youths proceeding to court and, ultimately, to detention. Warnings, cautions and YJCs are the diversionary options available under the framework of the Act. This study argues that youth diversion is being under-utilised and that the current diversionary system in NSW is failing due to a range of factors related to individual decision-making within specific institutional cultures and broader political contexts. Most significantly, it contends that youth diversion has not been realised in practice. The most recent statistics show that the percentage of children proceeding to court is as high as it has ever been since the Act was introduced.

Certain youth populations bear the brunt of the failures in youth diversion. The over-representation of Aboriginal and Torres Strait Islander young people (aged 10–17) in the criminal justice system—a consequence of colonisation's ongoing impacts, systemic racism, and continuing dispossession experienced by First Nations communities—represents one of Australia's most significant social injustices and a profound failure of the justice system. At the national level, during the period of 2022–2023, First Nations youth comprised only 5.8% of the Australian population aged 10–17 years yet accounted for 63% of those in detention on an average day (AIHW, 2024). In NSW during the same period, First Nations young people aged 10–17 years represented 65% of the youth in custody on an average day, despite comprising only 7.5% of the state's youth population (AIHW, 2024).

Historically, First Nations young people have not been afforded the same opportunities for diversion as their non-Aboriginal counterparts (Allard et al., 2010; Ringland & Smith, 2013). Data from this study[1] (Chapter 6) show that in 2024, 70.4% of First Nations young people who became persons of interest (POIs) to

NSW Police were proceeded against in court, 24% were dealt with by way of caution, and 5.5% through a JYC.[2] In contrast, among non-Indigenous young people, 51.7% were proceeded to court, 43% were cautioned, and 4.4% were diverted to YJC. These figures not only evidenced the systemic failure of diversion in NSW but also demonstrated the disproportionate impact of these failures on First Nations young people—evidence of systemic racism within the NSW diversion framework.

It has now been over twenty years since the introduction of the YOA and the NSW criminal justice system's commitment to the use of detention as 'a last resort'—a principle also enshrined in Article 37(b) of the UNCRC. The Act has been subject to several reviews over the past two decades regarding its implementation. However, this book argues that the current situation reflects long-term criminal justice reticence to fully implement the YOA and uphold the principle that detention should be 'a last resort' for young people. This is particularly evident for First Nations young people.

Drawing the threads together

Exploring decision-making processes in this study unveiled that the ambiguity of the legislation, combined with the broad discretion afforded to gatekeepers, results in varied interpretations regarding the appropriate level of intervention among police, magistrates and JJ personnel.

This book argues that key factors informing the interpretative lens of each individual decision-maker include welfare/justice pragmatism (often shaped by culturally institutionalised practices and/or community expectations), insufficient training or education on the Act, and prevailing attitudes toward diversion. In particular, a strong emphasis on recidivism and risk minimisation often leads to the abandonment of diversionary principles in favour of risk management strategies and a focus on community protection.

NSW police as decision-makers

The findings on the role of the NSW Police Force in the decision-making process regarding the diversion of young people under the YOA indicate that the success of diversion implementation in each Local Area of Command (LAC) extends beyond the control of YLOs. It hinges on the support for diversionary alternatives from all levels of the organisation—from management to arresting and general duties officers.

The findings reveal the existence of power conflicts and disparities in knowledge and attitudes toward diversion under the YOA among different groups within the NSW Police Force. These issues are largely attributed to a lack of training and education, as well as time constraints. It was noted that Senior Youth Officers (SYOs), YLOs, and general duties officers had varying levels of access to training on the Act, with general duties officers receiving the least. Although SYOs and YLOs are legislatively empowered to implement and administer the Act, the findings show that the final decision often rests with general duties officers. Discussions around these issues revealed that the high level of discretion allowed under the Act—particularly in applying the criteria for diversion—results in significant variation in its application. Decision-making is influenced by the level of knowledge and attitudes toward the YOA, potentially leading to *unequal* outcomes.

While discretion is necessary—since no legislation can account for every individual circumstance—in this context, it often becomes a mechanism for reproducing the norms and cultural tendencies of organisational cultures that lean toward conservative law enforcement and punitive practices. The findings illustrate that punitive discourses frequently guide arbitrary interpretations of the legislation, with the seriousness of the offence and the history of the offender often outweighing the eligibility criteria for diversion. Similarly, occupational culture(s)—such as the tendency to favour interventionist approaches—combined with punitive discourses, guide arbitrary decisions among decision-makers to impose informal limits on the number of YJCs, despite the legislation's clear instruction that referrals to YJCs are unlimited. A norm of allowing no more than two YJCs has emerged.

Furthermore, the findings indicate that the YOA's requirement for an admission of guilt continues to undermine diversion. The Protected Admission Scheme (PAS), introduced in 2014–2015 to overcome such issues, is viewed with scepticism and resistance by most police officers, and the scheme is rarely used. Interviews with YLOs in the NSW Police revealed that PAS is seldom applied. More significantly, the findings suggest that resistance to the scheme stems from a police culture in which the traditional value of an admission of guilt as evidence is strongly upheld and protected. This illustrates a disconnect between policymakers—who, while intending to protect young people, appear removed from the realities of youth experiences—and the attitudes young people encounter when brought into police custody. As a result, PAS, rather than serving its protective purpose (and despite its other flaws, such as concerns around due process), has generated further hostility among police, who perceive it as undermining their role.

Lastly, findings reveal frustration among YLOs regarding the incoherence and contradictions within the legislation, particularly the numerous offence exclusions that are seen as unwarranted (when compared to inclusions) and that prevent the diversion of children in cases they consider appropriate for such matters (see Chapter 4).

The magistracy as decision-makers

Findings on the NSW magistracy's perspective suggest that Children's Court magistrates express general support for the use of YJCs. However, closer examination of the data reveals underlying objections that cast doubt on the magistracy's genuine readiness to fully embrace diversionary alternatives, suggesting that their stated support may be somewhat conditional. The findings indicate that high expectations placed on diversionary outcomes, coupled with a strong focus on recidivism, contribute to a reluctance to make further referrals for the young people who have been diverted on prior occasions. In particular, there appears to be an unspoken, arbitrary limit among many magistrates, with two YJC referrals per individual often considered the maximum acceptable.

The findings also suggest that YJCs are frequently viewed as a sentencing tool rather than a *true* alternative to divert children away from the court system. Additionally, evidence of an urban-rural divide emerged, with disparities in justice practices, knowledge on the YOA, training, education and resource availability, all of which further undermine diversion efforts in rural areas. Community expectations were also found to play a significant role in decision-making, with a general perception among magistrates that YJCs are seen as a 'soft' approach within the broader community, which in turn diminishes the willingness to divert young people, at least for certain offences.

The findings disclose magistrates' concerns with YJC outcome plans, which are often perceived as insufficiently demanding in terms of accountability and responsibilisation of the young person. This perception further weakens support for referrals. Lastly, magistrates expressed frustration over the exclusion of certain offences from eligibility for diversion, viewing these exclusions as unwarranted barriers to diverting children in cases they consider appropriate. Some magistrates felt that the legislation should allow for greater judicial discretion, enabling judges to determine which offences are suitable for diversion, although this position was not universally shared among the magistracy (see Chapter 5).

Perspectives of youth justice personnel

The perspectives of youth justice personnel, as gathered through interviews, were triangulated with responses from other data sources, including police, magistrates and official statistics. The findings reveal a general commitment to the YOA, alongside resistance from both police and magistrates. The success of diversion implementation in each LAC appears to depend on several factors: support for diversionary alternatives at a management level, the attitudes and commitment of YLOs to the principles of the YOA, and the level of training and education amongst general duties police officers.

It was also found that localised approaches to managing diversion within Juvenile Justice NSW (JJ) result in varying levels of inter-agency consultation across different regions. Additionally, interview data from youth justice personnel strongly corroborated findings from NSW Police interviews, indicating that PAS as a scheme is very rarely utilised.

Lastly, the ambiguity of the legislation was found to lead to multiple interpretations regarding the appropriate level of intervention among JJ personnel. JJ provided evidence that suggests that, although the legislation allows for an unlimited number of YJCs, in practice, an arbitrary maximum of two is typically imposed by most gatekeepers. This finding was consistent with perspectives shared in interviews with both the NSW Police Force and the NSW magistracy.

YOA ethos: core concerns

In Chapter 2, the trajectory of juvenile justice highlighted the growing tensions between welfarism and punitivism in the treatment of children and young people within the youth justice system during the latter part of the 19th century. These tensions persist and are evident in the YOA, as the Act does not fully represent one philosophical position or another. Instead, the Act represents a compromise between these two contradictory philosophies. For instance, in line with a welfare-oriented perspective, the Act includes several guiding principles that advocate for the least restrictive form of sanction and discourage the initiation of criminal proceedings when alternative measures are available (YOA, s. 7(a); (c)). However, the scope of the Act excludes strictly indictable offences and a range of other offences (YOA, s. 8), thereby reinforcing more punitive, traditional justice-oriented practices.

The overarching principles of the YOA are further undermined by other legislation affecting young people, such as the *Bail Act 1978* (NSW), the *Children and Young Persons (Care and Protection) Act 1998 (NSW)* and the *Children (Criminal Proceedings) Act 1987 (NSW)*. These laws reflect a growing emphasis on law and order, 'tough on crime' policy shifts prioritising community protection over the welfare of the young person. Within this context, 'risk management' and concerns about recidivism (see Chapter 3) increasingly dominate decision-making processes. Interviews with the gatekeepers to diversion—that is, the discretionary decision-makers—reveal that these conflicted agendas coexist through out the system. This is significant, as it demonstrates that while there may be a commitment to the ethos of the YOA—to divert children and young people away from the formal court system—this commitment is often difficult to uphold when competing priorities take precedence.

Responsibilisation of young people

From the perspectives of key actors within youth justice, a central merit of the YOA is that it provides a better alternative to dealing with young people—an alternative that gives young people a chance to avoid getting caught in the system. One important finding was that individual actors pay lip service to the YOA because it provides an approach predicated on understanding the individual circumstances of the child and enabling welfare-based practices that recognise children as different from adults.

However, closer examination of police and magistrates' perceptions and decision-making processes reveals a persistent emphasis on the responsibilisation of young people. These actors, rightly so, stress that unless a young person consents and makes an admission, they are ineligible for a caution or YJC, and the diversion process cannot proceed. As admission is a legislative requirement, gatekeepers often view this aspect as *beyond their control*, thereby shifting full responsibility onto the young person. This perspective overlooks the challenges young people may face in navigating and engaging with the complexities of the YOA. The NSW

Police Force's limited efforts to facilitate young people's understanding and use of the PAS suggest that the issue is less about procedural constraints and more about a preference for preserving traditional justice-oriented values—particularly the emphasis on admissions of guilt and individual accountability.

Responsibilisation remains a core principle of the legislation. Consequently, cases involving non-admission proceed to court, and even those where young people fail to comply with caution or YJC requirements are referred back to police or court. This creates a clear risk of 'up-tariffing'—where cases escalate unnecessarily within the justice system. All interviewees acknowledged this dynamic. Given existing research highlighting the need to consider the complexities of young people's identities—including anti-authority attitudes and socio-economic factors (McAra & McVie, 2012)—the current emphasis on responsibilisation is problematic. At best, it undermines the goals of diversion; at worst, it expands the net of the traditional criminal justice system.

The findings also reveal that diversionary decision-makers often hold high expectations for 'outcomes plans,' particularly regarding the responsibilisation of the young person through punitive or deterrent measures. This has led to scepticism among some decision-makers about the adequacy of YJC outcome plans, which are sometimes viewed as insufficiently rigorous. Additionally, some gatekeepers expressed concern about the 'McDonaldization' (Bohm, 2006; Umbreit, 1999) of YJCs, noting that outcome plans tend to be formulaic and fail to address the individual needs of young people. As a result, YJCs are perceived as ineffective in addressing criminogenic needs and lacking the depth of intervention required to influence behaviour. These high expectations for YJC outcome plans to focus on deterrence and intervention have the potential to undermine diversion, particularly for young people seen as more likely to reoffend due to 'risk' factors—that is, those most vulnerable.

The findings further demonstrate a shared recognition that the quality of outcome plans is heavily dependent on the availability of resources and programmes, which are often limited. For gatekeepers seeking more punitive or interventionist outcomes, this scarcity can negatively influence their willingness to see diversion as an appropriate option. Related to this, the findings also indicate a widespread perception among police and magistrates that resource limitations are more pronounced in rural areas. This contributes to a broader rural-urban divide in diversionary decision-making. Accordingly, this study argues that dissatisfaction with outcome plans—particularly in non-specialist courts in rural areas—further undermines the use of diversion and exacerbates existing geographic disparities in youth justice practices.

The paradox of the YOA coverage

The scope of the YOA ultimately undermines its own foundational principle of court as a 'last resort.' The YOA does not apply to strictly indictable offences or a range of other offences that are explicitly excluded under Section 8 of the Act. Warnings are limited to summary offences, and certain offences—such as graffiti—are excluded by regulation, making them ineligible for police cautions (s. 18). Interviews with the decision-makers revealed widespread concern over the incoherence and perceived arbitrariness of these exclusions. This is significant for two reasons: first, from the perspective of gatekeepers, these restrictions limit the use of diversion in cases where it may be the most appropriate response; second, the perceived unwarranted and nonsensical nature of these exclusions undermines institutional commitment to the YOA and diminishes its perceived value. The findings show that there are further consequences to this, including difficulty in promoting the Act internally within the NSW Police, as its logic and coherence are frequently questioned, which leads to challenging the rationality of the legislation.

The findings also illustrate that the magistrates hold particular concerns about the exclusion of traffic offences. Under Section 8, Part 2(b), the YOA does not apply to traffic offences committed by a young person old enough to obtain a learner licence at the time of committing the alleged offence. While magistrates acknowledged that not all traffic offences are suitable for diversion, they emphasised that in many cases, a warning, caution, or YJC would be more appropriate than court proceedings. Moreover, they criticised the current practice whereby all traffic matters involving young people are heard in the Local Court rather than the Children's Court, arguing that it is inconsistent with the principles of the *Children (Criminal Proceeding) Act 1987* (NSW) and fails to recognise the developmental differences between children and adults. Ultimately, the Local Court's jurisdiction over traffic offences undermines the potential for diversion in appropriate circumstances.

Most sexual offences are also excluded from the YOA (s. 8, pt. 2(d)). The findings illustrate that there is a divide in judicial opinion on this issue. For some, a sense of duty to respond to community expectations for tough punitive responses to offences labelled as 'sexual' is sufficient reason not to include them under the legislation. Yet, the findings show that the majority of the magistrates highlighted that many sexual offences committed by children stem from developmental and experimental behaviours—such as a brief exposure, touching, or consensual sexual activity between peers of similar age. This book argues that, in appropriate cases, such behaviours could and should be addressed through the YOA. The blanket exclusion of sexual offences not only undermines the principle of diversion but also fails to account for the context and nature of youth sexual behaviour.

A similar concern was revealed by the findings regarding domestic-type offences. The YOA excludes offences under the *Crimes (Domestic and Personal Violence) Act 2007* (YOA, s. 8, pt.2 (e)). Magistrates noted that domestic violence cases in the Children's Court often differ significantly from those in the adult jurisdiction, typically involving sibling conflict or disputes between young people and their parents or carers. Many of these cases arise from the issuance of Apprehended Domestic Violence Orders (ADVOs), often in out-of-home care settings where police are called to manage behavioural issues that would otherwise be handled within the family. Both magistrates and police expressed concern that this practice neglects the welfare needs of children and is inherently punitive. Magistrates also reported that these practices increase the likelihood of ADVO breaches—often due to lack of understanding by the young person—leading to further criminalisation and 'up-tariffing.' Similar findings have been reported in a recent study by Gerard et al. (2023). The current approach to domestic violence offences undermines the YOA's diversionary intent and its principle of court as a last resort, with this discrimination particularly affecting the most vulnerable young people.

Graffiti offences, as noted previously, are also excluded from diversion under the *Graffiti Legislation Amendment Act 2012* (NSW). As a result, young people charged with graffiti offences are charged and proceed to court. Although courts technically retain the discretion to issue cautions or refer these cases to YJCs, interviewees reported that most young offenders are instead fined under the *Graffiti Control Act 2008* (NSW), which explicitly prohibits diversion under the YOA. This undermines both the principle and practice of diversion. As discussed in Chapter 5, fines disproportionately affect disadvantaged youth and have been shown to be ineffective in terms of deterrence and rehabilitation. In contrast, diversion offers more constructive responses, such as education and reparation. Youth justice personnel reported on YJC's outcome plans, which have included graffiti clean-up thereby allowing for rehabilitative opportunities that court-imposed fines cannot.

Finally, the findings show that significant concerns exist regarding the treatment of drug offences. The YOA excludes most offences under the *Drug and Trafficking Act 1985* (NSW), and eligibility for diversion in summary drug offences is determined by the quantity of the substance involved (YOA, s. 8, pt. 2 (e1; 2a)). Police interviews highlighted the complexity and inconsistency of these provisions. For instance, while an offence involving a small quantity of a prohibited drug other than cannabis leaf may be eligible for diversion, a young person found with more than half the small quantity of cannabis leaf is not. These inconsistencies were found to create confusion, leading to inconsistent diversionary decision-making among police officers, ultimately undermining effective and equitable application of diversion.

The findings from the interviews with magistrates demonstrate further concerns regarding drug offences. Noting that drug misuse is a significant underlying factor in the offending behaviour of many repeat young offenders, magistrates expressed frustration over the closure of the Youth Drug Court in NSW in 2012. Operating as a pre-sentence programme, the Youth Drug Court was viewed by the magistracy as a positive diversionary option that addressed the root causes of offending—particularly in cases where the YOA was not applicable. In the absence of this specialised court, and given the current restrictions within the YOA, magistrates reported feeling constrained in their ability to respond effectively to one of the primary drivers of youth crime. The lack of a focused approach to diversion and rehabilitation for young people charged with drug-related offences undermines the YOA's foundational principle of using the court as a last resort.

Implementation versus intent: reading the YOA

The findings in this study revealed that gatekeepers generally believe they are adhering to the guidelines and rules of the YOA throughout their decision-making processes. From their perspective, youth diversion is utilised to the fullest extent permitted by the legislation. A closer examination of these processes—particularly the application of the Act's rules and guidance—reveals a complex picture. In practice, certain provisions are prioritised over others, often depending on the individual attitudes of the decision-maker toward specific circumstances. This selective application can lead to two significant consequences: first, the under-utilisation of diversion; and second, the potential net-widening effect, whereby young people who might otherwise have had their cases dismissed in court are instead drawn deeper into the system through the diversion process itself.

This book argues that the hierarchical order of the legislation is not consistently followed, likely due to the Act's broad and, at times, ambiguous guidance. As outlined throughout the book, the YOA sets out several principles to guide its operation, including that the least restrictive sanction should be applied and that criminal proceedings are to be instituted only as a 'last resort' (YOA, s. 7(a; c)). In addition, the Act provides guidance on decision-making by identifying factors such as the seriousness of the offence, the level of violence involved, the degree of harm caused to any victim, and the young person's offending history (s. 37, pt. 3). It also allows decision-makers to consider 'any other matter the official thinks appropriate in the circumstances' (s. 37, pt. (e)).

The findings revealed that when police are assessing eligibility, offending history—particularly the number of times a child has been dealt with under the YOA—and the seriousness of the offence often outweigh other considerations in diversionary decision-making (see Chapter 4). Similarly, interviews with magistrates confirmed that offending history is a key determinant in their decision (see Chapter 5). The findings show that this emphasis on prior offending has led to arbitrary limits on the number of times a young person may be cautioned or referred to a YJC.

While the YOA stipulates that a child may receive a maximum of three cautions (s. 20, pt. 7), it places no limit on the number of YJC referrals (s. 34). Yet, interviews with police, magistrates and youth justice personnel unveiled an unspoken informal consensus that two YJC referrals are generally sufficient before escalating the next response for a young person. This cap is often justified by the belief that YJCs should reduce reoffending quickly. However, evaluating the effectiveness of YJCs solely on their capacity to prevent recidivism is misguided. The number of times that a young person reoffends does not negate their right to protection under the principles of the YOA. Rather, repeated offending may reflect systemic failures to provide adequate support, highlighting the need to review the level and quality of interventions available.

The findings in this book show that punitive attitudes can influence decisions to refer a young person to a YJC even when a caution might be more appropriate—particularly in cases involving no prior criminal history. These practices reflect broader institutional routines shaped by contemporary discourses of risk and actuarial governance, which prioritise control and prediction over welfare and rehabilitation (see Chapter 3). As such, they contribute to a punitive orientation in youth justice that undermines the YOA's foundational goals.

Inconsistent use of diversion across NSW

Based on interviews with youth justice personnel—including JJ Assistant Managers and ALS solicitors—the findings indicate significant concern about potential inconsistencies in the application of diversion. These concerns relate, first, to variation across LACs, and second, to differences between dedicated Children's Courts and Local Court settings. It is important to emphasise that these conclusions are not derived from statistical analysis, but rather grounded in qualitative empirical data, which provides the contextual landscape supporting these claims (see Chapters 4–6). Regarding the courts, interviews with the magistracy revealed that practitioners in generalist local courts—including legal representatives and magistrates—often lack familiarity with the YOA. This unfamiliarity is largely attributed to differences in training and experience in handling youth matters. As a result, the structure and function of the Local Court, present a challenge and may undermine the use of diversion in rural locations.

Regarding the variation in diversion practices across LACs, interviews with YOLs suggest several contributing factors. First, institutional support for YLOs and the YOA more broadly varies across different LACs. Second, disparities in diversion-related training and education among arresting and general duties officers appear to influence attitudes toward the YOA and, in turn, diversionary decision-making. The findings in this book indicate that the quality of training and education is closely linked to the strength of internal relationships between YLOs and frontline officers, as well as to the quality of external relationships with JJ Assistant Managers. Where these relationships are strong, peer consultation and informal training are more likely to occur, thereby enhancing the understanding and application of diversionary options.

How diversion decision-making discriminates against First Nations youth

As noted in earlier chapters of this book, one of the explicit objectives of the YOA is to address the over-representation of Aboriginal and Torres Strait Islander children in the criminal justice system through the use of warnings, cautions and YJCs (YOA, s. 3). The statistical data since the Act's introduction clearly demonstrate that this objective has not been met. First Nations young people have consistently been, and continue to be, less likely to be diverted than their non-Indigenous peers. This disparity contributes to more severe outcomes later in the justice process, including a significantly higher use of custodial orders for Indigenous youth (see Chapter 6).

The link between disadvantage, child protection (particularly children deemed at 'risk') and criminalisation—especially in Indigenous communities—was a concern raised by all interview participants in this study. There was consensus that current systems are inadequately resourced to respond to children and young people with complex needs. While participants emphasised the importance of expanding early intervention and support services to enable communities and young people to take responsibility for their actions, this emphasis reflects a broader neoliberal logic. Within this framework, responsibilisation is prioritised—placing the burden on young people to manage their own risks, rather than addressing the structural and social causes of crime. Overall, the responses in this study suggest that disproportionate representation of First Nations youth in the criminal justice system stems from systemic failures to engage with the specific needs of cultural groups. Notably, at no point did participants acknowledge that discretionary decision-making in diversion might itself contribute to this disproportionality.

A key aim of this research was to gain deeper insight into diversionary decision-making as it applies to First Nations children and young people. However, attempts to explore this issue were often curtailed. Both NSW Police and members of the magistracy asserted that 'everyone is equal under the law' and maintained that First Nations young people are assessed and offered diversion on the same basis as all others. This study argues, however, that equality in this context does not equate to equity. Treating all young people the same, without regard for historical and structural disadvantages, perpetuates systemic bias. As a result, First Nations young people—who are among the most socially and economically disadvantaged, as a direct result of colonisation's impacts, systemic racism, and ongoing dispossession experienced by their communities—remain disproportionately affected by the system.

The current trend of prioritising the offender's history in diversionary decision-making has particular adverse effects for First Nations youth, who are by far the most grossly over-represented population in Australian prisons (see Chapters 3 and 6). This aligns with Mirko Bagaric's argument that 'attaching less weight to prior convictions will ensure that every time such offenders are sentenced, their punishment will be no more than what is imposed on the affluent offender who has committed the same crime' (2016, p. 38). A focus on recidivism, therefore, is not only inappropriate but also counterproductive in efforts to divert First Nations young people. This is especially significant, given that the over-representation of Aboriginal and Torres Strait Islander children in detention in NSW has worsened: In NSW, for the 2022–2023 period, First Nations young people aged 10–17 years represented 65% of the youth in custody on an average day, despite making up only 7.5% of the state's youth population (AIHW, 2024). As explained in Chapter 1, it has been argued elsewhere that the increase in Aboriginal over-representation is likely an artefact of the decrease in incarceration of non-Indigenous young people (AIWH, 2017), which, in turn, suggests that diversionary measures may have been successful for non-Indigenous young people.

Another important factor emerging from this study noted earlier is the rural-urban divide. Since First Nations young people are more likely to come from remote/rural areas, they are more likely to appear before a non-specialist court. As has already been noted earlier in this chapter, the findings suggest diversion might be further undermined in rural non-specialist courts. This is due to comparatively lower levels of training/education, pronounced emphases on community expectations, and reduced confidence in the adequacy of outcome plans, particularly when contrasted with city-based specialist courts. Thus, it is argued that the rural/city divide undermines diversion overall, but more so for First Nations young people.

Bail legislation: a challenge for diversion

As noted in the early chapters, research on bail conditions in NSW highlights that children are most frequently remanded not for committing new offences, but for breaching bail conditions (see Wong et al., 2010). This concern was echoed by magistrates interviewed in this study, who expressed frustration that breaches of bail—often compounded by a lack of suitable accommodation—frequently result in children being taken into custody.

In NSW, where legal inconsistencies arise, the *Bail Act 1978* takes precedence over legislation specific to children's criminal matters (see Chapters 2 and 3). This legislative hierarchy has been criticised for undermining the spirit of the YOA, particularly as decisions made under the *Bail Act* do not reflect the YOA's guiding principle that arrest should be a measure of last resort (see Chapter 3; also, Stubbs, 2010 for a fuller discussion). Inappropriate bail conditions and the systemic failure to provide suitable accommodation not only draw children deeper into the criminal system and intensify the bifurcation between those classified 'low' and 'high risk' (Cunneen, 2008; see Chapter 3)—with the latter facing greater restrictions to diversion—but also contribute to the accumulation of offending histories. This accumulation of offending history, in turn, hampers their eligibility for diversion under the YOA, further entrenching their involvement in the system.

Where to from here?

The final section of this book offers suggestions for future practice and policy, grounded in the key themes that emerged from the findings on criminal justice perspectives regarding diversionary decision-making under the YOA.

The YOA emerged in the late 1990s as part of a broader shift in youth justice governance. Developed within a context of political, economic and structural change, the Act was designed to protect the rights of children and to ensure that detention would be used only as a last resort. Since its introduction, the YOA has undergone several reviews. However, there remains a notable gap in the literature concerning the decision-making practices of gatekeepers and the exercise of discretion. While past reviews have offered recommendations to improve the Act's implementation, there have been few—if any—substantive policy changes. Moreover, the implementation of the Act has remained largely static since its inception.

This book has explored the complexities of policy implementation under the YOA in NSW. Drawing on theories of police culture(s), the tension between welfarism and punitivism and frameworks of risk management and law and order politics, this study has examined how both micro- and macro-level contexts shape the application of the Act. Using youth justice in NSW as a case study, this book has identified the challenges of achieving the Act's aims, particularly in ensuring consistency across jurisdictions and equity for all young people.

Despite being in effect for over two decades, the YOA has not brought the system significantly closer to its foundational goal of using the court as a last resort. This book has shown that many of the barriers to full implementation are embedded within a complex system of youth governance, where the competing paradigms of welfarism and justice produce conflicting interests and outcomes. It has also demonstrated how institutional cultures tend to align more closely with one paradigm over the other, depending on how actors perceive their roles within the system.

Based on the findings of this study, this book puts forward a bold recommendation: to completely overhaul and rebuild the youth justice system in NSW, beginning with the legislation itself. The most effective path forward would be the introduction of a mandatory diversion model, under which alleged offenders under the age of 18 could not be prosecuted—except in the most serious cases, such as murder or manslaughter. In such a model, discretion would no longer be exercised in determining whether to divert but rather in selecting the most appropriate diversionary pathway. This approach would mirror the model successfully implemented in Aotearoa New Zealand.

New Zealand's youth justice is widely regarded as exemplary, having remained largely resistant to punitive trends (Lynch, 2012; Muncie, 2008). Its foundations rest on legislation that prioritises diversion and decarceration, encourages family and community involvement and maximises the use of community resources (see Cleland & Quince, 2014; Maxwell et al., 2004). Under the *Oranga Tamariki Act 1989* (formally known as the *Children, Young Persons and Their Families Act 1989* (CYPF)), police powers to arrest are strictly limited. Instead, responses include warnings, alternative action (ie. referral to a Youth Aid Officer who can arrange alternative measures like reparation or community work), and Family Group Conferences (FGC). When a young person is arrested and brought before the Youth Court, the court is required to refer the case to an FGC before sentencing can occur (Maxwell & Morris, 2006). A defining feature of the New Zealand model is that it positions FGC as the central decision-making forum for young people's cases, for more serious offences or young people with significant needs (Cleland, 2016).

The CYPF was designed to develop community alternatives to the traditional court system, with aims that include holding young people accountable for their actions, providing better support for families, responding more effectively to the needs of victims, enabling Māori participation in decision-making concerning their children, and reducing the number of young offenders appearing in court (for a fuller discussion, see, for example, Cleland & Quince, 2014; Maxwell & Morris, 1993).

Evaluations of New Zealand's youth justice system have been overwhelmingly positive (Cleland & Quince, 2014; Maxwell & Morris, 1993, 2006; Maxwell et al., 2004). First, police have shown increasing confidence in using diversionary warnings and cautions for minor offences (Maxwell & Morris, 2006). Second, research shows that young people are being made accountable, with as many as 95% of children being dealt with by FGC being made accountable in some way (Maxwell & Morris, 2006). Third, FGCs often include rehabilitative measures, with 60% of cases incorporating such outcomes (Maxwell et al., 2004). Fourth, although it has been noted that more can be done regarding culturally appropriate processes, FGCs are inclusive of some formal aspects of Māori protocols and are facilitated by individuals reflective of the young people's ethnicity (Maxwell & Morris, 2006). Thus, the FGC in New Zealand is more culturally appropriate as a process than the traditional justice processes are. Fifth, due to the stringent limits on police arrest, approximately 80% of young people in New Zealand are diverted rather than charged (Cleland, 2016; Cleland & Quince, 2014; Justice, 2010)—with the majority of these cases dealt with through diversionary mechanisms such as informal and formal police cautions or referrals to a Youth Aid Officer for an alternative action. Only a smaller percentage of the diversions of the most serious nature will proceed to an FGC. For instance, for 2022–2023, the proportion of children proceeded against who had an FGC or court action was 29% for all children and 36% for rangatahi Māori (New Zealand Ministry of Justice, 2024).

Thus, this system reflects the principles of the Beijing Rules and the UNCRC, which—as noted in previous chapters—state that responses to youth offending should further the wellbeing of the young person (Beijing Rules, r1.1, CRC Art. 3) and that young people should be diverted from formal criminal proceedings whenever possible (Beijing Rules, r11.1, CRC Art. 40(3)(b)).

It is important to note that the New Zealand youth model is far from perfect. In Aotearoa New Zealand, rangatahi Māori have regularly been over-represented among offenders sentenced to youth justice residences (Stringfellow et al., 2022). Nonetheless, the suggestion is to focus on the exemplary model of commitment to diversion, which is only possible due to its mandatory nature, but is framed within a participatory, problem-solving approach.

Focusing on diversion for young people acknowledges that not all young offenders are, or will become, dangerous criminals. Diversion offers an opportunity for young children to learn from their mistakes and have their needs met in supportive, rather than punitive, environments. For diversion to achieve its full potential, the system must be genuinely committed to protecting the children's rights and to using court as an absolute last resort. Formal court processing should only be used for the most serious incidents, such as cases of murder and manslaughter.

Accordingly, there is an urgent need to rethink the legislation and framework that guide diversion in NSW. Redrafting, enacting and implementing new policy of this sort requires a cutting-edge progressive political approach with a strong commitment against punitiveness and unnecessary interventions. Further, it requires a commitment to funding, ownership, and the strong provision of, and access to, community resources. Lastly, the system overall needs to be decolonised, enabling Indigenous communities to lead the design and implementation of diversionary responses for their young people. Such transformation would allow NSW to realise the full benefits of a truly effective and equitable diversionary system.

However, in the absence of the political will to pursue such comprehensive reform, the following section outlines a series of modest yet practical recommendations aimed at addressing some of the current barriers to the effective implementation of the YOA.

Alternatively: modest suggestions

The challenges identified in the findings can be broadly categorised into two thematic areas: internal (within institutions) and law-and-order challenges. Accordingly, proposals for moving forward will be framed within these two categories.

Responding to law-and-order challenges

Based on the findings of this research—and in response to the law-and-order themes emerging from interviews with NSW police and magistrates—this book puts forward the following recommendations to increase the number of referrals to diversionary alternatives under the YOA.

The scope of the YOA should be expanded to remove the exclusion of certain offences that currently prevent diversion in otherwise appropriate cases (as per magistracy assessment)—such as less serious sexual offences and offences under the *Crimes (Domestic and Personal Violence) Act 2007*. Similarly, all exclusions related to graffiti offences should be repealed, enabling police to divert such matters through warnings, cautions or referrals to YJCs. The legislation should also be amended to allow for the diversion of graffiti offences at both the police and court levels.

The current requirement for an admission of guilt should be replaced with a requirement that a child 'does not deny' the offence. This change would facilitate greater use of cautions and YJCs by police. Requiring a formal admission discourages participation and limits access to diversion. This shift would reflect a genuine commitment to the principle of court as a last resort and move away from traditional punitive practices. In addition, the legislative limit of three cautions should be removed, as a system genuinely committed to diversion should not impose limits on diversionary options. While some young people may re-offend, restricting their ability to re-engage with diversion programmes undermines the rehabilitative potential. This change must be accompanied by broader reforms that reduce the emphasis on recidivism and offending history in decision-making.

With regard to YJCs, the Act should include provisions requiring outcome plans to be individually tailored and culturally appropriate, incorporating components such as rehabilitation programmes, cultural activities, employment pathways, and access to health and substance abuse services. These plans should serve as a bridge to welfare-based responses, which currently fall outside the jurisdiction of the criminal courts. Addressing this gap will require further legislative and policy development to ensure that diversion is not only more widely available but also more effective in meeting the needs of young people. In addition, adequate resourcing must be allocated to support the development of comprehensive outcome plans, particularly in remote and rural areas where service availability is limited. This is especially critical for First Nations youth, who are disproportionately affected by systemic disadvantage. A government genuinely committed to diversion must take responsibility for funding and supporting these schemes, ensuring that their success is not dependent on the young person's capacity to comply but rather on the system's ability to provide meaningful and accessible support.

Furthermore, the evaluation of diversionary options should not rely solely on recidivism rates but instead consider broader indicators of success, such as improvements in education, employment pathways, and rehabilitation. Reoffending often reflects systemic failures in areas like housing, family support, and health, and should not disqualify a young person from continued access to diversion. The YOA acknowledges these risk factors and provides a framework for addressing them through outcome plans; however, this potential can only be realised through increased investment in community and government services. To support this, those responsible for diversionary decision-making—including magistrates, YLOs, SYOs, general duties police, and other stakeholders—must receive comprehensive training on the principles and intent of the YOA, as well as Indigenous cultural awareness.

Finally, while discretion remains a vital component of police and judicial decision-making, it must be exercised consistently and in alignment with the Act's objectives. This book recommends the establishment of a compliance monitoring mechanism—potentially housed within JJ or as an independent body—to oversee the use of discretion and approve outcome plans, thereby reducing inconsistencies and ensuring that diversion is applied fairly and effectively across the state.

Responding to institutional challenges

Institutional challenges are often more difficult to address, particularly those rooted in cultural and historical practices of youth governance. As demonstrated by the findings in this study, certain practices and frameworks are deeply entrenched within the occupational structures of institutions. Moreover, the aims and principles of the YOA frequently conflict with, or are undermined by, co-existing practices and legislative frameworks within the broader criminal justice system.

Some of these challenges—such as the interpretation of the legislation, including the over-emphasis on offending history, and prevailing attitudes toward the YOA—may be addressed through implementation of the recommendations outlined in the previous section on law-and-order changes. However, other issues will require targeted internal responses within institutions. This section focuses on those internal challenges, drawing on the findings of this study and addressing themes that emerged in relation to decision-making processes within the NSW Police Force and magistracy. The following recommendations aim to increase the number of referrals to diversionary alternatives under the YOA.

Those responsible for youth diversion must be adequately resourced to deliver a comprehensive and effective diversion system, supported by specialist decision-makers who prioritise the use of the YOA. Within the NSW Police Force, this includes ensuring that YLOs are available beyond standard business hours to provide oversight and consultation. This is critical, as YLOs currently hold the authority to oversee diversionary decisions. In the Children's Court, this necessitates that all matters involving children be heard by specialist Children's Court magistrates.

This is particularly important for First Nations youth in remote and rural areas. Where children's matters continue to be heard by local court magistrates, those magistrates should be required to undertake the training recommended in the previous section.

Finally, to address the inconsistent use of diversion across LACs, further evidence-based research should be conducted to identify areas requiring improvement and to determine the most effective strategies for achieving equitable outcomes. In addition, annual reviews should be undertaken to monitor the processing of young persons of interest across LACs. These reviews would help ensure that necessary changes are implemented and that equity in diversionary practices is achieved statewide.

Conclusion

This is the first research of its kind to examine the reasons behind NSW's failure to refer young people to diversion, focusing on both broader social and political dynamics as well as micro-level institutional factors. As such, this study is uniquely positioned to identify where meaningful changes should be made. It offers a significant contribution to the landscape of youth justice by highlighting where reform is most urgently needed.

The research presented in this book provides a detailed examination of the discretionary decision-making processes under the *Young Offenders Act 1997* (YOA) in NSW. By focusing on the institutions responsible for applying the Act, it explains the persistent failure to divert in NSW. Drawing primarily on qualitative data from in-depth interviews with experienced NSW police, magistrates and youth justice personnel, the book explores the competing perspectives on diversion and offers a credible analysis of the Act's implementation under-utilisation.

The findings demonstrate diversionary decisions made by police and magistrates are shaped by a complex interplay of individual, institutional (occupational cultures) and structural (legal and extra-legal) factors. These dimensions are deeply interconnected and inseparable, meaning that while decision-makers can influence diversionary outcomes, they do so within the constraints of institutional norms and broader socio-political parameters. The study confirms that prevailing ideologies—such as individual responsibilisation, risk-based strategies (with a focus on intervention) and punitive law-and-order approaches—form the backdrop to many decisions, often undermining the principles of diversion and the ideal of court, and ultimately detention, as a last resort. The implications of these findings for both theory and policy are significant.

Ultimately, the findings document a system in crisis: one marked by a lack of political will and bureaucratically entrenched practices that resist meaningful reform. Evidence of this resistance is the ongoing failure to raise the Minimum Age of Criminal Responsibility (MACR), which remains among the lowest in the world. Raising the MACR is the most fundamental and effective way to divert children from the criminal justice system altogether, recognising that very young children should not be subject to criminal prosecution or detention. However, while the MACR remains unchanged, it becomes even more critical to strengthen and expand other diversionary mechanisms—such as those provided under the YOA—to ensure that children are not unnecessarily drawn into the formal justice system. Urgent action is needed to implement a comprehensive diversionary framework that upholds the principle of court as a true last resort for young people in NSW.

While this book draws on insights from conversations that took place in NSW, it is not solely a NSW story. Rather, it offers a modest but critical exploration of how youth justice systems can fail to live up to their own principles when discretion, institutional culture, and punitive ideologies dominate. This book tells a broader story about the tensions between welfare and punishment and how these tensions are constructed and reproduced through everyday decision-making. In doing so, it contributes to international conversations on youth justice reform, offering insights relevant to jurisdictions around the world grappling with similar challenges. The lessons from NSW—particularly the need for structural change, cultural transformation, and a genuine commitment to diversion—resonate far beyond Australia's borders. It is hoped that this book may offer not only critical reflection but also practical guidance for other jurisdictions seeking to build more equitable, child-centred, and effective youth justice systems.

Notes

1 Data was outsourced from BOCSAR (File Reference KF25-24637) Live Dataset. In January 2022, NSW Police implemented mandatory identification protocols requiring officers to enquire about Aboriginal status for all offenders. This procedural change has resulted in increases in both the absolute number and proportional representation of Aboriginal offenders recorded in official statistics. Within this dataset, records are classified as relating to an Aboriginal or Torres Strait Islander person when at least 20% of an individual's police reports indicate Aboriginal and/or Torres Strait Islander identity. Due to these methodological changes, Aboriginality data reported here are not comparable with data generated prior to 2023.

2 Note that these figures do not add to 100% because of POIs recorded with 'unknown' Indigenous status.

References

Allard, T., Stewart, A., Chrzanowski, A., Ogilvie, J., Birks, D. J., & Little, S. (2010). *Police diversion of young offenders and Indigenous over-representations* (Trends and Issues in Crime and Criminal Justice, No. 390). Australian Institute of Criminology.

Australian Institute of Health and Welfare (AIHW). (2017). *Youth Justice in Australia 2015-2016. Bulletin 139.* Retrieved March 2017, from, https://www.aihw.gov.au/getmedia/b85be60c-9fef-436d-85df-82d8e5c5f566/20705.pdf.aspx?inline=true

Australian Institute of Health and Welfare (AIHW). (2024). *Youth justice in Australia 2022–23.* https://www.aihw.gov.au/reports/youth-justice/youth-justice-in-australia-annual-report-2022-23

Bagaric, M. (2016). Three things that a baseline study shows don't cause indigenous over-imprisonment; three things that might but shouldn't and three reforms that will reduce indigenous over-imprisonment. *Harvard Journal on Racial & Ethnic Justice*, *32*, 103–151.

Bail Act 1978 (NSW).

Bohm, R. M. (2006). "McJustice": On the McDonaldization of criminal justice. *Justice Quarterly*, *23*(1), 127–146.

Children, Young Persons and Their Families Act 1989 (NZ)
Children's (Criminal Proceedings) Act 1987 (NSW).
Cleland, A. (2016). Portrait of the accused as a young man: New Zealand's harsh treatment of young people who commit serious crimes. *The Round Table*, *105*(4), 377–387.
Cleland, A., & Quince, K. (2014). *Youth justice in Aotearoa New Zealand: Law, policy and critique*. Butterworths.
Cunneen, C. (2008). Understanding restorative justice through the lens of critical criminology. In T. Anthony & C. Cunneen (Eds.), *The critical criminology companion* (pp. 290–302). Hawkins Press.
Crimes (Domestic and Personal Violence) Act 2007 (NSW)
Drug and Trafficking Act 1985 (NSW)
Gerard, A., McGrath, A., Colvin, E., & Gainsford, A. (2023). *Children, care and crime: trauma and transformation*. Routledge, Taylor & Francis Group.
Graffiti Control Act 2008 (NSW)
Graffiti Legislation Amendment Act 2012 (NSW)
Justice, M. O. (2010). *Child and youth offending statistics in New Zealand: 1992 to 2008*. Ministry of Justice.
Lynch, N. (2012). Playing catch-up? Recent reform of New Zealand's youth justice system. *Criminology and Criminal Justice*, *12*(5), 507–526.
Maxwell, G., Kingi, V., Robertson, J., & Morris, A. (2004). *Achieving effective outcomes in youth justice: Final report to the Ministry of Social Development*. N. M. o. S. D. Wellington.
Maxwell, G., & Morris, A. (1993). *Family, victims and culture. Youth justice in New Zealand*. Social Policy Agency and Institute of Criminology, Victoria University of Wellington.
Maxwell, G., & Morris, A. (2006). Youth Justice in New Zealand: Restorative Justice in Practice?. *Journal of Social Issues*, *62*(2), 239–258.
McAra, L., & McVie, S. (2012). Negotiated order: The groundwork for a theory of offending pathways. *Criminology and Criminal Justice*, *12*(4), 347–375.
Muncie, J. (2008). The 'punitive turn' in juvenile justice: Cultures of control and rights compliance in Western Europe and the USA. *Youth Justice*, *8*, 107–121.
New Zealand Ministry of Justice. (2024). *Youth Justice Indicators Summary Report* N. M. o. Justice. https://www.justice.govt.nz/assets/Documents/Publications/Youth-Justice-Indicators-Summary-Report-December-2024_v1.0.pdf
Ringland, C., & Smith, N. (2013). *Police use of court alternatives for young persons in NSW* (Contemporary Issues in Crime and Criminal Justice, no. 167). NSW Bureau of Crime Statistics and Research.
Stringfellow, R., Tauri, J., & Richards, K. (2022). *Prevention and early intervention programs for Indigenous people in Australia and Aotearoa New Zealand*. I. J. Clearinghouse. *Oranga Tamariki Act 1989 (NZ)*.
Stubbs, J. (2010). Re-examining bail and remand for young people in NSW. *Australian and New Zealand Journal of Criminology*, 43(3), 485–505.
Umbreit, M. (1999). Avoiding the marginalization and 'McDonaldization' of victim-offender mediation: A case study in moving toward the mainstream. In G. Bazemore & L. Walgrave (Eds.), *Restorative juvenile justice: Repairing the harm of youth crime* (pp. 213–234). Criminal Justice Press.
United Nations. (November 20, 1989). *United Nations Convention on the Rights of the Child* (UNCRC). https://www.unicef.org.au/united-nations-convention-on-the-rights-of-the-child
United Nations General Assembly. (1985). *United Nations Standard Minimum Rules for the Administration of Juvenile Justice ("The Beijing Rules"): Resolution/adopted by the General Assembly* (A/RES/40/33). http://www.refworld.org/docid/3b00f2203c.html
Wong, K., Bailey, B., & Kenny, D. T. (2010). *Bail me out: NSW young people and bail*. Youth Justice Coalition. *Young Offenders Act 1997* (NSW).

Index

Note: Pages in **bold** refer to tables.